Film and Reform

Cinema and Society
General Editor
Jeffrey Richards
Department of History, University of Lancaster

Film and Reform

*John Grierson and the Documentary
Film Movement*

Ian Aitken

London and New York

First published 1990
by Routledge
11 New Fetter Lane, London EC4P 4EE

First published in paperback 1992

Simultaneously published in the USA and Canada
by Routledge
a division of Routledge, Chapman and Hall, Inc.
29 West 35th Street, New York, NY 10001

© 1990, 1992 Ian Aitken

Typeset in 10/12 Century Old Style by Laserscript Limited, Mitcham, Surrey
Printed and bound in Great Britain by TJ. Press (Padstow) Ltd., Padstow,
Cornwall

British Library Cataloguing in Publication Data
Aitken, Ian
  Film and Reform: John Grierson and the
  Documentary Film Movement. – New ed
  I. Title
  791.4302320924

Library of Congress Cataloging in Publication Data
Aitken, Ian.
  Film and reform: John Grierson and the documentary film movement
  / Ian Aitken.
    p.   cm. — (Cinema and society)
  Includes bibliographical references.
  1. Grierson, John, 1898–1972—Criticism and interpretation.
  2. Documentary films—Great Britain—History and criticism.
  3. Great Britain—Social conditions—20th century. 4. Social
  problems in motion pictures. I. Title. II. Series.
  PN1998.3.G75A48   1990
  791.43'0232'092—dc20   89–10901

ISBN 0–415–08121–1

Contents

General editor's preface

The pre-eminent popular art form of the first half of the twentieth century has been the cinema. Both in Europe and America from the turn of the century to the 1950s cinema-going has been a regular habit and film-making a major industry. The cinema combined all the other art forms – painting, sculpture, music, the word, the dance – and added a new dimension – an illusion of life. Living, breathing people enacted dramas before the gaze of the audience and not, as in the theatre, bounded by the stage, but with the world as their backdrop. Success at the box office was to be obtained by giving the people something to which they could relate and which therefore reflected themselves. Like the other popular art forms, the cinema has much to tell us about people and their beliefs, their assumptions and their attitudes, their hopes and fears and dreams.

This series of books will examine the connection between films and the societies which produced them. Film as straight historical evidence; film as an unconscious reflection of national preoccupations, film as escapist entertainment; film as a weapon of propaganda – these are the aspects of the question that will concern us. We shall seek to examine and delineate individual film *genres*, the cinematic images of particular nations and the work of key directors who have mirrored national concerns and ideals. For we believe that the rich and multifarious products of the cinema constitute a still largely untapped source of knowledge about the ways in which our world and the people in it have changed since the first flickering images were projected on to the silver screen.

Jeffrey Richards

Illustrations

Foreword

What this book amounts to is an extraordinarily expansive intellectual biography. It fills in areas that other books on Grierson ignore or skim over: the sources for the ideas on which his actions were based; the societal situations that permitted and restricted his actions. In tracking these origins and backgrounds Aitken provides an outline of influential philosophical, sociological, psychological, political, and economic positions of the first half of this century, useful far beyond an understanding of Grierson, and re-centering him in relation to them.

Those who already know something of Grierson's ideas and activities will be intrigued by the discoveries made in this archeological dig into their contexts. Those coming to Grierson for the first time will have a valuable guidebook to accompany his writings and the films for which he was responsible.

Aitken's major contribution, it seems to me, is to identify the philosophical basis for Grierson's programme and to demonstrate that it remained a constant azimuth throughout his wide-ranging career. Any subsequent writing about Grierson's significance in film theory and practice will have to incorporate these findings.

Jack C. Ellis

Professor of Film

Northwestern University

Acknowledgements

I would like to thank Vincent Porter of the Polytechnic of Central London for his assistance and friendship over the course of this research. I am also indebted to Professor Ben Pimlott of Birkbeck College, University of London; Raphael Samuel of Ruskin College, Oxford; Professor Stuart Hall of The Open University; Professor Ian Jarvie of York University, Canada; Professor Jack Ellis of North Western University, Chicago; and Jeffrey Richards and Steve Constantine of Lancaster University.

I would also like to thank John Offord, Sue Harper, Linda Wood, Robert Murphy, and others, for sharing their knowledge of film and history with me.

Thanks are also due to the following, for allowing me to interview them: the late Mr Alberto Cavalcanti, the late Mr Basil Wright, Mr H. Forsyth Hardy, and Mrs Marion Taylor. I am particularly indebted to Mr Cavalcanti and Mr Wright for granting me interviews whilst they were both ill. I would also like to extend my thanks to Mr Charles Dand; Mr Charles Oakley; Mr J. William Hess of the Rockefeller Archive Centre; Ms Brenda Parsons of McGill University; Jill McGreal, of Canada House, London; Michael S. Moss, of Glasgow University Library; and many others, for their correspondence and advice.

Appreciation is also due to the staff of the following institutions for their help: the British Library, the Public Records Office, the British Film Institute, the National Film Archive, the Imperial War Museum, the General Post Office Records Department, the University of London Library, the Polytechnic of Central London Faculty of Communication, and Research Administration Department. I would also like to thank the staff of Stirling University for their help and courtesy over the past few years, especially Professor Ian Lockerbie and Mrs Carolyn Rowlinson. Finally, I would like to thank the staff of Routledge, particularly Helena Reckitt and Julia Moffatt.

Last but not least, I would like to render sincere thanks to all who have given me support and encouragement over the years, especially Marian Whittome, and Bill, Eileen, Isabella, Moira, and Linda Aitken.

Ian Aitken
December 1989

Introduction

The term 'documentary film movement' refers to a group of film-makers and to a body of films and writings which appeared in Britain during the inter-war period. Between 1927 and 1939 the movement became established within two consecutive government film units: the Empire Marketing Board Film Unit (1927-33), and the General Post Office Film Unit (1933-39). It then became part of the Ministry of Information during the Second World War, when, as the Crown Film Unit, it produced propaganda for the war effort. In addition to its work for the State, the documentary movement also made films for a number of private corporate institutions, such as Shell, the BBC and the British Gas and Coke Company. But the documentary film movement did not only consist of a collection of films. It was also established to service a campaign for political and cultural reform, and it utilized film, written material, speeches, lectures, and other means of persuasion to that end.

The founder of the documentary film movement was John Grierson, who was born in Cambusbarron, near Stirling in Scotland, on 26 April 1898. From Cambusbarron Grierson attended Stirling High School, after which he was awarded a bursary which enabled him to matriculate with Glasgow University, reading philosophy and literature.[1] But before he could commence his studies war broke out, and he enlisted in the naval minesweeping service. He returned to Glasgow after demobilization in 1919, and graduated with a Masters Degree in philosophy and literature, before taking up an appointment as Assistant Registrar at Durham University in 1923. Whilst at Durham he was awarded a Laura Spellman Rockefeller Foundation scholarship to study aspects of public opinion and social psychology in the United States. He arrived in America in October 1924, and studied mainly in Chicago, New York, and Hollywood, before returning to England in January 1927.[2] On his return he took up an appointment as Assistant Films Officer at the Empire Marketing Board, where he remained until the Board was abolished by government decree in September 1933. After the abolition of the EMB Grierson took up an appointment as Film Officer with the newly established General Post Office Film Unit. He stayed at the Post Office until 1936, when he left to establish Film Centre, an organization dedicated to the development of sponsorship of documentary films. In 1939 Grierson was appointed as the first Film Commissioner of the National Film Board of Canada, and in 1946 he was appointed as Head of Information at UNESCO. He was awarded an honorary Doctorate in Law from Glasgow University in 1948, and an honorary Doctorate in Literature from Heriot-Watt University in 1969. From October 1957 to late 1967 he fronted *This Wonderful World* for Scottish Television. He made 350 programmes in the series, which, in January 1960, was in the top ten listed programmes broadcast by Scottish Television.[3]

Grierson was appointed Commander of the Order of the British Empire in June 1961; and a distinguished career finally ended when he died on Saturday the 19th of February, 1972.

Grierson was appointed as Assistant Film Officer at the EMB in 1927 by the then Public Relations Officer, Stephen Tallents. Prior to that appointment Tallents had convened a Film Committee at the EMB, which consisted of Walter Creighton, the EMB Film Officer; William Crawford, a prominent public relations expert; Frank Pick, previously Director of the London Underground; Walter Elliot, a relative of Stanley Baldwin; and several others.[4] The EMB Film Committee's first two productions were Creighton's *One Family* (1930), and Grierson's *Drifters* (1929). Creighton's film was a failure, but *Drifters* established Grierson and the EMB Film Unit as a significant force in film-making. On the basis of the success of *Drifters*, Grierson built up the Film Unit by appointing a number of film-makers who later went on to establish successful reputations in their own right. These included: (in order of appointment) Basil Wright, John Taylor, Arthur Elton, Edgar Anstey, Paul Rotha, Donald Taylor, Stuart Legg and Harry Watt.[5]

Between 1929 and 1933 the EMB Film Unit continued to expand, and, by October 1932, it had received 1,873 bookings for 4,380 film screenings.[6] A non-theatrical distribution and exhibition system was also established, and by 1932 an estimated 1,500,000 people – mainly school-children – had seen EMB films at the Imperial Institute Cinema.[7] 294 schools and seventy-three other organizations also used EMB films, making the Film Unit the largest supplier of films to educational institutions during the period.[8] This represented a considerable achievement for an organization only one year old in 1932.[9]

Despite this achievement, the expansion of the EMB Film Unit was restricted by a number of factors which were largely beyond the control of the film-makers. These included: an increasing public demand for sound films after 1927, which the Film Unit could not meet because it did not possess sound synchronization equipment; the lack of legislative protection offered to short films in the 1927 Cinematograph Films Act (and consequent recession in the short films industry);[10] and the shortage of suitable non-theatrical film projectors during the period. In addition, the EMB Film Unit had many critics, both within the Civil Service and within the film trade, and this contributed to its lack of success during the period.

In 1933 the EMB was abolished by act of Parliament, following the collapse of the policy of imperial preference, and the EMB Film Unit was also abolished at the same time.[11] However, Stephen Tallents, who had secured an appointment as Public Relations Officer with the Post Office, made his appointment conditional upon the Post Office taking over the Film Unit from the EMB. Consequently, the EMB Film Unit became the General Post Office Film Unit, and Grierson was appointed as its Film Officer.[12]

Like its predecessor, the GPO Film Unit achieved considerable national and international prestige during the 1930s. The movement continued to expand, and Grierson employed more film-makers, including Alberto Cavalcanti (1897–1983), Pat Jackson (1917–), Jack Holmes (1901–68), Len Lye (1901–85), and Humphrey Jennings (1907–50).[13] Some important films were also made, including *Song of Ceylon* (Wright, 1933), *Coal Face* (Grierson, Cavalcanti and others, 1935), *Night Mail* (Watt, Wright, 1936), *North Sea* (Watt, 1938), and *Spare Time* (Jennings, 1939).

The documentary film movement also contributed towards debates on the educational function of the mass media during the period. The journals with which the movement was associated: *Cinema Quarterly* (1932–6), *World Film News* (1936–8), and *Documentary Newsletter* (1940–7), published articles on the subject of socially purposive cinema, and contributed towards the rising status of the documentary movement. In addition, Grierson also furthered the aims of the movement by publishing articles in several contemporary journals, including *The Clarion, New Clarion, New Britain, Sight and Sound, Artwork,* and *Everyman,* and by maintaining contacts with sympathetic journalists on *The Times* (W. A. J. Lawrence), the *Daily Herald* (Ritchie Calder), the *Observer* (Caroline Lejeune), the *Daily Express* (Cedric Belfrage), the *Glasgow Herald* (William Jeffrey), the *Manchester Guardian* (Robert Herring), and the *Scotsman* (Forsyth Hardy).[14] Grierson also spoke at as many public meetings as he was able to and encouraged his film-makers to do likewise. Paul Rotha, for example, spoke in more than twenty-five major cities during his four month stay at the EMB Film Unit between January and May 1931.[15]

But despite the national and international prestige accumulated by the GPO Film Unit, and despite the campaign of self-publicity organized by Grierson, it remained subject to the same pressures and constraints which had undermined the effectiveness of the EMB Film Unit. As a consequence, Grierson left the GPO in 1936 to establish Film Centre, an organization dedicated to the promotion of non-governmental sponsorship for documentary films. He also became Production Advisor to the Films of Scotland Committee, and Film Advisor to the Imperial Relations Trust, before being appointed Film Commissioner to the National Film Board of Canada in 1939.[16] After 1936 the GPO Film Unit continued under the production control of Alberto Cavalcanti, until it was absorbed into the Ministry of Information during the Second World War.

The British documentary film movement, and Grierson in particular, had a considerable impact on film culture and theory in Britain and abroad from the 1920s to the present day. Various documentary film units, either directly initiated by members of Grierson's documentary film movement, or indirectly inspired by them, have come into being throughout the world. Speaking in 1983, John Sherman, who worked with the Crown Film Unit (the successor to the GPO Film Unit) during the Second World War, argued that during the 1950s 'Griersonite film technicians' travelled to many overseas countries, where they estab- lished national schools of documentary film-making.[17] In addition, Grierson's philosophy of documentary film-making influenced contemporary television documentary production, as well as various schools of realist and public relations film-making. Some film-makers, such as Lindsay Anderson and Karel Reisz, have reacted against the Grierson tradition, but have nevertheless been influenced by aspects of it; whilst others, such as Sir Denis Forman, who worked under Grierson at the GPO Film Unit – and was appointed as Managing Director of Granada Television in 1964 – have introduced Grierson's ideas into the heart of the contemporary media establishment.[18]

A large number of publications on and by the documentary movement have also appeared, both in Britain and abroad, and many educational institutions now carry courses on Grierson and the documentary film movement. A number of conferences on Grierson have been held in London, Stirling, and elsewhere, during the past ten years, and several events are planned to commemorate the 50th anniversary of his founding of the National Film Board of Canada in 1939.[19]

It is clear, therefore, that Grierson and the documentary film movement have had a significant effect on British film culture, and that there are considerable grounds for arguing that Grierson's ideas constitute the most historically important British contribution towards film theory. However, despite this pre-eminence, the historical origins and meaning of the documentary movement, and of Grierson's ideas in particular, have remained obscure, and a confused understanding of them has emerged.

Previous commentaries on Grierson and the documentary movement can be categorized according to their different approaches towards the subject. The first of these categories consists of writings by individuals who were once associated in some way with the documentary movement. In these writings the movement was frequently depicted as a 'heroic', socially purposive school of realist film-making, which contributed towards social equality by virtue of the positive representations of working-class experience which appeared in films such as *Drifters* (1930) and *Housing Problems* (1935).

This category of writings includes the work of Paul Rotha, and, in particular, his *The Film Till Now* (1930), *The Film Today* (1931), *Documentary Film* (1936), *Rotha on the Film* (1958), and *Documentary Diary* (1973). Rotha's writings were frequently critical and analytical, and also provided important biographical material on the documentary movement. However, they showed little understanding of the historical context within which the movement was located, and did not undertake a sufficiently thorough analysis of Grierson's ideas. Finally, they perpetuated an over-simplistic conception of the documentary movement, as a heroic and successful struggle by talented innovators.[20] Other works in this category include autobiographies and collections of interview material on or by major figures within the documentary movement. These included Stephen Tallents' 'The Birth of British Documentary' (1968), Elizabeth Sussex's *The Rise and Fall of the British Documentary Movement* (1975), Harry Watt's *Don't Look at the Camera* (1975), Eva Orbanz's *Journey to a Legend and Back* (1977), and James Beveridge's *John Grierson: Film Master* (1986). H. Forsyth Hardy has also published two edited collections of Grierson's writings: *Grierson on Documentary* (1946) and *Grierson on the Movies* (1981), as well as a biography of Grierson: *John Grierson, A Documentary Biography* (1979). As with the work of Paul Rotha, this body of literature contributes towards an understanding of the documentary film movement by providing essential biographical and empirical material. However, it also suffers from the same shortcomings. The writings of Watt, Wright, Tallents, and Hardy embody an often uncritical belief in the prestige and status of the documentary movement, whilst the edited reminiscences in Orbanz, Sussex, and Beveridge also reinforce a partisan conception of the movement. Few of these works address the shortcomings of the documentary movement in any meaningful way; nor do they address the question of how the movement was historically determined.

The most significant works in this type of literature are Rotha's *Documentary Diary* (1973), Forsyth Hardy's *John Grierson, A Documentary Biography* (1979), and, from a slightly different perspective, Rachel Low's *Documentary and Educational Films of the 1930s* (1979). Other works from earlier periods which generally represent a positive image of the documentary movement are: *The Factual Film* (Arts Enquiry, 1947), *The British Film Industry* (Political and Economic

Planning, 1952), *The Projection of England* (Tallents, 1932) and *Cinema* (Tallents,1945). Other more recent works which, whilst not being explicitly committed to a positive representation of the documentary movement, nevertheless assume the intrinsic value of its realist credentials, include: *The Documentary Tradition* (Lewis Jacobs, 1971), *Non-fiction Film* (Richard Meram Barsam, 1974), *Film and Reality* (Roy Armes, 1974) and *Documentary, A History of the Non-Fiction Film* (Eric Barnouw, 1974).

During the 1970s the inadequacies and contradictions within this tradition became increasingly apparent, and another body of literature on the documentary movement emerged. This was influenced by formalist and semiotic theory, and was critical of aesthetic forms (such as documentary) which suppressed the distinction between reality and the symbolic representation of reality in the art work. Documentary became criticised for its elevation of a particular system of representational conventions into an immutable 'realism', and for its suppression of the distinction between the signifying convention and the thing signified. This criticism was summed up by Bill Nichols, writing in *Screen* in 1976:

> We need then to examine the formal structures of the documentary film, the codes and units which are involved, in order to re-see documentary, not as a kind of reality frozen in the amber of the photographic image à la Bazin, but as a semiotic system which generates meaning by the succession of choices between differences, the continuous selection of pertinent features. Despite the denunciation of various cinematic realisms, this work has scarcely begun with documentary.[21]

The project which Nichols proposed was a valid one. An investigation into the means by which a documentary film mobilized a rhetoric of representational conventions in order to interpret and represent reality, has intrinsic merit. Such an investigation would also constitute an advance on the work of previous critics, such as Rotha and Barnouw, who have assumed *a priori* that the rhetoric of documentary cinema is more 'objective' than that of fiction cinema.

The central premiss in Nichols' argument was that film articulated, rather than recorded reality, and he rejected the claims of 'cine-verite' advocates, such as Richard Leacock, Donn Pennebakar, and Albert Maysles, who argued that film could achieve an unmediated represent-ation of reality.[22] But Nichols was wrong to imply that Grierson's theory of documentary film was of the same type as these philosophically untenable cine-verite ideologies.[23] Grierson's theory of documentary film was primarily an aesthetic of symbolic expression, which utilized documentary representation as a means to an end. Naturalist representation was subordinated to symbolic expression in order to express underlying, abstract realities. Grierson himself was also highly critical of cine-verite ideologies:

> You don't get truth by turning on a camera you have to work with it. . .you don't get it by simply peep hole camera work. . .There is no such thing as truth until you have made it into a form. Truth is an interpretation, a perception.[24]

But although Grierson's theory of documentary film was primarily an aesthetic of symbolic expression, it nevertheless expressed a belief in the relative objectivity of documentary, in relation to fiction cinema. That belief was primarily derived from a philosophical distinction between 'the real' and 'the phenomenal', in which the abstract and general (the real), was of greater significance than the empirical and particular (the phenomenal), but in which the empirical and particular constituted the best means of comprehending the abstract and general.[25]

Grierson's naturalist ideology consisted of a belief that the world, as it was perceived through the human sensory apparatus or through the camera lens, must constitute the basis of aesthetic representation, because it (the perceived world), was the empirical manifestation of underlying determining forces. Because of this, the film-maker, though at liberty to restructure actuality footage to some extent, must retain a commitment to naturalist representation. This ideology was fundamentally different from cine-verite theories of documentary, and was derived from completely different sources. However, it did share the cine-verite belief that the documentary image was less mediated, *vis-à-vis* reality, than was the image in a work of fiction. Nichols, and others, were correct to criticize this aspect of Grierson's thinking, but they failed to understand the precise nature of Grierson's empiricism, and consequently misinterpreted it.

Another criticism levelled at Grierson and the documentary movement during the 1970s and 1980s, was that the movement had been elevated into a tradition which obstructed the development of new forms of documentary cinema, and new forms of critical discourse on film. Paul Willemen argued that:

> Official film culture has enshrined the documentary film movement as the high point of the British cinema. This movement has been identified with the name of Grierson and both have now achieved the status of holy cows. . . . Consequently, criticism of the documentary movement and of the Griersonian ideology runs the risk of being regarded, not only as heresy, but as an attack on great artists and film-makers who oppose the industries monopolies.[26]

Alan Lovell expressed similar sentiments in 1983 when he argued that 'the basic thing is to break open the "prison" of Griersonism at the present'.[27]

The danger that the documentary movement might become a tradition which would obstruct the development of other traditions had been commented on as early as 1932 by Caroline Lejeune. She argued that Grierson had become a 'rather tiresome tradition.'[28] Similar sentiments were expressed fifty-one years later by Claire Johnston, who argued that the documentary movement had marginalized other types of documentary practice in the thirties, and continued to obstruct the development of new documentary forms in the 1970s and 1980s.[29]

These objections were valid in that the construction of a 'documentary tradition', by both the British film establishment and the documentary film movement, did have the effect of marginalizing other practices of documentary film-making during the 1930s. Films such as *Construction* (Workers Film and Photo League, 1935), and *Hell Unlimited* (Norman McLaren, 1936), deserved more recognition than they obtained, and the same was true of the work of the Progressive Film Institute, Kino, and the Workers Film Association. However, it is not sufficient to argue, as Johnston did, that these left-wing films and organizations were of greater significance than the documentary film movement, because they were more ideologically correct.[30] Such an argument does not address the fact that left wing politics had little public impact during the 1930s, nor that the documentary movement was associated with the major movement of reform during the period: the 'middle way' of social-democratic reformism. Johnston was also mistaken in arguing that Grierson's position 'could not, in any way, constitute the basis for any notion of an oppositional film practice.'[31] This argument assumed that what was progressive or reactionary in one period, would be so in all periods. From the particular historical conjuncture of the 1970s and 1980s, when the British post-war social-democratic consensus was disintegrating, it was understandable that Grierson, a social-democratic consensualist, appeared irrelevant to critics on the left. But in the historical conjuncture of the inter-war period, Grierson's social-democratic consensualism was a valid progressive 'oppositional film practice' (to use Johnston's term). This view of the documentary film movement as a progressive organization was not only held by film-makers within the movement, but also by those to the left of it, such as Ivor Montagu, Norman McLaren, Ralph Bond, and Sidney Cole (paradoxically, these were the same individuals who were later held up by Johnston and others in 1983, in preference to the film-makers of the documentary movement).[32]

Johnston's arguments, like those of Lovell, Willemen, and others, emerged during the early 1980s, when it seemed possible that the left could make an effective challenge for the centre ground of British politics. Set against that context, Grierson's social-democratic reformism seemed particularly inappropriate. However, by the late 1980s, when the left had been defeated during the Miners' Strike of 1984–5, and during the two General Elections of 1983 and 1987, Grierson's brand of social-democratic reformism seemed far less inappropriate.

The most significant criticism levelled at Grierson and the documentary movement during the 1970s and 1980s, was that Grierson's belief in the need to remain within the social consensus, the 'general sanction',[33] limited the role of the documentary movement to one of minor reform within existing norms. An associated objection was that Grierson's belief implied the subordination of individual expression to those norms. This belief in the necessity of working within the status quo has led to the exclusion of alternative practices and ideologies, and Lovell, Johnston and others have pointed out that the documentary movement has been used to exclude non-consensualist ideas. Similarly, Stuart Hood has also argued that, although Grierson's political philosophy did have a historical validity, his ideas have been used by contemporary television and film-making practitioners to institutionalize a doctrine of 'balance', which has reinforced political claims for the neutrality and fairness of established society and the mass media.[34]

These criticisms of Grierson and the documentary movement were valid and fully justified, but a great many of the disparaging reviews which appeared during the 1970s and 1980s were undermined by a lack of historical knowledge of Grierson, the documentary movement, and the context from which both emerged. This lack of historical knowledge was largely caused by the influence of structuralist and semiotic theories, which had a considerable impact on film theory in Britain during the 1970s. Semiotic theory distinguishes between 'synchronic' and 'diachronic' analysis, in which synchronic analysis: the analysis of the text as a system of codes, symbols, and relations, is given priority over diachronic analysis: the analysis of the text in relation to other texts and contexts. This implies that contextual analysis is subordinated to textual analysis.

The emergence of semiotic film theory in Britain during the 1970s was part of an attempt to establish a 'general science of semiotics', which would reorientate traditional fields of enquiry in the arts and social sciences.[35] The semiology of cinema was taken up in France by Christian Metz, in his *Film Language, A Semiotics of the Cinema* (1974); and in England, as early as 1969, by Peter Wollen in his *Signs and Meaning in the Cinema*. Semiotics had both a positive and a negative impact on film studies in Britain. On the one hand, semioticians tended to regard any non-semiotic theory as of little value. Paul Willemen, for example, believed that Jean Mitry's *Esthetique et Psychologie du Cinema* (translated in 1973) put 'a full stop after the pre-history of film theory.'[36] On the other hand, semiotics played a positive role in emphasizing the nature of film as an articulated system of codes, symbols, and relations:

> individual critics assumed that no knowledge was required other than the 'general culture' of the 'well educated gentleman/ gentlewoman'. Attempts to change this situation had been in terms of efforts to turn cinema into what it was not (yet): source material for the literary critic, sociologist, psychologist, historian, economist, moral philosopher. It always helps to know what one is dealing with *before* trying to integrate it into a particular discipline. No wonder that historians have very little idea of what attitude they should adopt *vis-à-vis* 'the film-as-document'; how are they to determine the validity of a text when they do not know how it functions?[37]

Willemen was correct to argue that semiotics provided a means of counteracting vague and impressionistic studies of film. However, he failed to recognise that it could also lead to a deprioritization of contextual, historical and empirical analysis. In Nichols' outline for a new project of documentary studies, for example, there is no reference to contextual analysis at all, and the project is defined entirely in terms of semiotic textual analysis.[38] This emphasis on textual analysis led to considerable misinterpretations of Grierson and the documentary movement. The range of evidence consulted on the movement was often narrow: consisting of the films themselves, the reminiscences of the film-makers, and the few examples of Grierson's writings published in Forsyth Hardy's *Grierson on Documentary* (1946).

Andrew Tudor misinterpreted Grierson in *Theories of Film* (Tudor, 1974), when he argued that Grierson rarely considered the medium of film 'per-se', and only considered it in terms of its use as an instrument of social persuasion. Tudor also argued that Grierson's theories had no implications for an aesthetic of film.[39] Neither of these arguments was correct. Grierson's conception of film as an instrument of social persuasion was actually derived from an aesthetic tradition based on philosophical idealism. His writings also contained an aesthetic philosophy which can be clearly distinguished from his social and political philosophy. Tudor went on to argue that, in Grierson's theory: 'aesthetics is reduced to morally prescribed social theory – purposive cinema emphasises the purposiveness at the expense of the cinema'.[40] Similar sentiments were expressed nine years later by Alan Lovell, who argued that Grierson subordinated aesthetics to social persuasion.[41]

This interpretation of Grierson's theory of documentary film as a doctrine which subordinated aesthetics to social and political instrumentalism was incorrect. It was derived from an inadequate investigation of the historical sources of evidence available, and from a tendency to concentrate attention on the social reportage films made by the documentary movement, such as *Housing Problems* (Anstey, 1935), and *Children At School* (Wright, 1937). The emphasis put on these social documentaries led to the marginalization of the more overtly aesthetic films which were made by the documentary movement, such as *Drifters* (Grierson, 1929), *Song of Ceylon* (Wright, 1933–4), and *Colour Box* (Lye, 1935).[42]

A study of Grierson's writings, from his youth to his final years, reveals that his theory of documentary film did not imply a subordination of aesthetics to social and political instrumentality. In fact, it implied that aesthetics and social purposiveness should have equal status. This interpretation has been substantiated by individuals who worked with Grierson in the documentary film movement,[43] and was also made explicit by Grierson himself in 1970:

> Most people...when they think of documentary films think of public reports and social problems and worthwhile education and all that sort of thing. For me it is something more magical. It is a visual art which can convey a sense of beauty about the ordinary world, the world on your doorstep.[44]

Inadequate investigation of the historical sources of evidence available on Grierson and the documentary movement can also be found in Lovell and Hillier's influential *Studies In Documentary* (1972). This book contained important critical work, but it also contained some misconceptions. In particular, it did not provide an adequate understanding of the historical, intellectual, and philosophical basis of Grierson's ideas. Lovell and Hillier were correct to point to the origins of Grierson's ideas in the tradition of philosophical idealism which dominated Glasgow University during the time that he was a student there.[45] However, they did not proceed from that starting point to investigate the substance of that philosophical tradition, or the precise nature of its influence on Grierson. They referred to three philosophers who might have influenced Grierson: F. H. Bradley, T. H. Green, and Bernard Bosanquet, and to Bosanquet in particular. But no attempt was made to prove any direct link between Grierson and these philosophers.

In fact, it was not Bosanquet but Bradley who had the greatest influence on Grierson during this period. Bradley was not a hegelian in the strict sense of the word,[46] and it would be a mistake to assume, as Lovell and Hillier have, that Grierson was the product of a neo-hegelian education. During the period of his studentship at Glasgow University, dominant neo-hegelianism was being eroded by a resurgence of neo-kantian philosophy,[47] and Grierson's student essays reflected that transition. In addition, Grierson acquired his knowledge of Bradley's philosophy through his (Grierson's) professor of Moral Philosophy, A. D. Lindsay, who interpreted Bradley from a neo-kantian perspective.

Grierson's ideas were derived from this synthesis of neo-hegelian and neo-kantian elements, and his general world view can be defined as a neo-kantian social-democratic version of Bradley's absolute idealist philosophy. His entire epistemology, aesthetic, and political philosophy was largely derived from this idealist synthesis, and it is impossible to give an accurate account of his ideas without understanding this. Failure to understand this has given rise to misinterpretations. For example, Lovell and Hillier argued that there was a contradiction between Grierson's 'naive realism', and his advocacy of dramatic montage.[48] But there is no contradiction when the idealist roots of Grierson's ideas are properly understood. A fundamental principle of both kantian and hegelian philosophy was the distinction between 'the real' and 'the phenomenal', in which the abstract and general (the real), is of greater significance than the particular and empirical (the phenomenal), but in which the empirical and particular constitute the best means of comprehending the abstract and general. There is, therefore, no logical contradiction – within the frame of reference set by philosophical idealism – between Grierson's advocacy of documentary naturalism and dramatic montage.

Lovell and Hillier also argued that, for Grierson 'the essential nature of cinema came from its ability to record the appearances of everyday life (this for him was 'the real world').'[49] But Grierson did not use the term 'the real' to refer to empirical reality, but to abstract underlying reality, and he believed that the essential function of cinema was to record this underlying reality, and not the superficial details of everyday life. This was the basis of his criticism of Walter Ruttmann's *Berlin* (1927). Lovell and Hillier argued that Grierson's criticism of the film was based on his belief that it was too 'artistic', but this was not the case. Grierson's criticism was not derived from a perception that the film was too artistic, but that it was too naturalistic, and that it failed to represent the underlying forces which affected the city of Berlin.[50] A better synthesis of textual and contextual analysis can be found in the work of Annette Kuhn, particularly her 'British Documentary in the 1930s and Independence' (BFI, 1980), and 'Desert Victory' (Screen, 1982). Stuart Hood has also published important work in his 'A Cool Look at the Legend' (Orbanz, 1977), and 'John Grierson and the Documentary Film Movement' (in Porter and Curran, 1983). Other useful work has been published by Bert Hogenkamp: 'Making Films with a Purpose' (in Clark and Heinemann, 1979), and by Jack Ellis: 'The Young Grierson in America' (Cinema Journal, 1968), 'Grierson at University' (Cinema Journal, 1973), and *John Grierson, A Guide to References and Resources* (USA, 1986).

During the late 1970s and early 1980s, a third body of criticism on Grierson and the documentary film movement emerged from a context of the increasing use of film as a form of historical document. Most of this work concentrated on the propaganda, newsreel, and fiction film as a form of documentation of historical events. Writings in this category included *Politics, Propaganda and Film, 1918-1945* (Pronay, 1982), *Feature Films as History* (Short, 1981), and *The Projection of Britain* (Taylor, 1981). Some PhD dissertations were also produced, including: *Official British Film Propaganda During the First World War* (Reeves, 1981), and *The British Documentary Film Movement 1926-1945* (Swann, 1979). A Journal, *The Historical Journal of Film Radio and Television* was also founded, and became associated with an international body: the International Association for Audio Visual Media in Historical Research and Education.

An important characteristic of this criticism in relation to previous traditions of film criticism, was that it viewed film primarily as a historical record, rather than as an aesthetic object. The nature of film as a signifying system was given less priority than its nature as a historical document. This approach had the advantage of bringing academic historiographical methodology into conjunction with a subject: film, which has frequently been investigated without reference to empirical and inductive norms. But this approach also had the disadvantage of failing to consult existing and prior traditions of film analysis, and of failing to engage with the question of how film functioned as a system of signification. Whereas the *Screen* school subordinated contextual to textual analysis, the *Historical Journal* 'school' subordinated textual to contextual analysis.

Most of the writing in this body of work touched on Grierson and the documentary movement indirectly, if at all. But Paul Swann investigated the subject directly in his PhD thesis: *The British Documentary Film Movement 1926-1945* (1979); and in two articles published, in the *Historical Journal*: 'John Grierson and the GPO Film Unit 1933-9' (Swann, 1983), and 'The Selling of the Empire, The Imperial Film Unit 1926-1933' (Swann, 1984). Although Swann's work has contributed towards a better understanding of the documentary film movement it suffers from a belief that only primary source material – usually held at the Public Records Office – constitutes the basis for an adequate understanding of historical phenomena. The bulk of the evidence which Swann investigated consisted of documents which were written by civil servants and politicians. These documents reflected the points of view of those who wrote them: they were ideological constructions, not objective records. But in assuming that these documents possessed superior objective value, Swann has given greater credence to the points of view expressed in them than he has given to the alternative points of view expressed in other forms of evidence, such as the writings of Grierson and the documentary film-makers.

The point of view expressed in many of those government documents was that Grierson and the documentary film movement antagonized potentially sympathetic civil servants, and flouted conventional Civil Service norms. This view was held by officials in the Treasury and in other government departments, and it has been upheld by Swann. Swann's argument was that, had the documentary film movement conformed more closely to Civil Service norms and practices, it would have prospered during the inter-war period. Swann also argued that the 'unsung heroes' of the documentary film movement were sympathetic civil servants who attempted to establish the documentary movement within the State, but were obstructed by the tactless behaviour of the film-makers, and by Grierson in particular.[51]

Given the nature of Swann's argument it is hardly surprising that his views have annoyed the surviving members of the documentary movement, whose recollections contradict Swann's interpretation fundamentally. Nevertheless, there is some truth in Swann's argument. The tactics adopted by the documentary movement were frequently misconceived and counter-productive, whilst Grierson's combative temperament inevitably made him enemies both inside and outside the Civil Service.[52] But there is no evidence to suggest that, had the documentary movement conformed more closely to standard Civil Service norms, a central state film unit, or even a more productive EMB or GPO Film Unit would have emerged. On the contrary, the evidence suggests that, even when Grierson left the GPO Film Unit in 1936, and it was reorganized in closer accordance with Civil Service norms, attempts by the Treasury to close the Film Unit down continued unabated.[53] No serious moves were made to establish a central state film unit before government officials were forced to establish such a unit, as a consequence of the run up to the Second World War. Had Grierson conformed to Treasury and film trade demands it is likely that no quality documentaries would have been produced, and that the documentary movement would have collapsed.

Swann's interpretation of the documentary film movement explains the evidence unsatisfactorily because it was primarily derived from one source of evidence: the views of upper-middle-class civil servants of conservative persuasion, in the Treasury and other government departments. The inevitable consequence of his approach was to switch the focus of attention from the originators of the documentary movement: Grierson and the film-makers; to largely anonymous middle ranking government officials.

The most important recent critical writing on Grierson and the documentary movement has come from Jack Ellis, and, in particular, from the 'Critical Survey' in his *John Grierson, A Guide to References and Resources* (1986). In the 'Critical Survey', Ellis grasped the importance of understanding the influence of philosophical idealism on Grierson's ideas, but he did not investigate how Grierson was influenced by particular idealist concepts or philosophers. A central argument of this book is that Grierson's epistemology, ontology, aesthetic, and political philosophy, were primarily derived from a tradition of philosophical idealism which he encountered at Glasgow University between 1919 and 1924. Philosophical idealism does not, however, entail totalitarianism, or even fascism. Nor does Grierson's dependence on idealism entail that he was an elitist totalitarian, as writers such as Morris have argued.[54] This book will make a clear distinction between the progressive and conservative tendencies within the idealist tradition, and will position Grierson within a context of social democratic reformist idealism.

This investigation of Grierson and the documentary film movement will, therefore, be structured around two interconnected objectives. One of those objectives will be to investigate the major influences on and development of Grierson's ideas, with particular reference to the influence of philosophical idealism. The other will be to investigate the parallels and relations between the documentary film movement and social-democratic reformism during the inter-war period. The existing confusion over the historical significance of the documentary film movement, and over the nature of Grierson's ideas, makes it essential that these two inter-connected problematics should be addressed together. Much of the confusion which has arisen over the historical role of the documentary film movement has arisen because the movement's origins and early history have not been adequately understood. This study will, therefore, concentrate on the origins and early history of the documentary movement. But before that investigation takes place it will first be necessary to examine the ideas and events which influenced the founder, and most significant individual within the documentary movement, John Grierson.

1   John Grierson

The historical and ideological context

The documentary film movement was founded and led by John Grierson, whose ideas were fashioned by the society within which he spent a significant proportion of his formative years: that of central Scotland between the turn of the century and 1924. The first step at arriving at a clear understanding of Grierson's ideas, therefore, will be to investigate their historical origins in that society.

By 1870 the Scottish economy, and that of the Clyde region in particular, where Grierson spent his formative years, was more closely integrated into the British imperial economy than any other region in Britain.[1] During this period the Clyde economy was the most dynamic sector of British capitalism, and the engine room of the British Empire, producing 60 per cent of British ships by the 1880s.[2] As a consequence of its function within the British economy, the Scottish economy was rapidly transformed into a predominantly capital-goods-based economy, until, by 1901, the heavy industry complex of iron, steel, engineering, and shipbuilding employed the majority of the national labour force.[3] This rapid transformation narrowed the range of diversification within the economy and resulted in a structural imbalance which left it susceptible to cyclical trade depressions. With little alternative industrial super-structure to rely on, it was periodically plunged into recession and unemployment.

These structural weaknesses were intensified by a continuous withdrawal of capital investment, and these factors eventually eroded processes of technological renewal, until, in 1920, 'the whole edifice' of the economy collapsed.[4] The economic problems which affected Britain as a whole in the post-war period appeared in Scotland 'in their starkest form.'[5] The volume of shipping produced on the Clyde between 1913 and 1920 dropped by 700,000 tons, and coal production dropped by one third.[6] Unemployment reached levels of over 70 per cent as the Clyde region, once the industrial centre of British imperialist expansion, plunged into a recession which created social deprivation on a large scale.

Such deprivation had always been a feature of the historical development of Scottish capitalism. As it developed, capitalism forced artisans, peasants and small scale craftsmen into the decaying urban centres, and created some of the worst social conditions in western Europe.[7] Between 1871 and 1931 the northern regions of Scotland suffered a net population loss of 580,000 through migration, and this led to a continuous depopulation of the Highlands.[8] At the same time immigration from Ireland increased, until, by 1881, there were 291,000 Irish immigrants living in central Scotland. These Irish and Highland migrants occupied the poorest sections of the decaying urban centres, thereby intensifying the already intolerable living conditions.[9] By 1861 Glasgow had some of the worst housing conditions in western Europe, and disease, alcoholism and illegitimacy were endemic.[10] By 1871, 41 per cent of all Glasgow families lived in single room flats. Even as late as 1931, 30 per cent of the population of Glasgow still lived in two rooms. Infant mortality rates were the highest in Britain, and expenditure on poor relief amongst the lowest in western Europe.[11]

It is against this context of severe crisis, poverty, and recession that Grierson must be placed. It was a context characterized by nascent class conflict, by the forced removal of people from ancestral homes into the decaying slum life of the inner cities, by an economy distorted because of its subjugation to the British economy, and by an unstable social order, consisting of different modes of production, ranging from the most modern state monopoly capitalist type, to medieval feudal estates. The period between 1870 and 1920 has been aptly described by Janet Glover as 'one in which unbridled capitalism grossly misused resources and amassed huge private fortunes. A period of intensive exploitation of working people.'[12] Although some sections of the population experienced varying degrees of affluence during this period, the majority of the population experienced substantial deprivation.[13]

However, despite this context of poverty and exploitation there was little evidence of any significant social protest.[14] A number of factors, some of which influenced Grierson, were responsible for this. The labour movement in Scotland was dominated by the respectable and moderate skilled workers, and they were usually opposed to radical policies. The Scottish labour movement defined its role in terms of an accommodating ideology, and worked within a political framework dominated by the Liberal Party: the party of *laissez-faire* capitalism.[15] The unskilled Scottish working class was impoverished, disorganized, and had little influence on the labour movement before 1900.[16] This resulted in a fragmented labour opposition, and a lack of co-ordinated social protest.[17]

Another factor which held back the development of an effective challenge to exploitative Scottish capitalism was the existence of a triad of ideological discourses: utilitarianism, economic liberalism, and calvinism. The philosophical basis of this triad was the economic liberalism of Smith and Ricardo, which formed the foundation of nineteenth-century liberalism.[18] From the 1870s onwards, Scottish capitalism's survival had rested upon the exploitation of overseas markets, and this had not only turned the Scottish middle class, but also large sections of the working and lower-middle classes, into dogmatic supporters of *laissez-faire*. For Scottish working people, whose livelihoods had come to depend on the export prospects of heavy industry, the ideology of economic liberalism had an 'apparently irrefutable logic'.[19] This popular acceptance of a profoundly capitalist doctrine effectively curtailed social protest.

The second ideological discourse within the triad was utilitarianism, which came in two phases, the first dominated by Jeremy Bentham, and the second by John Stuart Mill. Benthamite utilitarianism was closely connected to economic liberalism in that it stressed the thesis that the common good was inevitably promoted if every individual sought and increased his own individual happiness. Bentham did qualify this thesis by arguing that the common interest was not simply the sum total of the private interests of members of the community, and that therefore a 'harmonisation of interests' was required in order to attain the common interest.[20] The agent of harmonization could only be the State, and the concept of 'harmonisation of interests' logically entailed an acceptance of the need for State intervention in the economy and society. However, the economic needs of the class of which utilitarianism was an expression were such that Bentham's conclusions, which were logically entailed by his general theory, could not be achieved because they were not in the interests of that class. Instead of taking the doctrine of harmonization of interests to its logical conclusion, the Benthamites interpreted it in terms of the removal of barriers to individual enterprise. They argued that the market, if left free of monopoly, would lead to social and economic harmony, whilst State intervention, apart from restricting monopoly, would distort the market and contravene natural economic laws.[21]

The conservatism inherent in Benthamite utilitarianism's qualification of State intervention led to John Stuart Mill's reformulation of the doctrine of harmonization of interests to mean the 'harmonious integration of the individual's powers'.[22] This conception went beyond the traditional classical liberal advocacy of freedom from external influences to call for freedom of individual development and expression.[23] Mill believed that, in a situation where the right of freedom from external influence was used by some individuals to further their own interests at the expense of the interests of others, the State was justified in acting to protect the freedom of other individuals to find individual expression and development. Mill thus rejected the classical liberal economic argument of the 'hidden hand' of market forces, and sanctioned positive State intervention within society and the economy.[24] However Mill continued to espouse the orthodox liberal belief in the intrinsic dangers of a strong State, and advocated State intervention only as a last resort. In this respect, like Bentham, he was unable to pursue his theories to conclusions which were logically entailed by them, because those conclusions contradicted the contemporary consensus which had developed around the ideals of economic liberalism.

The other dominant ideological discourse within this triad was the established calvinism of the Church of Scotland. The function of calvinism in legitimating and reproducing capitalist relations of production has been well established by writers such as Weber, Tawney, and Thompson.[25] That function was particularly strong in Scotland because organized religion was such a strong social and cultural force there.[26] However, during the last third of the nineteenth century the hegemonic grip of religion in Scotland began to disintegrate. A number of factors were responsible for this. As the urban population expanded faster than organized religion's attempts to absorb it, the urban poor became increasingly excluded from established religious culture, and agnostic, atheist, and socialist thought took root.[27] Established calvinism also came under threat from the development of scientific knowledge, which increasingly questioned previously sacrosanct biblical presuppositions. Calvinism was especially vulnerable in this respect because it, more than almost any other Christian religious denomination, justified its creed upon intellectual premises based on a belief in the literal revealed truth of the Bible. The growth of scientific knowledge in the fields of geology, botany, biology, archaeology, anthropology, history, and physics, and the development of scientific biblical scholarship, all brought the intellectual basis of calvinism into question, until it 'collapsed as an intellectual system.'[28]

This dominant ideological synthesis of utilitarianism, calvinism, and economic liberalism declined in influence between 1870 and 1920, under the pressure of internal contradictions and external pressures of social reform. The period was one of change, in which old established values were being replaced by new ones. Raymond Williams, writing on the same period in England, characterized it as an 'interregnum', a period of transition between the Victorian period and the twentieth century.[29]

In spite of its decline, this consensus continued to exercise a substantial conservative influence, which retarded the development of political radicalism, and channelled social protest into reformist parameters. One of the reformist movements which emerged from this context was idealism, which played a significant cultural role in Scotland, and also had a significant influence on the ideas of John Grierson.

There were several forms of philosophical idealism, but the one which had the greatest influence on Grierson was Absolute idealism, which was associated with philosophers such as Hegel, Schelling, and Bradley.[30] Absolute idealists argued that 'ultimate reality' was neither empirical nor material, but essentially spiritual in nature. They argued that there was only one ultimately real thing: the Absolute, and that phenomenal reality was a contradictory and fragmentary representation of the Absolute.[31] The moral philosophy of Absolute idealism asserted that man must strive to achieve intimate knowledge of the Absolute, and, through this, intimate knowledge of his own nature as part of the absolute. Individual perfection lay in coming to an understanding of the underlying unity, which existed beyond the empirical.

The idealist movement in Britain was a reaction against economic liberalism and the exploitative nature of capitalism, and was also an attempt to adapt religious belief to new scientific knowledge. It was this latter characteristic of British philosophical idealism: the defence and reformulation of religious belief, which generated such considerable support for idealism in Scotland, and led to the triumph of hegelianism in the Scottish universities between 1870 and 1920.[32]

The historical and ideological contexts outlined above had a significant effect on Grierson, but before investigating the nature of that effect, it will first be necessary to examine the influence which his parental and family background had on the development of his ideas.

Grierson's father, Robert, was the son of a light-house keeper, and was born in Rhu Vaal, in the Inner Hebrides. All Robert's immediate forbears had been light-house keepers,[33] and John, writing in 1950, claimed that the line went as far back as Robert Stevenson's Bell Rock Light-House.[34] A light-house keeper was a person of considerable status, who, although necessarily isolated, nevertheless enjoyed middle-class social status.[35] The isolated nature of light-house keeping also produced a tradition of intellectualism and political awareness in Grierson's forbears, and this tradition of free-thinking rationalism was passed down to John's immediate family, where it influenced the atmosphere of family debate.[36] Another characteristic of the profession of light-house keeping was that it was a secure profession, and this marked it out from the widespread insecurity caused by rapid industrialization in Scotland during the nineteenth century.[37]

Despite the security afforded by the profession, Robert Grierson broke with the family tradition and became a teacher, thus becoming the first member of his family to enter the liberal professional middle classes. As John Grierson's mother was also a teacher, his parents were the first generation of his family to enter the liberal professions, and he and his brothers and sisters were the second.[38]

From Rhu Vaal, Robert Grierson moved to Boddam, a fishing village near Peterhead on the north-east coast. From Boddam the Griersons moved to Perth, and then to a number of locations within Stirlingshire, before settling at the small village of Cambusbarron – one and a half miles south-west of Stirling – in the summer of 1900.[39] John was born on 26 April 1898 in the village of Deanston, on the border of the counties of Perth and Stirling, and lived there until the summer of 1900, when the family moved to Cambusbarron. Robert Grierson was appointed schoolmaster in the village school on 14 August 1900, and John was enrolled there in November 1903.[40] He attended the school until he went on to Stirling High School in 1908.

Robert Grierson

In relation to the political and economic crisis which affected Scotland at the time, the Griersons enjoyed a relatively comfortable and secure existence. John's grandparents were from the lower middle class, his parents enjoyed secure professional employment, and he himself had a comfortable, if not luxurious childhood. However, the Griersons' immunity from the worst excesses of the Scottish recession did not result in a lack of consciousness of it. During the time that Robert was there, the small village of Deanston underwent the impact of industrial change, as the cotton mills – which had been the main source of employment for the villagers since 1785 – went into decline. The decline of the village, and the migration of the villagers into the industrial slums of nearby Glasgow, reinforced Robert's conviction of the need to protect communities from the negative effects of uncontrolled industrial development.[41] Cambusbarron was a mining village, and during the periodic strikes and lockouts, the Griersons played an active role in helping the destitute miners. Grierson's mother ran a soup kitchen, and was politically active on behalf of the miners. John himself was also involved, through helping his mother in the soup kitchen, and came into frequent contact with the miners.[42]

The cyclical trade depressions which afflicted the Scottish economy during this period were responsible for the periodic bouts of unemployment which affected Cambusbarron. However, although it was affected by the national economic recession, the village did not experience the kind of destitution which affected the large urban centres. Similarly, the Griersons did not directly experience, and were not consciously aware of, the full extent of the impoverishment of urban centres such as Glasgow: which was only thirty miles south-west of Cambusbarron. John Grierson, therefore, spent his formative years relatively isolated from the conditions of mass poverty which contemporary reformers such as James Maxton, William Gallacher, John Wheatley, and John Mclean had direct experience of, and this relative immunity influenced the character and composition of his opinions in later life.

As mentioned above, the Griersons did have some direct experience of poverty within the community in which they lived, and John's mother, Jane, responded to that in ways which were to the left of the accepted norm for a schoolmistress of that place and time. She was a 'socialist and a suffragette',[43] an extrovert individual who enjoyed debate and was politically active. She chaired election meetings for the Independent Labour Party MP Tom Johnston in 1918, was active during the ILP Election campaign of 1922, and ran a soup kitchen in ·Cambusbarron during the frequent mining disputes. All this was unusual for a woman in her position during this period.[44]

Jane came from a radical Ayrshire family, and her father was a small tradesman (a shoemaker) in Stewerton, Ayrshire. This maternal grandfather made a significant impression on John, to the extent that, some forty years later he started to write a book on the 'old Scots radicalism of grandfather Anthony'.[45] It is not clear what Grierson meant by the term 'old Scots radicalism', but it seems he was referring to the radicalism of the mid-to-late-nineteenth century, when the 'radicals' were a working-class section of the Liberal Party.[46] These radicals, who advocated, amongst other things, municipal socialism, limited measures of social reform, and limited measures of wealth distribution, also championed imperialism, free trade, and the fundamentals of capitalism.[47] The failure of this 'radicalism' to produce effective reforms – even after the Electoral Reform Act of 1884 had increased the number of voters by two thirds – led eventually to the formation of working-class labour and socialist groups in the 1880s and 1890s.[48]

The Grierson family outside the school house in Cambusbarron.
Front row (left to right) – John, Anthony, Margaret; centre – Nancy,
Mrs Grierson, Ruby, Dorothy, Mr Grierson; back – Janet

This radical tradition, which influenced Grierson through his grandfather, must be distinguished from the republican radicalism of the Chartists, and the revolutionary radicalism of John Mclean and others. It was a reformist radicalism which occupied a position on the left of the Liberal Party, and flowed naturally into the reformist socialism of

Fabianism, and into Keir Hardie's movement for independent labour representation. Jane Grierson passed this reformist radicalism on to the young John, and he remained influenced by it for many years.[49]

John was also strongly influenced by his father's liberal idealism. Robert was a person of status in the village: a schoolmaster, lay preacher, and village elder.[50] Unlike his wife, he was primarily concerned with questions of religious value and belief, though, like her, he was also socially and politically conscious, and believed in the value of education and debate.[51] Robert supported the village institute at Cambusbarron and gave lectures there on Carlyle and Ruskin.[52] According to John 'The basis of his educational philosophy was deeply rooted in Carlyle and Ruskin and the natural rights of man. The wind of the French Revolution still blew behind it. But it was strictly individualistic'.[53] John also read Carlyle, Ruskin, Coleridge and Byron at Cambusbarron, and became immersed in the idealist tradition which these writers represented.

Although idealism has been generally seen as a conservative phenomenon, because it advocated medieval systems of social, cultural, and political relations, it was, in fact, a progressive discourse in relation to existing ideologies of economic liberalism and utilitarianism. These two discourses legitimated the absolute control which the capitalist class held over the relations of production. The idealist discourse, on the other hand, which emerged from the dissident and marginalized liberal bourgeoisie, questioned the wisdom of such a concentration of power, and proposed a programme of reform. The progressive nature of British idealism lay in its critique of capitalist social relations, and in its call for social reform.[54] This progressive aspect, with its emphasis on the reformist function of the State, influenced the thinking of the young John Grierson. Writing in 1919, he argued that 'The central authority, the state, must be truly representative of the community for economic and spiritual purposes'.[55] And again, 'The state ensures security of life for the individual'.[56] These organic conceptions of the State were idealist, in that they stressed the organic inter-relation of the State and the individual within a totality.[57]

As mentioned earlier, the popularity of idealism in Britain stemmed primarily from its defence of religious values, and from its success in adapting religious belief to new scientific knowledge. This was also important to Grierson, who wrote:

> There are two sides to the knowing mind, the subjective and the objective. There are also two traditions: the mystical and the scientific. These are inseparable because of the two sides of the mind .... This means that religion is not supplanted by philosophy (or science), both are aspects of our attempts to understand the world.[58]

This quotation illustrates the influence on Grierson of the central idealist belief in the need to provide a viable, intellectual justification for religious belief.

This use of idealism as a defence of religion, can be found in two of the earliest idealist thinkers to influence Grierson: Coleridge and Carlyle. Both believed in a distinction between scientific knowledge and a 'higher reason', a distinction which corresponded to the central idealist distinction between phenomenal reality and a transcendent reality. Coleridge believed that 'intuitive reason' could comprehend realities which transcended the senses, whilst Thomas Carlyle argued that nature was a veil of illusion which obscured a 'suprasensible reality.'[59] Coleridge and Carlyle were also critics of the social inequalities produced by industrial capitalism, and, writing from the standpoint of the educated liberal middle classes, they called for a reform of the governing class of landowners and industrial capitalists.[60] Carlyle went further, and called for the replacement of this governing class by an elite of 'cultivated persons' who would emphasis the 'highest values' at which society must aim; values which transcended the class values of free enterprise culture.[61] This broader range of values was to be propagated through a comprehensive system of popular education, which would draw the individual into a national consensus.

John Grierson read Carlyle and Coleridge before he left home in 1916, at the age of eighteen. This reading was influenced primarily by his father, but it was also influenced by the 'Duchess': a nickname given to one of the cleaning ladies who worked at the schoolhouse in Cambusbarron.[62] She had read 'every book in the old village institute library',[63] and had introduced Grierson to Carlyle, Coleridge, Ruskin and Byron before he was ten years old. Grierson identified with Carlyle's emphasis on the importance of education in expanding the consciousness of the individual,[64] and he also identified with Carlyle's call for a national sense of mission to realise the fullness of the individual and the nation. In a service given to a small presbyterian congregation in 1920, he talked in terms of life as a mission:

> Those who take no part in the fight never realise, and the whole secret of it is that each one of us must take part in the establishment of good things, before good things can come to pass. . . it is for each of us to live and live strongly for the community of men, and to act according to the light that is in us.[65]

This passage reflected the synthesis of individual and social duty which was such a strong theme within British idealism.

These idealist themes of individual development, education and social responsibility were also central to the ideas of another thinker who influenced Grierson: John Ruskin. Grierson was impressed by Ruskin's critique of the ways in which capitalist work processes and relations impoverished the quality of human craftsmanship, and by Ruskin's assertion that such impoverishment contradicted the intrinsic human need for personal development.[66] These human needs were seen by Ruskin, and by other idealist thinkers, primarily in terms of spiritual and ethical needs; rather than in terms of material benefits. This prioritization of the spiritual and ethical over the material and physical also influenced Grierson, when he asserted that the purpose of existence was more than material security. Grierson argued that existence was a 'life search' for 'the principle in which man had his being.'[67] Although he admitted that 'life's fullness depends largely upon a measure of economic welfare', he went on to argue that the political should be subordinated to the ethical and spiritual, because of man's belief in the supremacy of his moral nature.[68]

The 'supremacy of the moral nature' was hardly the central concern of those social reformers working in the poverty and destitution of inner Glasgow, and other urban centres. Grierson's subordination of material to ethical welfare reveals his middle-class idealism clearly, and differentiates his beliefs from those held by social reformers whose primary concern was the alleviation of poverty.

Idealists such as Carlyle, Coleridge, Byron, and Ruskin disapproved of the free enterprise culture of the industrial middle classes, and believed in the need to establish a 'clericy' of cultivated persons who would draw attention to the highest values at which society should aim.[69] This British idealist tradition was most clearly expressed in Matthew Arnold's *Culture and Anarchy*, the 'most influential work in the whole tradition.'[70] Arnold believed that none of the existing social classes was capable of governing society wisely. He argued that, in each class, there was a 'remnant', capable of placing 'the love of humane perfection above their class spirit,' and he argued that these remnants should form a cultural and political clericy, which would act as the guardians of national values.[71]

The British idealist prioritization of the spiritual over the material was also reflected in Arnold's conception of 'culture', which he conceived to be the study of 'harmonious human perfection.'[72] Arnold's phrase 'the love of humane perfection' was similar to Grierson's phrase 'the supremacy of the moral nature,' and both reflected the idealist prioritization of the spiritual and ethical over the material and political.

The British idealist tradition provided Grierson with a frame of reference, which enabled him to develop a critique of capitalist society, and which provided him with a means of opposing the dominant ideological triad of utilitarianism, economic liberalism, and established calvinism. Although he admired utilitarianism's stress on the 'rational use of experience for the attainment of happiness,'[73] he also argued that the theory of undifferentiated psychological hedonism which underlay utilitarianism was inadequate, and that 'the struggle for life was paramount.'[74] By this, he meant that the individual should seek, not merely an undifferentiated happiness, but, in J. S. Mill's phrase 'the highest and most harmonious development of his powers.'[75] This conception was distinct from Benthamite hedonism, and implied the need to insert pleasure within a hierarchy of values.

In the above quotation, Grierson did not use the term 'life' to mean material pleasure, but to mean spiritual fulfilment. Benthamite psychological hedonism legitimated capitalist entrepreneurial activity. The doctrine of the pursuit of happiness and utility corresponded to the central assertion of economic liberalism that each individual should act in his own interests, and that external interference with the rights of the individual should be kept to a minimum. The inherent moral poverty of these prescriptions was recognised by Grierson, brought up as he was within a Scottish idealist tradition which emphasized spirituality, reformism, and state regulation of capitalism. Grierson believed that the State had a legitimate right to interfere with individual liberty, because man was a social animal 'man can not live unto himself. . . only in community is life at all.'[76] Consequently, the State had a right to interfere with individuals who threatened the interests of the community.

Grierson argued that the true function of the State was to regulate community life in accordance with the fundamental principle of full free individual development 'the principle in which man had his being.'[77] He defined this principle in both an individual and a social sense, as an individual quest for self-realization, and as a collective quest for social unity and harmony. The true function of the State was to create and sustain the conditions within which these goals could be fulfilled. Grierson's belief in an active interventionist State caused him to reject utilitarianism as a philosophical doctrine, and turn towards idealism, because ' That doctrine as it had appeared in England had always stressed the content of life and the part played by the state in that content.'[78]

Idealism also provided Grierson with a means of opposing the conservative teachings of established calvinism. Although the Griersons were a religious family, and members of the Church of Scotland, they were not orthodox calvinists. John Grierson's father, Robert, had been connected to the Wee Free sect in his youth.[79] The 'Wee Frees' were a puritanical sect attached to the Free Church, who split formally from the Free Church in 1900, when it became the United Free Church.[80] Robert Grierson reacted strongly against this tradition of calvinist puritanism, and turned instead to a more liberal form of presbyterianism, which was influenced by idealist thought. John was educated within this liberal form of presbyterianism, and was influenced by its idealist features. Like his father, John turned against orthodox calvinism, and described its entrenched support of the status quo as the 'conservatism of death.'[81] In addition to enabling him to oppose the conservatism of established calvinism, idealism also enabled him to find a place for religious belief within an intellectual system capable of defending religion against the subversive force of scientific materialism. This is clear from his assertion that religion was not inferior to philosophy.[82]

Idealist thought continued to exercise a significant influence over Grierson's ideas till late in his life. However, that influence, which came to him through his father, was not an overwhelming one, and must be seen in conjunction with the influence of a politically-conscious radicalism which he inherited from his mother.[83] Both parents had an equal degree of influence on him, and his ideas – at least until 1919 – were the product of these combined influences. Grierson's ideas, during and after this period, were a synthesis of these two discourses: a middle-class liberal idealism, and a radical – though not revolutionary – socialism. That synthesis can be seen expressed in a letter, written by Grierson, in the 1940s:

> The basis of his (Robert Grierson's) philosophy was deeply rooted in Carlyle and Ruskin and the Natural Rights of man. The winds of the French Revolution blew behind it. But it was strictly individualistic. Education gave man a chance in the world. It put him in good competitive standing in a grim competitive world. It fitted men to open the doors of a spiritual understanding in literature and philosophy. But it was in the name of a highly personal satisfaction. Behind it all was the dream of the 19th Century, the false dream, that if only everyone had the individualistic ideas which education taught, free men in a free society, each in independent and educated judgement, would create a civilisation such as the world had never seen before. The smashing of that idyllic point of view has probably been the greatest educational fact of our time. I saw it smashed right there in my village. I saw the deep doubt creep into the mind of that school-master that everything he stood for and strove for was somehow wrong. What were the delights of literature when a distant judgement by a distant corporation could throw a man into six months of economic misery? What were the pleasures of Shake-speare and *A Midsummer Night's Dream* in the evening schools, when industrial conditions were tiring the boys to death? What was the use of saying that a man was a man for a' that, when you were dealing day in and day out with a war of economic forces in which only armies counted and where the motivating powers were abstract and unseen? Before my father finished teaching the true leadership in education passed to other shoulders. Passed to the miners themselves and the economists among them. They read

their Blatchford and Keir Hardie and Bob Smilie; they attended their trade union meetings; and the day came when they elected their first Labour Member of Parliament.[84]

This letter implied that the socialist commitment which Grierson had inherited from his mother had taken precedence over the liberal idealism which he had inherited from his father. However, the letter must first be set in context: it was written in 1942, during the 'people's war', when idealism had long since been abandoned in British intellectual circles, and when liberal intellectuals like Grierson had been radicalized by the war. One would, therefore, expect criticism of idealism in a letter written on that subject during that period. However, despite this, the basis of Grierson's argument in the letter: that 'distant corporations' threatened the realization of individual potential, was very much part of the idealist philosophy. Grierson used idealist notions to criticise idealism, and this shows that, even in 1942, he was still influenced by idealist philosophy. His argument revealed a nostalgia for the idealist vision, and implied a synthesis of idealism with some form of liberal humanist socialism.

John Grierson's political philosophy, 1916–19.

In July 1915 Grierson left Stirling High School, and in October was awarded a bursary to attend Glasgow University. But before commencing classes at the University, he volunteered for military service. His enthusiasm for the war effort was not surprising, given his immersion in the heroic idealism of Carlyle and Byron, and given the widespread public support for the war in 1916. He applied for munitions work in the Vale of Leven, south of Loch Lomond, then lied about his age in order to join the Royal Navy, and entered the Royal Naval Volunteer Reserves on 7 January 1916 as an ordinary telegraphist. He was posted to the wireless telegraphy station at Altbea on Loch Ewe, and then joined the crew of the minesweeper HMS Surf, after which he was transferred to the minesweeper HMS Rightwhale, where he remained until his demobilization on 17 February 1919.[85]

Grierson remained committed to the ideals of the war up till 1918; after which he adopted a more critical position.[86] His support for the war between 1914 and 1918 was partly due to the fact that he did not encounter its worst excesses: he was not a foot soldier, and did not experience the horrors of trench warfare. Although his posting as a telegraphist on board a minesweeper had its moments of danger, these did not seriously traumatize him, and his overall experience of military service was a rewarding and fulfilling one.[87] His immersion within the idealist traditions of service to community and State led him to identify closely with the regulated and disciplined life in the armed forces. 'I was scared to leave the disciplined, co-ordinated and harmonious life of the navy... (where)... for your well ordered duty you received in return a well ordered security.'[88] Although this sense of anxiety and displacement produced by the experience of demobilization was common to many at the time, Grierson was particularly susceptible to it because of his idealist background.

The early knowledge of advanced communications technology, which Grierson's employment as telegraphist gave him, may well have influenced his later interest in the mass media, and in documentary film.[89] His experiences on the minesweeper also led him to form a romantic attachment for the sea, and to the Scottish coast.[90] However, this romantic attachment did not lead him to a political involvement with Scottish nationalism, or with specifically Scottish issues. He was always primarily concerned with national, as opposed to regional politics, a concern strongly influenced by the idealist emphasis on the 'nation state'.[91]

Although the war reinforced Grierson's idealism, its aftermath also reinforced the more radical political views which he had inherited from his mother. In an essay on Byron, written in 1922, he wrote of 'The era when squirearchy and industrialism divert the masses with entire success by a series of interconcessions.'[92] In another essay from the same period, he argued that the First World War was the 'reductio ad-absurdum' of the view that the State inevitably incorporated the will of the people,[93] whilst, in another essay, he criticised the 'glorification of the state in hegelianism'.[94] These statements indicated a subordination of ethical idealism to a more radical political commitment. However, that subordination was not total, and idealist thought continued to influence him during this period.

When the First World War ended, Grierson, in common with many others who had hoped for post-war reconstruction, were disappointed. This general sense of disappointment at the pace of reconstruction was widely felt:

> When the war ended in November 1918, there were few who did not hope that the losses and sufferings it had brought might be redeemed in a better world, a happier society at home, the nations of the earth living in peace and unity. The history of the twenty years between the two world wars is the history of the disappointment of these hopes.[95]

Similar sentiments were expressed by Grierson, in a pamphlet written in 1945:

> I came back, as I thought, to an alien world of dreary people who were doing the same old things... as though this war of ours had made no essential difference to the world. ... The war had made a

profound difference to the world and to ourselves. We were a new kind of generation with a new and directly personal concern in the problems which nearly killed us. The world was entering into a new phase of development of a crucial sort in which it would be decided whether or not wars between people could be prevented. It was wrong to treat us as schoolboys, to try to accommodate us to the old ways as though nothing had happened.[96]

This quotation reflected a widespread sense of frustration which was felt particularly strongly in Scotland, where the economic problems which beset the British economy as a whole in the post-war period appeared 'in their starkest form.'[97] The structural imbalances within the Scottish economy were intensified by the war. The diversion of production to meet the demands of the war effort lost Scottish industry many traditional overseas markets, until, by 1916, the export trade to neutral countries and the colonies had largely ceased.[98] The immediate post-war period in Scotland was characterized by large reductions in industrial output, the closure of industrial plant, and the drift of plant and management into England. By 1920 unemployment in Glasgow averaged 16 per cent, and by 1923 that figure had risen to 25 per cent.[99] Within the space of one generation, the Scottish economy, and the economy of the Clyde in particular, had declined from being the 'engine room' of the Empire, and the most important sector of the British war economy, to become one of the most severely depressed regions of western Europe.

This post-war economic and social crisis soon led to a corresponding cultural and political crisis, in which a number of radical organizations and discourses emerged to challenge the crumbling ideological consensus of economic liberalism, utilitarianism, and established calvinism. Grierson's response to, and participation within, this period of social and cultural upheaval, must be investigated. In particular, his involvement in the politics of 'Red Clydeside' needs to be examined closely, in order to dispel the mythology which has developed around his – often assumed – involvement, in this so-called revolutionary moment in British history.

An example of this mythology was Grierson's alleged attendance at the reception organized to celebrate the release from prison of John Mclean, the Marxist political leader and war-time dissident. It has been claimed that Grierson had been one of the group who organized Mclean's reception,[100] yet, at the time of Mclean's release from Peterhead Prison on 3 December 1918, Grierson was still in the Navy – at Harwich – and was not demobilized until 17 February 1919. This suggests that he could not have attended Mclean's reception, let alone organized it. It is possible that Grierson was able to obtain leave at the time, but there is no evidence of this, and he has spoken elsewhere about being kept idling in Harwich until his demobilization.[101]

Several close colleagues of Mclean did organize a reception for him on his release from prison. William Gallacher has written that:

> We had a horse drawn carriage there waiting to receive him. . . .
> Crowds surged around the carriage and mounted it to shake hands
> with him or slap him on the back. Never in the history of Glasgow
> was there such a reception as John Mclean got that night.[102]

Who were the 'we' to whom Gallacher referred, and was Grierson involved in any way, either in respect to Mclean's reception, or in any other respect?

Gallacher was the deputy candidate for Mclean when the latter stood as Labour Party candidate for Glasgow Gorbals during the 'Coupon Election' of 14 December 1918.[103] At the time both Gallacher and Mclean were members of the British Socialist Party (BSP), which had been formed during the war by Mclean, on the basis of his refusal to participate in what he saw as an 'imperialist struggle'.[104] Gallacher and others in the BSP would certainly have been involved in the organization of Mclean's reception, as would Arthur MacMannus, one time member of the Socialist Labour Party (SLP) and BSP, and founder member, along with Gallacher, of the Communist Party of Great Britain. Most of the radical groups on the Clyde also participated in the Clyde Workers Committee (CWC), whose Chairman was Gallacher. This was an umbrella organization which included Labour Party and Independent Labour Party (ILP) groups. All of these groups were active in the Red Clydeside movement, and all of them would have been involved in some way with celebrating Mclean's release from prison. As the official Labour Party candidate for Glasgow Gorbals, Mclean commanded a wide range of support, from the social democratic centre to the revolutionary left.

Even if it is accepted, hypothetically, that Grierson was present at Glasgow railway station on 3 December 1918, at 4.30 pm, there is still no evidence that he played any part in the organization of a reception for John Mclean. In all the literature on the Red Clyde, there is not one single reference to Grierson; and this suggests that his contribution to that political phenomenon was minimal. In fact, Grierson's political activity during this period was limited to political discussion groups within Glasgow University.[105] An active member of the University Fabian Society, he was nevertheless instrumental in disbanding that society in 1921, in order to replace it with the New University Labour Club. Like many of the other students, he felt that Fabianism was no longer relevant, and that it was important to align more closely with the Labour Party.[106] However, the New University Labour Club had little concrete connection with either the Labour Party, or the ILP, and was limited to political activity within the University.[107]

Despite his lack of involvement in the political events of Clydeside,

Grierson did have strong political convictions, and, in a Preface to Paul Rotha's *Documentary Film* (1952), he commented on his political beliefs at the time:

> The Clydeside cult was the most humanist in the early socialist movement. This was its deep political weakness, as Lenin himself pointed out, and men like James Maxton came to practically demonstrate. But while recognising this, as one must, the overriding humanist factor did not lose its ultimate validity as the harder forces of political organization have taken control of the thoughts we had and the sympathies we urged. For myself, I shall only say that what I may have given to documentary – with the working man on the screen and all that – was simply what I owed to my masters, Keir Hardie, Bob Smilie and John Wheatley.[108]

The 1952 Preface positions Grierson precisely within the spectrum of ideologies which evolved in response to the Scottish post-war crisis of 1920-22. In the Preface he named his political masters as Keir Hardie, John Wheatley and Bob Smilie, and, in doing so, identified himself with the tradition of moderate reformism which these figures represented.

Hardie and Wheatley had a particularly strong influence on Grierson. Hardie was born in 1856, and began his political career as a trade union organiser in the coal mining districts. In 1886 he founded the short lived Scottish Labour Party, and was instrumental in establishing the Independent Labour Party in 1893. His socialism was moral and emotional rather than intellectual, and was inspired by the Bible, to the extent that he claimed socialism to be the 'embodiment of Christianity in the industrial sphere.'[109] He was not a Marxist, and was profoundly hostile to the Marxist conception of class struggle. His belief in reform as a 'new faith', or as a modern religion, was close to the central principles of the British idealist tradition; and it is not surprising that Grierson, himself an idealist, should have identified so closely with Hardie's ideas. Like Grierson, Hardie had read idealist authors like Carlyle and Ruskin, and he also held to the idealist belief in the organic unity of society: a belief inimical to the Marxist belief in class conflict.

Like Hardie, John Wheatley, an Irish Catholic, also wished to make religious morality the foundation of political and social life. Like Hardie, Wheatley rejected the Marxist doctrine of class war, and worked for the synthesis of catholicism and socialism. To this end he founded the Catholic Socialist Society in 1906. He joined the ILP in 1907, fourteen years after it had been founded by Keir Hardie, and went on to become an influential parliamentarian in the first Labour Party government of 1923-4.[110]

The moderate reformism represented by these figures found its institutional embodiment in the Independent Labour Party, which, though originally founded as a working-class party, had always attracted middle-class support. In Glasgow, ILP members included teachers, clerics, businessmen, professional people, and middle-class Fabian socialists, as well as skilled and unskilled trade unionists.[111] This heterogeneity enabled the ILP to take up a number of positions to the left of the Labour Party, which was dominated by the more hesitant and cautious skilled trade unions. The ILP's tradition of moderate socialist opposition, its cross-class character and appeal, and its opposition to both Marxist theory and the over-cautious reformism of the 'labour aristocracy', all led Grierson to identify closely with it.

The political programme of the ILP was centred on a strategy of increasing working-class representation within Parliament in order to transform the system from within. This strategy was opposed by other groups on the left, who believed that only extra-parliamentary revolutionary action could result in a socialist transformation of society. These groups included the Social Democratic Federation, led by H. M. Hyndman, which advocated a brand of dogmatic mechanistic Marxism; the Socialist Labour Party, which split from the SDF in 1903 under the leadership of John Mclean and James Maxton – and which advocated a brand of industrial unionism; the British Socialist Party, which was founded in 1905 by Mclean as a national extension of the Socialist Labour Party, and which split formally from the SLP in 1913 over Mclean's opposition to the coming war;[112] and the Clyde Workers Committee, an umbrella organization whose Chairman was Gallacher, and whose policies consisted of a combination of industrial unionism, syndicalism and anti-imperialism.[113] These organizations were joined in August 1920 by the Communist Party of Great Britain, which was founded from a union of the Socialist Labour Party, the British Socialist Party, and Sylvia Pankhurst's Workers Socialist Federation.[114]

Grierson could not have identified with the Marxist, syndicalist, industrial unionist, and guild socialist theories which these groups advocated, because of their emphasis on workers' control, revolutionary action, class conflict, and (except in the case of Marxism) a reduction in the power of the State. Grierson's idealism and reformist socialism led him to believe in the indispensability of representative parliamentary government, and in the need for a strong State. It also led him to reject the argument that capitalist society inevitably produced class struggle and inequality.[115] On the other hand, he identified strongly with the idealist and religious beliefs of the ILP, and with its emphasis on issues of poverty and social inequality, as opposed to the class politics of the groups mentioned above.[116] The ILP was, in addition, by far the largest of the left wing groups in Glasgow at the time. By 1920 it had a membership of 45,000, compared with Communist Party's 10,000, and, in the General Election of 1922, the ILP won ten of the fifteen seats in Glasgow. Given that it was the most popular left wing political party in the Clyde region during this period,[117] it is not surprising that Grierson associated with it – even if only in spirit.

In addition to the influence of Hardie, Wheatley and the ILP, another major influence on Grierson's political ideas during the early twenties was Bertrand Russell.[118] Two of Russell's books were important to him, and remained on his bookshelves for years. These were: *Roads to Freedom* (1918) and *Principles of Social Reconstruction* (1916). Born in 1872 – sixteen years before Grierson – Russell was influenced by idealist theories in his youth, and these two early books contain clear evidence of that influence.

At the beginning of *Principles of Social Reconstruction* Russell proposed a doctrine of human nature in which creative and natural-human impulses were regulated by the objective and impersonal powers of mind: 'Mind enables us to decide what impulses need to be suppressed or diverted because they conflict with other impulses or because the environment makes it impossible or undesirable to satisfy them.'[119] Later in the book he qualified this model by arguing that both 'instinct' (or 'impulse') and mind were regulated by 'spirit', 'the principle of impersonal feeling which enables the individual to transcend personal satisfaction by serving some supra-human end, ie. a mission of some sort.'[120] Russell argued that such transcendence was essential to the development of the human character 'if life is to be fully human it must serve some other end which seems, in some sense, outside human life.'[121] This argument contained two postulates: (a) that human impulse and desire should be allowed freedom to develop as fully as possible, and (b) that it should be subject to regulation by the social imperatives of 'mind' and 'spirit'.

In these books Russell tackled the classical contradiction between individual desire and social determinism by stressing the need for freedom of impulse and desire, and by stressing the need for that freedom to be integrated, via the social categories of mind and spirit, into a unity. Russell's postulate of a synthesis of individual freedom and social necessity enabled him to avoid the conclusion that the former should be subordinated to the latter, and also enabled him to construct an argument which contained strong libertarian elements. This was particularly clear in his view of education, when he argued that 'The integration of an individual life requires that it should embody whatever creative impulses a man possess, and that his education should have been such as to elicit and fortify these impulses.'[122]

Russell argued that the integration of individual freedom and social necessity within the individual should also exist within society, and that 'men and women should work together towards some common life, some common purpose, not necessarily conscious, in which all members of a community find a help to their individual fulfilment.'[123] These organic conceptions of individual and social unity were idealist in origin, as was the conception of human life as the synthesis of a quest for individual perfection and social duty. Russell argued that the principal agent for realizing this synthesis was the State, which was the social manifestation of the regulative integration of instinct, mind, and spirit. Although he argued in favour of the hegelian theory of the State as an impartial arbiter of conflict within civil society, he qualified that argument with the traditional British idealist opposition to a too-powerful State. His solution to the problem of State power was also the same as that adopted by other British idealists: that of distributing power within the liberal professional bourgeoisie, in order to counter-balance capitalist exploitation.

However, Russell's belief that the solution to the problem of State power lay in the greater distribution of that power into civil society led him to propose a degree of distribution which went far beyond anything contained within the traditional political philosophy of British idealism. In *Roads To Freedom*, he advocated workers' control of production, free provision of basic essential commodities, the nationalization of land and capital, and the establishment of a guild socialist system of political power, which would be divided between Parliament and large industrial unions.[124]

Russell's emphasis on the social function of spirit, and on the need for social commitment within a 'mission of some sort'[125], was shared by Grierson, and Grierson also shared Russell's emphasis on organic conceptions of individual and social unity and harmony.[126] In addition, like Russell, Grierson also argued that the principal instrument for achieving this synthesis on the social level was the State.[127] However, like Russell, Grierson also shared a common British idealist hostility to an over-dominant State 'For if the state be an end in itself... anything may become justifiable which is done in its name.'[128] Grierson's position on this stemmed from his identification with the traditional British idealist belief that the State was, currently, an instrument of class, rather than national purpose.[129]

Although Grierson identified closely with many of the ideas expressed in these two books, he did not identify with them all. Whilst he agreed with Russell's stress on the importance of the social, he did not agree with the anarcho-sensualist view of individual freedom proposed by Russell. Grierson conceived individual freedom in terms of moral development, rather than in terms of individual existential satisfaction. His Scottish and calvinist background made it difficult for him to adopt the latter position.

Russell's criticism of the State was also much stronger than Grierson's. Grierson believed in the idealist distinction between the 'agents of the State', and the State itself. Whilst the agents of the State might use it for class purposes, the State itself was the highest level of social organization, and must, therefore, be protected from radical change. Russell's more radical views led him to propose a radical restructuring and redistribution of State power in terms of guild socialist and anarcho-syndicalist principles and to argue that representative parliamentary government was fundamentally undemocratic.[130] Grierson, on the other hand, was opposed to guild socialism because of the reduction which it implied, in the power of a unified State:

> From this point of view, relegating the State to a purely economic function with the guild socialists for example, becomes impossible ... in the State alone, as it fulfils its function in the world organization is security of life for the individual, in the State alone, as it co-ordinates the various associations within it for fullness of life, is the happiness of the individual.[131]

Grierson believed that, under guild socialist, industrial unionist, or anarcho-syndicalist systems of government, the State would lose its power to represent and express the general will, and, as a result, would not be able to organise an integrated society.

In conclusion, it is clear that Grierson was influenced by Russell when the latter remained within the British idealist tradition, or within the tradition of moderate socialism represented by Hardie, Wheatley, and the ILP. When Russell went beyond these traditions, his influence on Grierson grew less.

Grierson, Glasgow University, and the influence of idealist philosophy, 1919-24.

Russell's books were an early influence on Grierson, but of even greater significance was the education which he received at Glasgow University between 1919 and 1923. The theories and ideas which he encountered during this period eventually formed the basis of his mature ideology.

Grierson left Stirling High School with high academic marks, and, in June 1915, sat a bursary examination for Glasgow University. In October he was awarded the John Clark Bursary for 'the sons and daughters of Protestant parents', which was tenable for four years at the University's Faculty of Arts.[132] In 1919 he matriculated on to the ordinary degree course (MA) in the Faculty of Arts. This was a broad-based degree which had been restructured in 1908 to include subjects from four departments: Language and Literature, Philosophy, Science, and History and Law.[133] The central discipline was philosophy – which was compulsory – and had been a central feature of Scottish schools and university curriculum for centuries.[134] The centrality of philosophy within a broad-based curriculum was also a characteristic of the Scottish high school system, whose syllabus consisted of Greek, Latin, Logic, Maths, Moral Philosophy, Natural Science, and Literature and Language.[135]

Grierson was a recipient of this philosophically-based education both at Stirling High School and at Glasgow University. At the University he took classes in Logic and Metaphysics, Moral Philosophy, English Literature, Comparative European Literature, and Botany.[136] He did well, and, in his first year, won the Buchanan Prize for English Literature, and a first class certificate in Italian Language and Literature. In his second year he was awarded fourth prize for Ordinary Moral Philosophy, and took Honours in Moral Philosophy and Logic, and Metaphysics.[137] He studied for four years, and graduated as Master of Arts at the end of the 1922–3 academic session.[138]

Grierson received his education at a university which was at the forefront of academic achievement in the field of philosophy. In addition to its record of academic achievement, Glasgow University also doubled its student intake from 2,000 to 4,000 between 1900 and 1920, and played a prominent part in the 'renaissance' of Scottish culture which took place between 1900 and 1930. This renaissance included figures such as Charles Rennie Mackintosh, John Buchan, J. M. Barrie, Erik Linklater, Hugh MacDiarmid, A. J. Cronin, Lewis Grassic Gibbon, James Maxton, and John Mclean – many of whom were associated with Glasgow University.[139]

From 1880 to at least 1925 the dominant philosophical doctrine at Glasgow University was philosophical idealism – a form of neo-hegelianism and neo-kantianism. There had been a tradition of idealist philosophy in Scotland dating from the early nineteenth century, and the first attempt at critical interpretation of Hegel in Britain was made by the Scottish philosopher J. H. Stirling (1820-1909) in his *The Secret of Hegel* (1863). Stirling regarded Hegel as the intellectual champion of the Christian religion – and it was this widespread belief in hegelianism as the intellectual foundation for Christianity, which shaped that doctrine's enthusiastic reception in a country whose established religion – orthodox calvinist presbyterianism – was in need of new intellectual foundations.[140]

One of the principal means by which Scottish hegelians endeavoured to provide an intellectual foundation for calvinism was through the reconciliation of religious belief and scientific knowledge. This was a central concern of Edward Caird (1835-1908), who held the Chair in Moral Philosophy at Glasgow University from 1866 to 1894,[141] and of his brother, John Caird – a presbyterian theologian and Professor of Divinity.[142] Edward Caird played an important role in establishing neo-hegelian philosophical idealism in Britain, as did T. H. Green, who was probably the most influential philosopher in Britain between 1880 and 1914.[143] Although Green was not as much of a hegelian as Caird and the school of Caird, he fully accepted what he took to be Hegel's central idea:

the existence of an organic totality: 'There is one spiritual self-conscious being, of which all which is real is the activity or expression'.[144] However, although Green believed in this central axiom of hegelianism, he was as much a kantian as he was a hegelian; and his synthesis of kantian and hegelian philosophy was characteristic of a more widespread shift from Hegel to Kant during this period.[145]

Kant's philosophy developed as a reaction to the inherent subjectivism and scepticism of eighteenth-century empiricism, which achieved its most extreme position in Berkeley's doctrine that men only have knowledge of their own minds and ideas, and cannot have knowledge of the external world.[146] Kant countered this doctrine by arguing that men do have knowledge of external reality, of 'things in themselves', as well as knowledge of their own subjective internal reality.[147] However, the external reality to which Kant referred was not that of the phenomenal world, but that of the 'noumenal realm of value' or 'supra-sensible substrata': a structure of laws, principles, and universals, within which individual 'noumena' (a noumena being the idea of an object apart from its physical appearance) were subsumed, then integrated into general laws.[148]

Kant believed that, in order to comprehend nature as fully as possible, the individual subsumed particulars within general laws, in order to construct a system of inter-related rules. This process was guided by the belief that nature was an intelligible unity.[149] Kant did not believe that there was an organic unity, but that man's reflective judgement was such that empirical enquiry into nature was dependent upon him assuming the existence of an organic unity.[150]

Kant also argued that aesthetic appreciation enabled the individual to see, in both works of art and nature, a 'phenomenal expression' and manifestation of the 'noumenal realm of value': a realm of value which was conceived by the viewing subject, as an intelligible and satisfying unity.[151] Kant believed that a revelation of unity was the basis of our judgement of what was, and was not, beautiful, and he argued that aesthetic appreciation was intuitive and emotional, rather than rational and conceptual. Aesthetic ideas, which were the counterpart of rational ideas, could not, therefore, be made fully intelligible through language, and this implied a certain superiority of the visual and musical arts over the written arts.[152] The function of the artist was to extract aesthetic ideas and laws from nature, through intuition, and then to objectify them, in order to promote 'social communication and the mental powers.'[153]

Kant therefore believed that the basis of aesthetic experience and general cognitive experience was the perception of complex connection and organic unity. However, he did not believe in the actual existence of an organic totality. Hegel, on the other hand, did believe in the existence of an organic totality: the Absolute. He argued that all the individual things of which the world was composed were aspects of the Absolute, and were seen to be such when viewed properly. He viewed the universe as an animate being, with a soul, goals, and intentions,[154] and argued that every manifestation of being was intelligible only as a manifestation of the Absolute.[155] He also believed that the monolithic architecture of the organic totality could be comprehended, in different ways, using art, religion, and metaphysical philosophy.[156]

Grierson's writings during the mid-twenties reveal a confused understanding and application of these kantian and hegelian concepts. For example:

> The mind demands coherence – and the phenomenal world is perceived through the mind, therefore there is a desire for coherence and unity.[157]

> The notion of an ultimate synthesis is a conception of the mind necessary to itself. However the notion is inconceivable except inasmuch as it is *an ideal of mind*. It is an *is* because it is a must of the mind, and reality can be conceived in no other way.[158]

These two quotations expressed a kantian conception of totality, but in the following quotation Grierson clearly identified with hegelian Absolute idealism:

> The ultimate, which must be self caused and self sufficient. . . is a coherent and dynamic unity which eternally makes itself explicit through and in space and time. . . as it was in the beginning, is now, and ever shall be.[159]

The evident contradictions between these different conceptions indicate the inconsistent nature of Grierson's ideas at the time. In certain passages within the 1919-22 writings, he clearly endorsed Kant's aesthetic philosophy, whilst in other passages he argued that the Kantian aesthetic had been transcended by that of Hegel: 'Kant's aesthetic was not a finished product, and therefore is not to be accepted in its entirety'[160]; 'Kant's aesthetic is, taken as a whole, entirely unsatisfactory. . . the most important thing about Kant's aesthetic is that it is not to be taken seriously.'[161] Grierson also argued that hegelianism 'resolved the difficulties contained within that aesthetic'.[162] One of the difficulties which he found in Kant's aesthetic, was a belief in the existence of immutable aesthetic forms. Grierson argued that all aesthetic forms were mutable: 'Every age produces its own morality and its own art according to its own particular insight into the conditions of human life.'[163] This belief in the need for a new art form to match a new age, was partly responsible for his enthusiasm for cinema and the documentary film.

These undergraduate writings of Grierson's are, unsurprisingly, confused and contradictory. They reveal the transitional nature of his thought at the time, which consisted of a synthesis of kantian and hegelian ideas. This synthesis was formulated under the influence of a theorist who had a great effect on Grierson at the time: F. H. Bradley.

A considerable degree of uncertainty has always surrounded the question of Grierson's influence by hegelianism. However, Grierson's early writings reveal the clear influence of Bradley. This has also been substantiated by the recollections of Grierson's younger sister, Marion Taylor.[164] According to Mrs Taylor, Grierson spoke of Bradley frequently, and also retained a lifelong interest in Indian mystical philosophy, an interest which culminated in his visit to India in 1971. Bradley's philosophy was also influenced by Indian philosophy, and, in particular, by the Hindu doctrine of Maya: the world as illusion[165] – a doctrine which is similar to the idealist distinction between the empirical and the 'real', and which was at the centre of all Grierson's thinking, from the 1920s onwards.

The philosophy of F. H. Bradley must be broken down into five categories in order to examine its influence on Grierson. These five categories are: the theory of the Absolute, the aesthetic theory, the ethical theory, the theory of the State, and the theory of history.

Like Hegel, Bradley argued that there was a universal order which encompassed all existence. This universal order, which Bradley called the Absolute, transcended the world of phenomenal appearance, and was a 'seamless whole, comprehensive and harmonious, in which all contradictions and antinomies are overcome.'[166] The Absolute was the totality of appearances, and everything which existed was part of the Absolute.[167]

The individual experienced this transcendent reality during the period of time prior to the growth of self-consciousness. The experience was 'a basic sentient experience which underlay the emergence of distinctions between subject and object.'[168] But this 'immediate experience' of the Absolute was undermined by the development of self-consciousness, which caused the 'world of the manifold' to appear as external to the subject.[169] The undermining of immediate experience, and the perception of externality, were reinforced by the development of thought, language and reason, all of which articulated and fragmented the organic totality.

Bradley argued that, in spite of this irreversible dissection of the Absolute, immediate experience could be re-experienced by the subject at certain moments when the externality of thought to being was overcome. But because thought was part of the relational world of appearance and contradiction, it could not be the means of realizing that objective.[170] According to Bradley, the true goal of knowledge is: 'a complete apprehension of the universe in which every partial truth would be seen as internally, systematically and harmoniously related to every other partial truth in a self-coherent whole'.[171] The procedures of scientific and rational understanding develop by connecting isolated phenomena within increasingly comprehensive explanatory models. However, Bradley argued that such 'relational thought' was unable to grasp ultimate reality, because it cannot encompass all the terms and relations which constitute reality, and because relational thought and experience was part of the world of appearance and contradiction.[172]

Bradley's philosophy amounted to an uncompromising criticism of thought, when considered as an instrument for comprehending reality.[173] Although he derived his doctrine of immediate experience from Hegel, he rejected the hegelian idea that dialectical thought could reveal the nature of the Absolute. In this respect his philosophy was deeply irrationalist. For example, he believed that only intuition, or 'the feeling experience' could comprehend ultimate reality.[174] He also believed that 'states of mind' through which the organic totality was comprehended recurred in the mature subject through forms of religious and aesthetic experience. Because these forms of experience were essentially intuitive, they were capable of penetrating the veil of appearance and contradiction, and of comprehending the organic totality.[175]

In his doctrine of the concrete universal Bradley argued that the Absolute was universal – without being devoid of content – because it contained all content within itself.[176] The Absolute was, therefore, a 'concrete universal': a term used by Bradley to denote a category of phenomena, where a community of individual entities was 'richer' than any of the individual entities within it. Bradley argued that human society was a concrete universal, and that the category of individuality was an abstract one, compared to the more 'concrete' category of 'the social'.[177] However, the category of the social was itself relatively abstract compared to the Absolute, which was the ultimate concrete reality.

Bradley's assertion that social reality was more concrete than individual reality led him to assert that the individual must subject himself or herself to 'the morality already existing, ready to hand, in laws, institutions, social usages, moral opinions and feelings.'[178] This subjection of the individual to the social leads, according to Bradley, to a correspondence of individual and social will, which in turn leads to the self-realization of the individual, as he or she achieves understanding of their true relation to social reality. However, this self-realization of the individual is not completed until he or she achieves an understanding of his or her relation to ultimate reality. When this is achieved, 'the essence of man is fully realised.'[179]

Although Bradley argued that the individual must subject himself or herself to the social will, he also argued that, in different societies, the social will was at different removes from the 'universal will'. As social formations achieved a closer relation to the Absolute, they increasingly exhibited the characteristics of the Absolute: harmony, and absence of internal contradiction. These conditions were realised through successive stages of historical evolution:

> History is the working out of the true human nature through various incomplete stages towards completion... the essence of realisation is evolution through stages.[180]

This evolutionary conception of history rested on both hegelian historicism and social darwinist evolutionism. Bradley also emphasized the autonomy of societies, and of the Nation State. His emphasis on this autonomy contradicted his central thesis: that of the existence of the organic totality. Despite this, he placed considerable emphasis on the autonomy of individual Nation States, and on the relativity of culture and morality.[181] Although he qualified this principle of relativism through his doctrine of societies evolving to a closer correspondence with the Absolute, he remained firm in his belief in the autonomy of the Nation State.

Hegel's nationalistic historicism led him to conceive the feudal Prussian State in which he lived as the embodiment of spirit, just as Bradley's nationalistic historicism, when combined with his belief that some societies were in a closer relation to the Absolute than others, led him to a belief in the supremacy of the Christian West. However, this conclusion was not logically entailed by the premiss that some societies were in a closer relation to the Absolute than others. The same premiss could imply that societies other than those of the West were in a closer relation to the Absolute. Bradley's theory, therefore, contained a potential critique of western bourgeois capitalist society, despite the fact that he himself was a conservative.

Another potentially radical component within Bradley's philosophy was his distinction between the agents and institutions of State, in which the agents of State could corrupt the institutions of State in order to serve class interests. As with the theory of societies in different relations to the Absolute, this distinction contained the potential for a critique of existing society. Even so, Bradley never questioned the value of the existing institutions of State, because he believed them to be the culmination of historical evolution towards the Absolute. Despite the radical potential within his philosophy, he was a reactionary 'An implacable enemy of all utilitarian or liberal teaching, he could not abide... any belief in the natural equality of man.'[182] He found democratic ideas 'degenerate', and his philosophy was radically cut off from the ordinary enquiries of humanity.[183]

Many of John Grierson's philosophical ideas during the early twenties were influenced by Bradley's philosophy. Like Bradley, he argued that there was a universal order which encompassed all existence 'the ultimate... is a coherent and dynamic unity which eternally makes explicit through and in space and time.'[184] Grierson also reflected the influence of Bradley's theory of 'immediate experience', when he argued that the subject had an initial experience of the Absolute prior to the emergence of self-consciousness, and that that emergence interposed self-consciousness between the subject and its experience of the Absolute. ' The process of thought is seen as a constant differentiation of an initial whole whose unity pervades its particulars.'[185]

Following Bradley, Grierson argued that the true goal of knowledge was a comprehension of the universe as an organic totality. He also argued that relational thought could not achieve that goal, because it could not encompass all the terms and relations which existed in the Absolute, and because it was itself part of the phenomenal world of contradiction: 'Presupposing thought, it (the Absolute), is yet different in kind from thought, and finally unattainable in thought.'[186] Because the phenomenal world was encompassed by, and contained within, the Absolute, and because reason was part of that phenomenal world, reason must also be contained within the Absolute. However, reason did not exist within the Absolute *as such*, but, like 'goodness beauty, and truth', was 'transmuted into a function within the Absolute.'[187] This transmutation took place because reason was corrupted by virtue of its existence within the phenomenal world, and, consequently, was transmuted into an uncorrupted 'function' within the Absolute. This argument that all phenomena were transformed within the Absolute implied that the Absolute was also 'supra-logical', because logic itself was part of the phenomenal world 'the Absolute is not a logical harmony... it is supra-relational, beyond space and time.'[188]

Grierson also restated Bradley's assertion that the ultimate harmony could only be comprehended intuitively, through forms of religious and aesthetic experience:

> Philosophical enquiry is lower than the imaginative power of the poet and the prophet to reach God at the first leap.[189] Religion is of the emotions, art is the expression of emotion, and religious utterance is therefore artistic. . . . The artistic faculty means above all the power to see, the power to grasp from among the dross of time and place, the hidden harmonies of man and nature.[190]

Similarly, Grierson also used Bradley's theory of the concrete universal to emphasize that social and collective realities were superior to individual realities, and that, because of this, the individual must submit to existing social norms:

> The degree of general sanction is. . . the degree of sanction allowed by all parties of Parliament or Congress. . . . This of course imposes

a clear limit on the creative artist...(but he must) do his utmost within the limitations set.[191]

Grierson's well-known phrase 'the degree of general sanction', has often been used by his critics to emphasize the implicit totalitarianism in his ideas. In a pamphlet written for the Canadian Association for Adult Education in 1941, Grierson rejected these charges:

> I am not going to pretend that I do not realise how 'totalitarian' some of my conclusions seem, without the qualification I have just noted. You can be totalitarian for evil and you can also be totalitarian for good. Some of us came out of a highly disciplined religion and see no reason to fear discipline and self denial. Some of us learned in a school of philosophy which taught that all was for the common good and nothing for oneself and have never, in any case, regarded the pursuit of happiness as anything other than an aberration of the human spirit.[192]

The 'qualification' which Grierson referred to in this quotation, was that 'information work both ways and we should insist that new local organizations of every kind have constant and active representation at the centre.'[193] This would constitute 'a fundamental safeguard against discipline and unity turning into something else.'[194] However, Grierson never indicated how the public were to make their views known to the State, or how information would 'flow both ways'. Given this, and his constant emphasis on the need for a strong State, the charge of totalitarianism has some justification.

Like Bradley, Grierson believed that in different societies the 'social will', and social structures, were at different removes from the 'universal will' and universal social structures of the Absolute. Like Bradley, he argued that social formations could evolve to a closer relation to the Absolute, and so increasingly manifest the characteristic features of the Absolute. However, unlike Bradley, Grierson was sceptical of the view that western society was closer to the Absolute than other societies:

> It may be questioned here whether the process is an evolution from a less perfect to a more perfect completion... it would seem to be an odyssey in which there is in no real sense, a progress.[195]

Grierson also adopted Bradley's distinction between the institutions of State and the agents of State, and he emphasized the critical potential within this distinction by criticising the exploitative basis of class government in Britain.[196]

Bradley's intuitionist philosophy had a considerable influence on Grierson. However, in Grierson's later university writings there is evidence of an increasing reinterpretation of bradleyan ideas from a kantian perspective. This was influenced by the teachings of Grierson's professor of Moral Philosophy at Glasgow University: A. D. Lindsay.[197] Lindsay acquired the Chair in Moral Philosophy in 1922, and held it till the summer of 1924, when he left to become Master of Balliol College Oxford.[198] He was one of the leading figures in the Workers Education Association, along with William Temple and R. H. Tawney, and was active in the Independent Labour Party in Scotland. Although a socialist, he was opposed to 'Marxist fundamentalism.'[199] He was also a kantian – even though he had been a pupil of the hegelian philosopher Edward Caird – and he was also influenced by intuitionist philosophers such as Bergson, Croce, and Bradley.[200] Although, unlike Bradley, he did not believe in the existence of an organic totality, he shared the latter's belief that underlying reality could only be experienced through intuition and aesthetic experience. He also shared Bradley's belief in the importance of the State, and in the intrinsic value of existing constitutional structures.

Lindsay differed fundamentally from Bradley in advocating egalitarian theories of political democracy, which he derived from concepts of Christian individualism, and from Rousseau's conception of the 'general will'.[201] However, he did not interpret egalitarianism in terms of the will of the majority, but in terms of 'right and reasonable group decisions.'[202] In other words, representative parliamentary government, rather than popular government.

At Balliol, Lindsay became closely involved with the Fabian movement, and tried to bring academic studies closer to the contemporary experience by instigating the Modern Greats school, which examined relations between art, philosophy, and contemporary society.[203] Like other British idealists, he was interested in questions concerning the social role of religious belief and art. He believed in the trained imagination as an aid to moral insight, and interpreted the novels of Dostoyevsky, of which he was particularly fond, in terms of the moral insight which they contained. He was also a social reformer, and believed in the 'dignity of labour'.[204]

The deviation from bradleyan theory in Grierson's later university writings is explainable by reference to the influence of Lindsay. Grierson's criticism of 'the old idealism which led to the conservatism of death, and to the atrocities of the Great War,'[205] was derived from Lindsay's strong criticism of conservative idealism, as well as from Grierson's own experiences of the war. His cultural relativism was also similar to Lindsay's interest in comparative religion. Similarly, Grierson's belief in the intrinsic value of existing constitutional structures stemmed from both Lindsay and Bradley – but his endorsement of egalitarian liberalism stemmed from Lindsay, not Bradley.

From early youth Grierson had been influenced by two, often contradictory influences: a liberal idealism which he inherited through his father, and a more radical socialist commitment which he inherited through his mother. These contradictory influences were reinforced at Glasgow University when he was influenced by both neo-hegelianism and the socialism of the Independent Labour Party. The importance of Lindsay for Grierson lay in the fact that, in Lindsay, these contradictory influences were integrated into a coherent philosophy which combined idealist and reformist-socialist elements. Lindsay's ideas became the model upon which Grierson structured his own synthesis of those elements into a relatively coherent ideology.

By 1924 Grierson's ideas consisted of a synthesis of social democratic constitutional reformism, and an idealist philosophy which had been derived from Kant and Bradley, and formulated under Lindsay. This formed the conceptual core of what was later to become his theory of documentary film. In the next chapter I will investigate how these influences shaped the ideas on film and cinema which he developed in America, between 1924 and 1927.

2 John Grierson and the influence of American scientific naturalism 1924–7

In 1924, John Grierson was awarded a research fellowship to undertake social science research in America, and the four years he spent there had a crucial influence on the evolution of his ideas. In America he encountered a number of conservative, often anti-democratic ideologies, which he had to contend with, and which influenced his ideas on political democracy and the documentary film. The influence of these ideologies on Grierson will be the subject of investigation in this chapter.

At the end of the 1922–3 academic session Grierson graduated from Glasgow University with a Master of Arts degree in Moral and Metaphysical Philosophy, with distinctions in English Literature, Italian Language and Literature, and Moral Philosophy.[1] This successful graduation enabled him to obtain a teaching post at the University of Durham. Dr. J. R. Peddie, the Advisor on Studies at Glasgow University, sent Grierson with a recommendation to Dr. J. Y. T. Greig, the Registrar at Armstrong College Newcastle-upon-Tyne, part of Durham University. The Registrar was an ex-Glasgow graduate, and this Glasgow connection, together with references given by Professor R. W. Renwick – who had taught Grierson at Glasgow and then had moved to Armstrong College in 1921 – was instrumental in obtaining an appointment for Grierson as Assistant Registrar at Durham.[2]

In mid-1924 Grierson applied for a Laura Spellman Rockefeller Foundation fellowship to undertake social science research in the United States. The Foundation had a British selection board, whose Chairman was Sir Geoffrey Young of Cambridge University. One of the prominent figures serving on this board was Sir Theodore Morison, who was also the Principal of Armstrong College. At the end of June 1924 Grierson was awarded a fellowship to study 'Immigration and its effects upon the social problems of the United states'.[3] His fare to, and tuition in, America were covered, and he was awarded a stipend of 1,800 dollars.[4]

Grierson arrived in America in 1924, and his first place of study was the University of Chicago, where, from November 1924 to June 1925, he was tutored by Professors Merriam and Park. During this period he modified his subject of study to include research on 'Public opinion, social psychology and newspaper psychology.'[5] This enabled him to travel around America investigating the editorial and reporting practices of local and national newspapers. He stayed in New York from July to October 1925, and then, from October, travelled to over twenty-five different cities, before returning to New York. He finally left America, for Britain, on 31 January 1927.[6]

Grierson was one of the first overseas students to win a fellowship to undertake research in America. This was a 'pretty privileged thing at the time,'[7] and it seems incongruous that he, a graduate in speculative philosophy from a university well known for its emphasis on speculative idealist philosophy, should be awarded a scholarship to undertake quantitative empirical research at Chicago University: then the centre of quantitative methodological research in America.[8] However, although Grierson studied speculative idealist philosophy at Glasgow, an analysis of Glasgow University Library records reveals that he had also read American pragmatist authors such as James, Dewey, Ellwood, and others.[9] He had also been influenced by the pragmatist idealism contained in Bertrand Russell's *Principles of Social Reconstruction* (1916) and *Roads to Freedom* (1918), and by the pragmatist-influenced teachings of A. D. Lindsay.[10] He was, therefore, familiar with American pragmatist ideas to some extent, and had some awareness of contemporary American social theory.

Grierson applied for and was awarded a scholarship in a subject not of his choosing, and in a discipline with which he was unfamiliar, because he wanted to expand his experience by travelling abroad. This was a feature of the Scottish academic tradition, and Grierson was encouraged to travel by his friends, teachers, and family.[11] At university he had gained a knowledge of modern art through an American magazine called *The Dial*, and had argued that, whilst Russia was the home of political revolutionaries, America was the home of aesthetic revolutionaries.[12] He was drawn to Chicago in particular, because of the influential cultural figures who lived in the city then. These included: Vachel Lindsay, an author, poet, and troubadour; E. E. Cummings, a writer and poet; Sherwood Anderson, a novelist and essayist; Carl Sandburg, a poet and critic; Upton Sinclair, a writer and social reformer; and Frank Lloyd Wright, the architect.[13] He was also drawn to the 'maelstrom of Chicago'[14] because of the 'social reality of the immigrant melting pot there,'[15] and because social change appeared to be occurring there at a rapid pace. From his familiarity with idealist and pragmatist ideas he derived the notion that each new age produced its own forms and values, and he saw America, and Chicago in particular, as representative of the new age.

Given the above, Grierson's application for a Rockefeller scholarship becomes understandable. What was less understandable was the Rockefeller Foundation's acceptance of Grierson – a student who had no experience of the positivist methodology which the Foundation funded and promoted. Part of the answer lies in the role played by the Rockefeller Foundation, and the University of Chicago, within an intellectual movement which attempted to redefine key aspects of American life.

The intellectual discipline within which Grierson found himself in Chicago, was dominated by four central influences: empiricism, positivism, hegelianism, and social-darwinism.[16] The empiricist heritage emphasized the belief that particular, rather than general phenomena, should be the object of study. It also emphasised the notion that the individual's knowledge of the external world was subjective, by virtue of its dependence on sense data, and that objectivity was an unattainable ideal.[17] However, although these two principal foundations of empiricist ideology significantly influenced twentieth-century American intellectual discourses, a third foundational concept of eighteenth-century empiricism – that the world was a fixed and immutable system[18] – had no comparable influence. This lack of influence was in turn influenced by the dominance of idealist and social darwinist theories of evolution, which held that reality was dynamic and mutable.[19] However, the dominant academic discourse which influenced the intellectual tradition within which Grierson found himself, was positivism: the theory that the natural sciences provided the methodological basis for academic research, including that undertaken in non-scientific fields, and that all social phenomena could be subjected to scientifically established invariable laws.[20] The positivist ideologies which emerged in America after 1900 deprioritized disciplines which did not conform to the imperatives of scientific methodology, reinforced the particularist and nominalist trends inherited from empiricism, and questioned the validity of speculative value judgements.[21]

These four major influences on American thought produced a shared body of assumptions which was positivist and particularist, which emphasized the concrete and the practical, which stressed the mutability of social reality, focussed on group conflict and the 'survival of the fittest' as the generative motors of social change, and emphasized the effects of a theory, rather than any intrinsic truth which it might contain.[22] When this body of assumptions was applied to the new social sciences of sociology and psychology, the effect was to produce disciplines which were empiricist, quantitative, and positivist. This effect was reinforced by the use of the 'correspondence theory of truth', which was based on the premiss that an idea was true, not if it reflected the reality of its object, but if it produced useful results.[23] All of this turned social science away from speculative generalization, and towards empirical descriptions of material processes. This in turn led to the exclusion of certain moral and political questions on the grounds that those questions were outside the province of the social scientist; (who was only concerned with the scientific analysis of observable, quantifiable data).

The positivist and social-darwinist basis of this discourse emphasized the natural superiority of educated thought, and the inevitability of social inequality. These ideas became integrated into a critique of democratic theory, and academics such as William Sumner argued that scientific method had exposed major weaknesses in traditional conceptions of democracy.[24] Two of the most important weaknesses which Sumner felt had been exposed concerned beliefs in the rationality of human behaviour and the practical possibilities of popular government.[25] The belief in egalitarian democracy was also criticized by political scientists such as Merriam and Lasswell, who lectured to Grierson at Chicago, and who argued that a central reality of society was the ability of small groups to dominate and control the majority of the population.[26] These arguments led to the development of a political science which interpreted political events in terms of the struggle between influential groups, and which restricted analysis to an account of the tactics employed by those groups.[27] The underlying assumption behind this political science was that the community of equally franchised democratic citizens was an unattainable myth.[28]

This underlying assumption was also reinforced by the emergence of a sceptical attitude to the belief in the rationality of human behaviour. This scepticism was influenced by events during the First World War, when propaganda revealed the extent to which manipulative procedures could be employed by dominant social groups,[29] and when empirical intelligence testing on recruits revealed that 70 per cent were of 'low intelligence'. Many concluded from this that the tests proved the irrationality of democracy as a form of government. The influx to America in the 1920s of European psychological theories, by Freud, Piaget, Jung, and Janet, which deployed concepts of the unconscious and the irrational, further reinforced this sceptical view of human rationality.[30]

As psychology developed in America, the theory which quickly became dominant was behaviourism. The problem for American positivists interested in psychology, was how to construct a positivist psychology. Their answer was to construct a psychology which examined objectively verifiable data, and which excluded notions of 'consciousness' from its terms of reference.[31] Behaviourists argued that man was an organism reacting to an environment. Consciousness, and the mental, were reduced to specific types of response to an object or environment.[32] The origins of this materialist psychology lay in the physiological psychology of Pavlov, and particularly in his principle of the conditioned reflex:

Given a reflex according to which a stimulus B produces a reaction
C, and given that a certain animal has frequently experienced a

stimulus A at the same time as B, stimulus A will produce the reaction C even when B is absent.[33]

Pavlov's theory was repeatedly echoed in behaviourist literature. 'The behaviour of all individuals and groups must be considered as a mechanically formulable resultant of the stimulus response cycle.'[34]

The behaviourist postulate of man as a mindless automaton, reacting blindly to manipulative stimuli, reinforced the positivist and social-darwinist conviction that democratic government was undesirable. Combined with positivist sociology and political science, behaviourism formed part of a broad based anti-democratic discourse. One of the most significant factors responsible for the growth of this discourse was the expansion in size and influence of the American lower-classes. Although one-man one-vote had existed in America before it existed in Britain, genuine democratic government, in which the lower classes had a significant say in the process of government, had been an ideal rather than a reality. However, between 1820 and 1930, 37,000,000 people, mainly from southern Europe, emigrated to America, and during the early 1900s the American labour movement began to organize more effectively.[35]

This newly expanded lower class threatened middle-class control of the political process, and sought, in some instances, to actualize the democratic ideals enshrined within the American constitution. It was against this context that anti-democratic theories began to appear. Many of these anti-democratic theories were connected to big business, and functioned ideologically on behalf of corporate interests, in stressing the need for an efficient, modern society, in which elites governed the majority.[36]

One of the most influential anti-democratic theorists of the period was Walter Lippmann. Lippmann drew on positivist and behaviourist assumptions to argue that the form of cognition common to the mass public was based on generalized subjective judgement, and that, because of this, it was inferior to rational and scientific modes of cognition, which were based on objective empirical analysis.[37] He argued that the public relied on sources of inadequate information, rather than on direct personal experience of social issues and events. From these inadequate sources the public constructed a 'mental image' or 'pseudo-environment', from which 'fictions' emerged, which determined ideas and actions.[38] Lippmann also believed that democracy was intrinsically flawed because it did not conform to the imperatives of the scientific method, and argued that 'nowhere is the idyllic theory of democracy realised.'[39] In *Public Opinion* (1922), he argued that there was some hope for an elite-controlled democratic system, but no hope for any kind of mass democratic system. However, in *The Phantom Public* (1925), he argued that there should be no popular involvement in government at all, and that democracy should be abandoned.[40]

John Dewey argued that Lippmann's work constituted 'perhaps the most effective indictment of democracy as currently practiced ever penned.'[41] Yet Lippmann's work was not original, but was, on the contrary, derived from the pragmatist, particularist, positivist, and social-darwinist thinking of James, Dewey, Peirce, Sumner, and others.[42] Nevertheless, Lippmann was an influential and prominent spokesman for a cultural movement which was often virulently anti-democratic, authoritarian and racist. Harold Lasswell, whom Lippmann quoted frequently, and from whom most of the ideas in *Public Opinion* were derived, argued that political protest was often a symbol of individual psychological disturbance 'a hatred of the father projected on to a hatred of the state.'[43] Other theorists echoed Lasswell, who lectured to Grierson at Chicago, in arguing that individuals with 'non-consensual opinions' were in fact mentally ill.[44] Others also argued that scientific tests should be applied to distinguish between capable and less capable citizens; the object being to arrive at a limited disenfranchisment, probably along racial lines.[45] In 1935, the President of the American Political Science Association argued that: 'The ignorant, the uninformed, and the anti-social. . . should be excluded from the franchise, and government controlled by. . . an aristocracy of intellect and character.'[46] This summed up Lippmann's ideology at the time, and a wide gulf existed between that ideology and Grierson's idealist, social-democratic constitutionalism.[47] This was made clear at the time by Grierson: 'I met Lippmann, who is the high priest in public opinion hereabouts, we disagreed a whole lot about it. And I never thought much of Lippmann to begin with.'[48]

The 'objectivist'[49] discourse within which Lippmann and others operated was often sponsored and funded by private corporate institutions such as the Rockefeller, Guggenheim and Carnegie institutes.[50] These institutions, which were all connected to big business, were instrumental in encouraging the use of positivist methodology in the social sciences,[51] and, by 1927, had given 8,000,000 dollars to social science research.[52] The Laura Spellman Rockefeller Foundation, which funded Grierson's research programme, was, like the other foundations, committed to a policy of funding research which was objectivist and non-political:

> The Spellman Fund has no political objectives, it is interested in helping only to provide experience and wisdom in executing public programmes which have already been adopted, and which are no longer matters of political controversy.[53]

But despite this claim of political neutrality, the Spellman Fund did have political objectives. Their argument that they encouraged objective empirical research, rather than subjective political opinion, was the same as that used by objectivists and positivists as a means of disregarding the reactionary implications of their research. The Spellman Fund's claim that they avoided 'matters of political controversy' was disingenuous: in reality, they were happy to work within an academic status quo in which positivism had become the dominant discourse.

Although Grierson was sponsored by the Spellman Fund, his research was tutored at the University of Chicago.[54] By the early twenties the University of Chicago had emerged as the leading centre of sociological research in America, and also employed some of the most prominent academics in the country. Lasswell, Merriam, Park, and White all taught there, and Merriam and White – whose *New Aspects of Politics* served as a manifesto of objectivist methodology in the discipline – supervised Grierson's research project.[55]

In 1923, White, Merriam, Lasswell, Park, and others, collaborated with Beardsley Ruml, the Director of the Spellman Fund, to initiate a sociological project to investigate aspects of social behaviour in Chicago. The group sponsored a variety of research projects into social processes, ranging from population movements, to the formation of political factions. The objective was to turn Chicago into a 'social laboratory' in which causal factors and empirical results were scientifically scrutinized,[56] and in which 'facts could be built up fact by fact like a brick wall.'[57] Not all of this scholarship was based on positivist, objectivist methodology. Chicago sociology also had a progressive aspect, derived from the muck-raking tradition of yellow journalism, and from studies of the underlife of a large, ethnic city. However, it was the objectivist aspect of the Chicago School which influenced Grierson.

The Chicago Project drew in scholars from overseas, as well as from America. It had a British selection board, on which sat the Principal of Armstrong College, where Grierson worked as Assistant Registrar, and it was this selection board which awarded Grierson his scholarship to research into 'Immigration and its effects upon the social conditions of the United States'.[58] The subject matter reflected the interests of conservative positivism in America, and Grierson was probably expected to produce a 'scientific analysis' of the ways in which immigration was exposing the inadequacies of traditional democratic concepts.

As I have argued, Grierson could not have identified with the aims of such a project. By 1924 his ideas consisted of a combination of idealism and social-democratic reformism, which fully accepted the democratic franchise as an essential element of western societies. However, he was influenced by certain aspects of this American objectivist discourse. He had been familiar with the writings of Dewey, James, and other American pragmatist theorists since his university days,[59] and was particularly influenced by the pragmatist distinction between knowledge which did and did not lead to useful results.[60] This distinction provided the model for his own distinction between 'judgements of knowledge' and 'judgements in purpose' – the latter being the superior form of judgement.[61] He also absorbed Lippmann and Lasswell's thesis that the citizen was incapable of comprehending a complex variety of social data, and argued that education should teach a knowledge of the factors which generated change, rather than 'teach man to know everything about everything all the time.'[62]

Although there is evidence that Grierson was influenced by pragmatist theory, there is no evidence that he ever identified with the more extreme forms of positivist ideology then current in America. In fact, he was opposed to the 'empirical approach':

> There were the universities and the begoggled academics. I expected them and survived them, and left them as gracefully as I could a long time ago. They completed my education in filing systems and called it sociology and the empirical method. I sat quiet for perhaps a couple of months. Gave birth to a little filing system of my own to show how humble I was.[63]

Far from being associated with Lippmann's reactionary elitism, Grierson was closer to more liberal strands of objectivist thought then current in America. These liberal objectivist theories had their source in anxieties concerning the effects of corporate capitalism and 'mass society' on the liberal middle classes, the traditional guardians of national values.[64] The writings of Dewey, James, Ellwood, and others reflected these anxieties concerning the status of the middle classes, against a context of rapid economic and social change.[65] The expansion of corporate capitalism threatened to turn many self-employed middle-class citizens into wage labourers, whilst the growth of working-class power threatened middle-class interests in numerous ways.[66] Consequently, writers such as Dewey sought a middle way between elitist and democratic development.

Dewey criticized corporate expansion, but at the same time, he rejected the socialist analysis that capitalist society was an arena of class conflict, and he also regarded socialism as a 'theology'.[67] He argued that society consisted of a plurality of interest groups, and that the function of the State was to arbitrate between conflicts of interest. This arbitration was to be achieved through use of the scientific method and 'intelligent co-operation between social elements so that scientifically guided action could replace class conflict.'[68] Scientifically guided action was to be developed by an elite of social scientists and legislators, whose brief was to resolve conflict between immutable habits, and mutable social forces.[69] This argument was identical to that expressed by Grierson in his 1922 essay, and reveals the influence of Dewey.[70] Dewey's definition of knowledge as a minor form of experience,[71] also paralleled Grierson's notion of the 'little thinking man' as an abstraction from the 'whole man',[72] and his distinction between abstract and pragmatic judgement was also paralleled by Grierson's distinction between 'judgements in knowledge' and 'judgements in purpose'.[73] Finally, like Dewey, Grierson was also concerned with the need to preserve the role of the liberal middle-class intelligentsia against a context of the growth of corporate capitalism and mass society.

However, although Grierson identified with some aspects of Dewey's thought, he also disagreed with others. One such was Dewey's instrumentalist theory of truth, which was based on a positivist redefinition of science as method and process. This redefinition emphasized the efficiency and practicability of theories, rather than any inherent 'truth' which they might contain. Dewey also defined the moral as 'intelligent conduct', and equated the moral with the efficient and the pragmatic.[74] He believed that there were no sacrosanct ethical truths, and that the individual should surrender 'political and moral dogmas' to the test of consequence and verification.[75] Grierson's ideas at the time were far removed from these notions. He believed, contrary to Dewey, that there were sacrosanct ethical truths, and that moral imperatives transcended the imperatives of efficiency and pragmatism.

Contrary to common misconception, Grierson's views were not close to those of Lippmann. They were closer to those of Dewey, and even closer to those of writers such as C. A. Ellwood. Although there is no record of Grierson having met Ellwood, he must have been familiar with Ellwood's writings and reputation, and an analysis of Ellwood's ideas provides helpful insights into the ways in which American pragmatism and positivism influenced Grierson's ideas at the time.

C. A. Ellwood was a devout Christian, opposed to behaviourist sociology, who argued that positivist social science had destroyed religious belief without providing a suitable substitute.[76] He argued that the nature of human society made a qualitative, rather than quantitative approach to the understanding of social problems necessary. He was part of a movement dedicated to turning the social sciences back from positivism and towards speculative philosophy, and argued that metaphysics had a role to play in the construction of a scientific ethics.[77] However, Ellwood also believed that quantitative methods could be used to interpret social problems, and argued for a theory of historical evolution, based not on social-darwinist premiss, but on ideas drawn from Dewey's instrumentalism, and from other pragmatist sources.[78] He believed that customs and habits must be negated by the inevitability of change, but he rejected Spengler's assertion that all civilizations had a definite life cycle, and were faced with eventual decline.[79] He also argued that religion provided civilization with a morale, with which to halt the process of decline by negating the corrupting effects of 'luxury and self-indulgence', and that socio-cultural institutions could perfect themselves as they evolved through time.[80]

It was Ellwood's ideology, and not that of Lippmann, which was closest to Grierson's at the time. Grierson was also a devout Christian, opposed to positivist sociology, and he too believed that science threatened religious belief without providing an adequate alternative.[81] He also believed that religion provided civilization with a 'morale' which could combat 'over-sophistication and self-indulgence,'[82] and that metaphysical and ethical questions could not be reduced to instances of material processes. He agreed with Ellwood's belief in the inevitability of change, and in the ability of civilization to stave off the cyclical decline predicted by Spengler. Finally, like Ellwood, he was influenced by Dewey's instrumentalism, by pragmatist ideas in general, and by a belief in the value of quantitative and scientific method in interpreting socio-cultural issues.[83]

Despite his involvement with Lippmann, Lasswell, and the Rockefeller Institute, Grierson did not identify with the anti-democratic ideas promoted by many American academics at the time. He rejected the argument for an elite leadership as a replacement for universal franchise, and argued instead that the 'technocrats and managerialists' were under an obligation to explain how their prescriptions differed 'from those of fascism'.[84] He also rejected ideas which he described as 'the intellectuals case against the people', because they failed to address the central problem of the age: that of creating a 'mature citizenry.'[85]

However, Grierson did absorb some of those ideas, and his writings reveal a scepticism regarding the practical possibilities of popular-based democratic government. He described the belief in democratic equality as 'romantic and impracticable,'[86] and stated that egalitarianism was 'an anarchic and dangerous doctrine... (which)... threatens the disciplines of a community.'[87] In a 1922 essay he set out two different definitions of popular sovereignty:

> only the right of the people to choose whom they will serve, and on the other hand, it may imply the right of the people to perpetual control of government and involve such extreme things as universal suffrage and absolute freedom of speech.[88]

It is evident that his sympathies lay with the first, rather than the second definition.

This scepticism regarding the practical possibilities of popular-based democratic government originated from two sources. The first, was the middle-class liberal idealism inherited from his father, the ILP, Bradley, Lindsay and James. The most important formulation of this was Lindsay's integration of bradleyan idealism and social-democratic constitutionalism into a conception of democracy as 'minority consensus'.[89] The second source of Grierson's scepticism was the American positivist and pragmatist criticism of a key postulate of democratic theory: that of the 'rational citizen.' Academics such as Lippmann, Sumner, Lasswell, and Merriam argued that the 'average citizen' had an inadequate grasp of the facts, and should not, therefore, play a role in the process of government. Grierson was influenced by this argument, and it led him to reject the 'nineteenth-century liberal ideal of education', which rested on the postulate of the rational citizen, and to argue that the average citizen had to be addressed using non-rational means.[90] This in turn led him to argue for a distinction between a 'rational' and a 'mature' citizenry.[91] A mature citizenry could be created by informing people about the significant generative forces in society, and this could only be achieved through the development of a mass communications practice which could function at an intuitive and non-intellectual level. These ideas were primarily derived from Bradley and Lindsay, but they were also predicated on a positivist belief in the irrationality of the average person.

It is clear, therefore, that although Grierson found himself in an intellectual context which was often dominated by conservative and anti-democratic ideologies, he consciously distanced himself from these ideologies, and associated himself with more liberal pragmatist and positivist ideologies. His ideas at the time were much closer to those of Ellwood and Dewey than they ever were to the ideas of Lippmann and Lasswell. However, he *was* significantly influenced by the fashionable belief that society must be governed and guided by elites, and this belief can be found in many of his writings, from the twenties to his final years. This belief had a formative influence in shaping his views on democracy, and on the role of the mass media within democratic societies. It also had a formative influence on his aesthetic of film, and it is to an analysis of that aesthetic that this investigation will now turn.

Although Grierson is best known for his theory of documentary film, that theory was in fact derived from an earlier theory of 'epic cinema', which was primarily concerned with feature-length fiction films. That theory has since become largely forgotten, yet an analysis of it, and of the evolution of Grierson's ideas between 1924 and 1927, reveals all the basic themes and ideas which reappeared in his later theory of documentary film. It is therefore important to understand the evolution of Grierson's ideas over this period, and to reconstruct his forgotten theory of epic cinema.

Grierson's Rockefeller research led him to conclude that the best way of resolving the social problems caused by immigration was through the use of forms of mass communication which were accessible to the immigrant population.[1] This led him to examine the methods of the popular press. The Rockefeller research fellows were encouraged to travel, and Grierson needed little persuasion, given his disapproval of the positivist sociology practised at the University of Chicago. He spent from July to October in New York, and then travelled back to Chicago in November, passing through New England, Albany, Buffalo, Toronto, Toledo, Cleveland, and Ohio en-route. At each place he stopped to talk to local newspapermen in order to examine editorial and reporting practices. Between December 1925 and July 1926 he travelled to a further nineteen cities, before returning to New York.[2]

During his visits to newspaper offices Grierson frequently contributed articles, some of which were published. The most important of these were a series of articles on modern painting written for the *Chicago Evening Post* between 1925 and 1926.[3] In the early twenties Grierson was as interested in the arts as he was in politics and education. His 'principal guide' to modernist aesthetic theory was an American journal called *The Dial*, and he regarded America as 'the great homeland of aesthetic revolutionaries in our time.'[4] He claimed he had 'elected for Chicago', but he had little choice in the matter, as the academic project which the Rockefeller Foundation was sponsoring was based at Chicago University. Nevertheless, he quickly immersed himself in the artistic and cultural life of the city, and made influential contacts in the process. One of these was Samuel Putnam, the art critic of the *Chicago Evening Post*, who invited him to write a series of articles on modern art for his newspaper.[5] These articles were significant because they illuminated the continuity and development of Grierson's ideas, and showed how the primarily visual aesthetic which he had derived from Kant, Bradley and Lindsay, constituted the foundations of his ideas on cinema and documentary film.

In these articles Grierson made a distinction between aesthetic representation of the 'phenomenal' and the 'real' world.[6] This distinction was derived from three idealist sources: Kant's distinction between 'noumena' and 'phenomena', Bradley's distinction between 'the Absolute' and the 'phenomenal world', and Hegel's distinction between the 'spirit of the age' and the flux of transient events.[7] Grierson argued that the purpose of art was to represent the real world, and not the 'bank holiday of frenzied events.'[8] According to him, aesthetic representation of the real occurred when two important aspects of the human condition were represented: the 'essence of the age', and a canon of immutable ethical values. So, by the term 'the real', Grierson did not mean the material or the physical, but a complex of generative historical forces (both concrete and abstract), and a universal morality.

In these articles Grierson defined the ethical values which he declared to be immutable as 'strength, simplicity, energy, directness, hardness, decency, courage, duty, upstanding power.'[9] At the same time he also defined a canon of negative ethical values, such as 'sophistication, senti-mentality, lounge-lizards, excessive sexuality, homosexuality, nostalgia, bohemianism, status-seeking and social climbing.'[10] This grouping of positive and negative ethical values was influenced by his Scottish presbyterian upbringing. It was a stoic and masculine set of values, in which qualities normally regarded as 'feminine' were given a negative status.

In addition to these immutable ethical values, the other aesthetic prerequisite for representation of the real was the 'spirit of the age'. By this Grierson meant the underlying historical forces which determined the empirical. He believed that the central characteristic of contemporary culture was 'the feeling for movement and change which is the only verifiable distinction which our twentieth century possesses,'[11] and he also argued that the 'power and energy' of modern life, in a world of 'turbines and dynamos', constituted the spirit of the age.[12] Grierson believed that if art represented these contemporary phenomena, it would then take on a contemporary significance, and would escape the insignificant 'ivory tower of art for art's sake.'[13] However, the contemporary phenomena which Grierson argued art should represent was of a general and abstract kind: that which related to the human condition, rather than to concrete political, social, and class conditions. He did not believe that art should represent specific concrete phenomena, the 'frenzy of events', but that it should represent the 'essence and spirit of things.'[14]

Grierson argued that the act of aesthetic judgement, or experience, occurred when the spectator intuitively comprehended the 'spirit of the painting.'[15] That spirit was manifested through the 'significant form' of the painting: that form which expressed (Grierson's) canon of positive immutable ethical values. The spectator comprehended the spirit of the painting, through the painting's significant form, by converting the canon of ethical values which it connoted, into an abstract 'personality complex':

> the spectator comes to know the painting as he would a close friend; after it has been lived with, suddenly, as when fire leaps up and light kindles, . . . one can only understand pictures as one can people, by entering into comradeship with them.[16]

Grierson's use of the term 'spirit of the painting' was clearly a reformulation of his belief in the existence of an immutable pantheon of positive values. The spirit of the painting was an individualized configuration of that canon. Grierson argued that the spectator's contemplation of a painting was dictated by an intrinsic desire to perceive that configuration as an expression of the mind of the artist 'we go to paint because there are great men behind it. That, I feel, is very near the heart of the matter.'[17] A painting, he argued, was significant, inasmuch as it provided the spectator access to the mind of its creator, and inasmuch as its creator's mind embodied those values which Grierson held to be particularly significant.

Grierson believed that the best artists were those who expressed these values. He described Gauguin, Cézanne, Matisse and Van Gogh as 'simple and hard'[18] artists who expressed with 'emotional impact', a 'vision which registers itself back into life with the intensity of revelation.'[19] He also argued that those painters who did not reflect his ethical discourse were of lesser value. He referred to the impressionists, who 'beguiled and titillated'; to Oscar Wilde, who justified 'dirt' (homosexuality); and to Whistler and Walter Pater, who produced 'emotionally shallow works', and whose doctrine of art for art's sake 'was a doctrine of personal impotence.'[20] These painters produced paintings for a privileged elite, and their work was, according to Grierson, of little social value.

This distinction between the positive and negative social function of art, also provided the basis for the distinction which Grierson made between the major and the minor arts. He believed that the true social function of great art was to express cultural values which then became integrated into the value system of the spectator.[21] However, the minor arts and 'mere crafts' were unable to penetrate beneath the level of superficial events, because they did not express significant values, or represent the 'spirit of the age'.[22] This meant that the minor arts and crafts were unable to play a significant role in integrating the spectator within a system of socio-cultural values. On the contrary, they could actually delude the spectator by propagating a superficial – and therefore false – ideology.

Despite his repeated emphasis on the need for representation of positive values, Grierson also contended that the social function of art would be best fulfilled if it reflected negative, as well as positive aspects of contemporary life. However, he believed that positive representation should always dominate negative representation. This argument revealed his aesthetic to be instrumentalist and prescriptive, rather than strictly realist.[23] Grierson also argued that a central characteristic of the modern age, was a continuous process of change and experimentation, and that this had both negative and positive aspects.[24] On the one hand, it resulted in reform, but on the other hand, it could result in 'anarchy and dangerous egalitarianism.'[25] Although he admired the energy and 'full-bloodedness' of contemporary life, he regarded the tendency, particularly in the arts, towards continuous experimentation, with apprehension.[26] He described this tendency as 'self indulgent license', and believed that experimentation with the formal language of art should only be practised in order to establish the 'significant form' which that language should use. Once that significant form had been established, it should be consolidated, and experimentation should cease.

This was the basis of Grierson's criticism of Picasso, whom he called the 'everlasting experimenter'. It was also the basis of his criticism of modernism: 'And the more obstreperous friends of modern art have never made it quite clear where this flip flap of morning papers and pajama patches ended and where art began.'[27] However, Grierson did treat one modernist movement, the vorticist movement, with unqualified approval. Vorticism was an English avant-garde movement, based on Italian and Russian Futurism, whose most influential practitioner was the English artist Wyndham Lewis. Lewis and the vorticists developed an aesthetic based upon a perception of the world as dominated by machinery 'we considered the world of machinery as real to us, or more so, as nature's forms.'[28] Grierson felt that the American version of vorticism upheld correct ethical values, that it had 'upstanding power and expressive simplicity', and that it accurately represented the spirit of the age:

> They have caught something of the power and energy of modern life and wanted to express it. They have wanted to tear away the confusions, see through the details to the essentials, and make an art a little worthy of turbines and machines.[29]

In retrospect, it seems odd that Grierson should have eulogized a minor and short-lived artistic movement like Vorticism so uncritically. The vorticist painter Rudolph Weisenborn, whom Grierson acclaimed most frequently, has now faded into total obscurity. The masculine dynamic, and purposive style of Vorticism did correspond to Grierson's views at the time, but it is unlikely that he would have acclaimed the movement as he did, had he not built up a close friendship with Weisenborn.[30] Weisenborn's influence on Grierson has probably been underestimated. Grierson claimed that Weisenborn taught him much: Weisenborn was 'excited by the thing in itself . . . by the images of action everywhere. . . . the effects of light on the new materials. . . . The concrete and the glass and the aluminum and the steel and the synthetic materials.'[31]

Grierson believed that Vorticism was part of the 'solid body of understanding and progress which only a fool would fail to see in modern painting.'[32] He also argued that excesses had been perpetrated in the name of art, and that, in order to avoid those excesses in the future, art should communicate to a 'larger public', which would exercise restraint upon 'bohemian excess'.[33] However, Grierson did not believe that art should communicate to the general public, but to a minority public of social scientists and academics who searched for fundamental truths by different means: 'It does not matter if the strange result is a formula in X's and Y's and a far away theory of relativity, or, on the other hand, the impossible proportions of an eastern design.'[34] The fundamental truths which were sought by these different means were those underlying historical forces which shaped contemporary events:

> Modern logic and modern philosophy, modern psychology and modern political science, they too are vorticist. They have all registered the same element of the living and growing element in things. The art that is really modern is doing nothing very original, nothing that has not been sensed by thousands of people in their own fields of endeavour. It merely expresses the mental feeling of the time and there is no great mystery about it.[35]

Grierson believed that these thousands of social scientists and academics could exercise a moderating influence on artistic excess, by helping artists to consolidate the 'significant form' which best expressed the 'mental feeling of the time': 'Only the long attention of ordinary people with level heads will clear from modern art the over-enthusiastic and quite uncritical fog which surrounds it.'[36] These 'ordinary people' – social scientists and academics – understood the 'vorticistic' nature of contemporary intellectual disciplines, and could play a part in consolidating artistic practices by communicating that understanding to artists.

Grierson also rejected the idea that modern art could be made accessible to the masses, because he believed that art could only ever have a minority appeal. His arguments in this respect were mainly derived from Lippmann and Lasswell's belief that the masses were incapable of sustained rational thought.[37] Even though Grierson believed that the act of aesthetic judgement was an intuitive, rather than a rational act, he did not believe that the public – whose general mode of cognition was 'intuitive' – could grasp the aesthetic significance of modern painting.

This scepticism regarding the ability of the public to comprehend modern artistic forms was derived from his belief that the public could only respond to a language of forms which was familiar and conventional. This belief was, in turn, derived from his belief that the lower-class and middle-class public 'thought' in different ways, and from his belief that the masses could not play any significant role in the process of government.[38]

Many of these ideas were influenced by the American pragmatist and positivist criticism of traditional democratic theory and practice, and they reveal the extent to which Grierson was influenced by that criticism. Although his argument that the masses would find few points of appeal in modern painting has a basis in common sense, it was also based upon the explicitly stated premiss that the masses thought 'or something'[39] differently from the way in which the middle classes and intellectuals thought. This premiss, which was restated in the distinction which he made between a 'rational' and 'mature' citizenry,[40] has clear anti-democratic implications. It was because of his wish to steer clear of these implications, that Grierson placed such an emphasis on the value of intuitive knowledge, and of a mature – if not rational – citizenry.[41]

Although Grierson's writings on modern art were of secondary importance in relation to his Rockefeller research on the problems of immigration, they did help to shape that research, and to influence his writings on the cinema, and it is to an analysis of those writings that this investigation will now turn.

Grierson's theory of epic cinema.

As already mentioned, Grierson's investigations into the immigration problem led him to conclude that the most effective means of integrating immigrant communities, was through an understanding and command of the popular mass media. Consequently, he altered the terms of his research project to accommodate an investigation into the reporting and editorial practices of the 'yellow press'.

The yellow press emerged from the social changes which affected American society during the first decades of the twentieth century. During this period large numbers of immigrants from southern Europe arrived in America, until, by 1910, 40 per cent of the population of New York was of recent immigrant status.[42] At the same time, the native white American population also expanded. For example, the new lower-middle class of clerical and office workers grew from 756,000 in 1870, to over 5,000,000 in 1910.[43] Big business also expanded, until, by 1900, the American economy was virtually dominated by corporate monopoly capital. By 1904 1 per cent of American companies produced 38 per cent of manufactured goods,[44] and the largest corporation, US Steel, incorporated over 158 smaller companies.[45] This process of rapid corporate expansion and monopoly control led to the formation of anti-trust pressure groups, organized across a broad class spectrum, and this in turn led to the appearance of the 'yellow press', which focussed on issues of corporate corruption.[46] This new popular press was able to communicate to the recently expanded population because of the introduction of new printing technology, which enabled newspaper output to be increased.

One of the most influential of these crusading popular journals was the *New York World*. This newspaper had been bought by Joseph Pulitzer in 1883, and had been immediately targeted at two social groups in particular, both of whom were in search of status and identity: the recently arrived immigrant working class, and the upwardly-mobile suburban lower-middle class. The *New York World* employed a story-based reporting style, rather than an information-based style, and focussed on issues of crime, scandal, and sensationalism, in order to foster a petit-bourgeois sensibility dominated by consumer status values.[47] The style and politics of the paper contrasted starkly with established newspapers such as the *New York Times*, which employed an information-based reporting practice, and was targeted at the middle and upper-middle classes. The *New York Times* supported corporate and monopoly expansion, and often criticized the *New York World*'s anti-corporatist and sensationalist style.[48] Nevertheless, the *New York World* eventually became one of the most widely read newspapers in America, and its sensationalist approach influenced many other journals.

In July 1925, Grierson went to New York in order to study the reporting and editorial practices of the *New York World*, and other journals of the yellow press.[49] He also wanted to meet Walter Lippmann, who was then editor of the *New York World*, and whose book *Public Opinion* (1922) had made him, as Grierson put it, 'a high priest'[50] of public opinion. Grierson wanted to discover the 'deeper principles beneath the sensationalising' of news in popular journalism.[51] However, at a meeting with Lippmann which had originally been arranged to discuss questions relating to popular journalism, Lippmann argued that Grierson's research would be more productively directed at investigating popular cinema:

It was Mr Lippmann himself who turned this educational research into the direction of film. I talked to him one day about the labour involved in following the development of the yellow press through the evanescent drama of local politics. He mentioned we would do better to follow the dramatic patterns of the film through the changing character of our times, and that the box office records of success and failure were on file. I took his advice and a young man called Walter Wanger opened up the necessary files. A purely educational theory became thereby a theory involving the direct use of films. That directive use was based on two essential factors: the observation of the ordinary or the actual, and the discovery within the actual of the patterns which gave it significance for civic education.[52]

Although Grierson disagreed with Lippmann's anti-democratic views, he found his advice to investigate cinema 'very very helpful,'[53] and, over a period of time, switched his attention from the press to cinema.

From late 1925 to mid 1926, Grierson travelled around America visiting local newspapers and developing his interest in the cinema.[54] In Denver he contacted Ben Lindsay, a veteran judge of the juvenile court, who had expressed concern in public about the relationship between films and juvenile delinquency.[55] Lindsay was one of many at the time who wished to place constraints upon the rapidly increasing influence of the cinema. The origins of cinema as a working-class and *lumpen* form of entertainment had always led some middle-class opinion leaders to view it with apprehension, and, after the First World War, the media increasingly depicted Hollywood as a kind of modern Babylon. A movement of patriotic and women's societies, with membership in the tens of millions, mounted vigorous campaigns for movie censorship, and eventually forced the film industry to organise its own regulatory body.[56] This was the Motion Pictures Producers and Distributors of America (MPPDA), which was otherwise known as the Hays Office, and was formed in 1922 in response to threats of external censorship.[57] However, despite the establishment of the Hays Office, belief in the negative influence of cinema still existed in 1925-6, and Lindsay's concern with the relationship between juvenile delinquency and film must be viewed in that context.

After meeting Lindsay, Grierson wrote an article on the subject of juvenile delinquency and the cinema entitled *Flaming Youth of North America*.[58] This paper, which is now lost, received a favourable reception within the film industry. A copy was passed to Jesse Lasky, head of film production at the Zukor-Lasky Famous Players Lasky Corporation.[59] Zukor had been one of the main forces behind the formation of the MPPDA in 1922, and Famous Players Lasky also kept detailed box office and audience reaction data. There were two main reasons why these records were kept. Between 1919 and 1927 Zukor had attempted to gain virtual control of the American film industry, to the extent that, in 1927, Famous Players Lasky was found guilty of breaking anti-trust laws by the Federal Trades Commission.[60] Through employing virtually all the top movie names of the time – including Mary Pickford, Gloria Swanson, Douglas Fairbanks, D. W. Griffiths, C. B. DeMille, and Mack Sennett –

Zukor ensured that Famous Players Lasky was the most successful film corporation of the period. However, in 1919, his attempt to take over First National, which employed Charlie Chaplin, failed, and, later that year, Pickford, Fairbanks and Griffith left Famous Players Lasky in order to form United Artists with Chaplin.[61] Against this background of increased competition, Zukor found it necessary to keep detailed records of box office returns and audience tastes.

The other main reason why these records were compiled was that, after 1922, the system of production whereby a superstar dominated each major film began to decline. Soon, films made by well known directors, without major movie stars, were making more money than films made by Fairbanks or Pickford. As a result, film producers began to search for new and more sophisticated, formulae for film production. Cecil B. DeMille, who worked for Famous Players Lasky, succeeded with a formula based on high society costume dramas, which functioned as a showcase for consumer goods, and for clothes in particular.[62] The emergence of these new types of film, and the decline of the older models, stimulated Famous Players Lasky to keep detailed box office and audience response records, in order to keep track of the audiences' growing sophistication.

Walter Lippmann knew of Famous Players Lasky's box office records, and may have been instrumental in passing Grierson's article on juvenile delinquency and the cinema to Jesse Lasky.[63] Lasky then sent a copy of the article to Walter Wanger, his general production manager at Hollywood. During the First World War, Wanger had worked on propaganda production at the American Embassy in Rome, under C. E. Merriam, who later taught Grierson at Chicago.[64] Wanger was also a close friend of William Randolph Hearst, whose journalism Grierson so admired, and was also regarded as a 'liberal intellectual' within the film industry.[65] At Famous Players Lasky, he was instrumental in raising the technical and 'artistic' level of production, through his policy of hiring top professionals from the fields of fashion, design, photography, and literature.[66]

When these correspondences of outlook and experience between Wanger and Grierson are taken into account, and when Famous Players Lasky's need to use their box office data to determine future production policy is also considered, it is not surprising that Grierson – the student of Merriam and disciple of Hearst – should be invited to Hollywood by Lasky in order to draw conclusions from the company's audience response data. Although Grierson later tried to portray Wanger's invitation as purely altruistic, Wanger and Lasky expected practical results from Grierson's investigations, as Grierson soon began to realise:

I got in with the Famous Players people and cornered their audience reaction files. Travelled from Keokuk to Kanka-Kee and back again with all the Swansons and Dixies on the inventory. But for my side of the bargain I found myself lecturing to the managers on how to swindle the public and to movie actresses on the psychology of stardom, with grave interludes on the mythology of the process and other nonsense. That wasn't so good. Heavy American headlines that describe you as a 'celebrated English showman' who has just been instructing managers on 'how to haul the coin to the bank' play hell with the respectabilities of 61 Broadway.[67]

Nevertheless, Grierson was able to draw on his Famous Player Lasky research for a series of seven important articles published in *Motion Picture News*, between 20 November and 18 December 1926. In these articles, Grierson expressed his ideas on how the cinema should develop into a socially purposive medium. The articles dealt with four areas: the 'crisis' in the film industry, and the need to develop new types of film to meet that crisis; definition of these new types of film, and of the thematic material they should contain; the development of cinema technique and craftsmanship in order to express that thematic material to best advantage; and the obstacles which prevented the construction of this new cinema and means by which those obstacles might be overcome.

Grierson argued that the cinema's nature as a popular medium entailed a curtailment of tendencies towards experimentation, in order not to alienate the public. He also argued that, because the cinema had gained a degree of maturity, it was better placed to 'realise how great is its destiny in the modern world.'[68] Grierson felt that some Hollywood films, such as *The Big Parade* (1925), *Ben Hur* (1926), *The Gold Rush* (1925), and *Beau Geste* (1926), had 'that extra quality in them of inspiration, of power, which separates a special picture from an ordinary one.'[69] But he also felt that most Hollywood films were sub-standard, because they contained stereotyped, one-dimensional characters, and because they allowed 'hokum' and 'sentimentality' to erode the 'dignity of noble themes.'[70]

In his *Chicago Evening Post* articles on modern art, Grierson argued that paintings did not reproduce the real, but articulated it, through a manipulation of the intrinsic properties of the medium. In the *Motion Picture News* articles on cinema he also argued that film was not an intrinsically mimetic medium, but one which articulated its immanent properties in order to convey an illusory impression of mimesis:

Visual storytelling... involves a manipulation of character and acting and stage as in legitimate drama, it involves a manipulation of visual composition as in painting... it involves a manipulation of tempo as in music;... it involves a manipulation of visual suggestion and visual metaphor as in poetry. Beyond all that it involves a manipulation of such effects as are peculiar to itself. This includes (under camera) the manipulation of dissolves, double exposures, trick shots etc., etc.; (under continuity) the manipulation of long shots, close ups, medium shots, truck shots and so on, and of recurring visual themes as in music.[71]

All these processes, if cinema is being handled properly, ought to be utilised in the deliberate and coherent manipulation of the spectator's emotions.[72]

Grierson believed in the existence of an underlying reality of generative forces, which shaped empirical reality. It was this belief which caused him to reject the idea of film as mimesis. If film could reproduce empirical reality, then it could not, at the same time, reproduce underlying reality. But Grierson also believed that film could not reproduce empirical reality either, because it was fundamentally different from the empirical world which it represented. He believed that the cinema articulated contemporary reality through material aesthetic processes intrinsic to itself, and he rejected the view, which was prevalent at the time, that cinema could reproduce external reality. Grierson's film aesthetic was, therefore, fundamentally different from later cine-verite aesthetics which argued that film could reproduce the real.[73]

Grierson also believed that some cinematic processes were more important than others, and that the most important one was narrative construction:

So the first point about visual composition is that, unless it is complementary to the spirit of the action and at all times subservient to it, it is a dangerous affair to play with and is very likely to spoil things. . . . First and last, the composition must help the story, the story is paramount.[74]

This belief was drawn from Grierson's experiences of the popular press, and from Lippmann's critique of 'liberal education'. Lippmann argued that traditional liberal educational and democratic theory was inadequate, because the public could not absorb all the facts of a complex modern world. However, Grierson believed that the Hearst press and the movies filled this 'gap in educational theory in a practical way', by using techniques of persuasion to reduce the inaccessible multiplicity of facts to accessible 'dramatic patterns'.[75]

The most important of these techniques of persuasion was dramatic narrative, but Grierson also believed that 'the dramatic' was a fundamental characteristic of reality itself. Reality evolved constantly 'a world on the move, a world going places,'[76] within an endless process of growth and decay which revealed the 'dramatic nature of the actual.'[77] The dramatic patterns used by the mass media were, therefore, an ideal means of representing the dramatic processes which generated change and development within society.

Grierson argued that the dramatic narratives employed by the popular press and the movies fulfilled an important socio-cultural function because they represented a system of values with which the spectator could identify. This process of identification occurred as a consequence of the spectator's identification with the central characters within the diegesis. Grierson argued that people needed to escape temporarily from everyday reality into a more fulfilling reality, in which they could imaginatively experience dramatic events, and identify with fictional heroes.[78] The basis of this imaginative experience was the spectator's 'suspension of disbelief' in the unreality of the fictional world represented. But whether or not the spectator was able to suspend his or her disbelief depended on the efficacy of the illusion presented, and Grierson argued that the cinematic processes from which the film was constructed must reinforce that efficacy. Although he recognised that film interpreted reality, and was not mimesis, he did not believe that the average spectator should share that recognition, and believed that a convincing illusion of reality was essential in order to make the narrative as powerful as possible.[79]

Grierson's main criticism of the German cinema was that, in many German films, cinematic processes worked to weaken this illusion of diegetic reality:

> The Germans, on the other hand, have tended to studio mania, and they have become theatrical in the bad sense of the word. . . the dramatic atmosphere of the sets was so deliberate, and the visual composition so conscious, that the action was overshadowed and lost.[80]

In contrast, he pointed to American films such as *The Covered Wagon* (1923), and *The Big Parade* (1925), which, although 'carefully composed', also looked 'natural', and therefore enabled the spectator to suspend his or her disbelief in the unreality of their fictional diegesis. Grierson attributed the use of naturalist representation in these films to two factors. German films, such as *The Last Laugh* (1924) revealed a knowledge of film aesthetics which Grierson believed had not yet been attained in the American film industry, and, in fact, he believed that the success of the American films was due to their 'very ignorance of aesthetic matters.'[81] This lack of knowledge had led to the production of less technically sophisticated films than had been made in Germany, and this had in turn encouraged the trend towards more naturalist film production. But Grierson also believed that American films were more closely in tune with the wishes and aspirations of the public than were German films, and he argued that this led to the production of naturalistic films, because of the public's psychological and sociological need for naturalism:

> The American feeling for the open air and for action, and the hatred at the box office for things artificial and introspective and morbid, have combined to lead the American tradition of cinema aright. Pictures like *The Covered Wagon, The Vanishing American, The Iron Horse, The Big Parade, What Price Glory*, etc., etc., and cinematic stars like Fairbanks, Pickford, Swanson, Vidor, Adoree, Dix, Colman, Mclaren, etc., indicate its essential rightness. Even the Russians, who might be expected to approach cinema with the same preoccupations as the Germans, have been very conscious of the superior naturalness of American cinema, and their latest efforts (if rather more intense) are in the American manner.[82]

Grierson argued that the American cinema was naturalist because the American public wanted a naturalistic cinema, whilst the German cinema was expressionist because it was made for the German intelligentsia, and was alienated from the German public.[83] He believed that expressionism was a product of the alienated relations which existed in Germany between the intelligentsia and the public; alienated relations which were in turn the product of alienated social and cultural conditions in post-war Germany. In contrast, he believed that social and cultural conditions in America were becoming increasingly harmonious and integrated, and that this was reflected in the adoption of a naturalist style of film-making.

The argument that, when an artist becomes alienated from society, artistic production ceases to fulfil any useful social function, was identical to an earlier argument expressed by Grierson in a 1922 essay entitled, *Byron and his Age*:

> Byron is the reflection of his own age's dissonance. . . he is the poet of those who protest rather than the poet of those who with a clear vision before them seek to mould life in its image.[84]

> The earlier period is essentially an era of dramatic unities and disciplined forms generally and it is full because society which it reflects is whole. When that wholeness passes we find the harnessed couplet of Pope passing into thinness and futility and the first signs of the spirit of Romanticism. . . in this sense Romanticism is always the sign of disease and it is a disease of individual dreams and chaotic longings because first and foremost it is a disease of the body politic.[85]

These arguments were derived from the Marxist thesis that, in periods of class conflict, artists become alienated from society, and artistic production becomes decadent. In *The Formalist School of Poetry and*

Marxism (1920), Leon Trotsky criticized the Russian Futurist and Formalist movements, by accusing them of an 'abortive idealism' through the elevation of form over social content. He argued that this distortion of aesthetic priorities reflected the Formalists' alienation from the real needs of society.[86] In an article entitled *On Art for Art's Sake*, Georgei Plekhanov, leader of the Menshevik section of the Russian Communist Party, asserted that 'the belief in art for art's sake arises wherever the artist is out of harmony with his social environment.'[87] Plekhanov argued that the nineteenth-century Romantics were opposed to the bourgeois establishment, but had no contact with the proletariat, and so rejected the concept of a 'socially useful art'. This argument was virtually identical to Grierson's assertion that Byron and the Romantics were rebels without a cause.

Grierson was 'an admirer of Lenin and Trotsky'[88] and had read both these and other Russian communists whilst at university. Plekhanov was also well known in Britain at the time. Some of his writings had been translated and published by the Social Democratic Federation, who were based around Glasgow; and it seems likely that Grierson would have had access to essays such as *On Art For Art's Sake*, or *On the Social Basis of Style*, whilst he attended Glasgow University.[89]

In addition to his influence by the Marxist critique of formalism, Grierson was also influenced by the Marxist theory of critical and social realism. This theory argued that, besides truth of detail, it was important to represent typical characters under typical circumstances, in order to represent as full an account as possible of individual and social relationships. This was close to Grierson's model of an epic-naturalist cinema, which represented the interaction of social and individual forces.

Grierson was initially drawn to Marxist theory because many of its most fundamental premises were drawn from hegelian idealism. The extent of the idealist influence can be seen in the way in which he ascribed terminology normally used to diagnose the condition of a biological entity, to an institutional structure of social relations and practices. This tendency to personify material social relations and practices, was typical of hegelian epistemological methodology. Grierson ascribed the healthiness of the American cinema to the intrinsic vitality of the American world view, which, according to him, emphasized qualities such as 'optimism', 'sunshine and achievement', 'youth', 'enthusiasm', and 'light and open air'.[90] On the other hand, he ascribed the deterioration of the German cinema to the moral atrophy of the German world view, which emphasized qualities such as 'pessimism', 'failure', 'drabness of scene', 'tragedy and despair', and 'psychological obsessions'.[91]

In ascribing the difference between the American and German cinemas to a difference between optimistic/healthy and pessimistic/unhealthy cultures, Grierson ignored the influence which more material and concrete factors had in determining that difference. The historical causal forces which he believed caused historical difference, bore no relation to the industrial, institutional, social, and economic determinants which ensured and maintained the ascendancy of the American cinema. A central characteristic of idealist theory was its tendency to attribute causal determination to mental phenomena, and to subordinate the status of material phenomena as a causal agency. Grierson's arguments were fundamentally idealist, in that they mobilized mental categories such as 'national pessimism' and 'national optimism' to explain differences between America and Germany, and in that they neglected to take account of more concrete causal factors.[92]

The dominance of the American cinema was founded, not on any representation of 'immutable fundamental needs',[93] but on the extensive size of the American market, which enabled film producers and investors to undercut foreign competition.[94] American films were able to cover their costs in America, and overseas sales counted as profits. As a result, American film costs for overseas distribution and exhibition were reduced to the point where they undercut other national film industries, and this eventually led to the predominance of American films in those industries.[95]

The dominance of the American cinema during this period was a good example of a central characteristic of corporate capitalist societies, i.e., that a dominant corporate capitalist economy will subjugate lesser economies and relocate them within economic practices and relations, which ultimately benefit the interests of the dominant economy.[96] Grierson's lack of awareness that this, and the other social and economic factors mentioned above, played an important role in enabling the American film industry to dominate other film industries, reveals the extent to which idealist epistemological premises influenced his ideas on cinema, and distorted his understanding of historical determination.

That distortion was also apparent in his analysis of the origins of changes which occurred in film formats. He attributed the appearance of films such as *The Covered Wagon* (1923) and *The Big Parade* (1925) to the cinema's 'realisation of its destiny in the modern world.'[97] Again, we see the attribution of an abstract ahistorical personification, rather than an understanding of the social, economic, institutional and cultural determinants which influenced the production of these, and other films. The changes in production methods in the mid-twenties, which resulted in the making of films such as those mentioned above, were the product of increased competition within the industry, and of the decline of the star system.[98] Technological innovations, new labour relations practices, and external political forces also played a role in the development of these 'special feature' films.[99] Despite this, Grierson attributed the development of the special feature film to abstract, unverifiable causes only.[100]

Idealist preconceptions also shaped Grierson's understanding of the yellow press. He argued that the dramatized reportage style of the Hearst press fulfilled a human need for dramatic forms which operated within a didactic framework.[101] The epistemological basis of this argument was influenced by the platonist theory of ideas: that ideas and truths were abstract entities which possessed an independent existence.[102] This argument influenced Grierson when he asserted that 'the dramatic' was an abstract ideal, which individual dramatic assemblages should correspond to.[103] It was significant that Grierson did not find a contemporary representation of the 'dramatic ideal' in the contemporary theatre, but in the yellow press and the cinema.

Grierson hardly, if ever, referred to the material forces which contributed to the success of the yellow press. The fact is that the yellow press expanded, not because of the need to fulfil a platonist 'idea' but because of the expansion of the mass market in general in America.[104] A central driving force in capitalist development is that, when markets become over-produced, capital seeks to expand into new markets, in order to protect profit margins.[105] American newspapers were particularly susceptible to the imperatives of continuous market expansion because of their reliance on advertising revenue.[106] Other factors which also contributed towards the expansion of the yellow press, were the growth of the population through immigration, and the development of new printing technology. Grierson seems to have been unaware that these factors, and not some abstract 'dramatic ideal', were primarily responsible for the expansion of the yellow press.

Grierson also failed to situate the yellow press within its principal context: the growth of corporate capitalism in America.[107] Corporate capitalism, with its twin creations of organized capital and organized labour, was perceived as a threat to traditional middle-class political, economic, and cultural hegemony. The lower-middle class felt threatened by corporate capitalism, and newspapers such as Hearst's *New York World* fed on that fear. Grierson seems to have been largely oblivious to this anti-capitalist, petit-bourgeois aspect of the yellow press. He spoke about it in terms of its 'democratic value', and not in terms of its very real hostility to big business. All of this shows the extent to which idealism influenced, and distorted, Grierson's understanding of contemporary society.

Although Grierson argued for a naturalist cinema, he also argued that it was necessary to develop sophisticated cinematic techniques, in order to construct an effective naturalist cinema. His study of the formal language of cinema was influenced by the work of Eisenstein, Flaherty, D. W. Griffith, the American western, the German cinema, and Chaplin.

One of the strongest of these influences was that of Eisenstein, whose film *Battleship Potemkin* reached American cinemas in 1926.

However, prior to the screening of *Potemkin*, Grierson had seen two other Soviet films in America. These were *The Peasant Woman of Ryassan* (1920) and *Polikushka* (1920). *Polikushka* was the first film made by the Artistic Collective of Russ, a film co-operative set up by Anatoly Lunacharsky, the People's Commissar for Education in Russia. It was an adaptation of a short story by Tolstoy,[108] and Grierson described it as the first 'proletarian movie' shown in America.[109]

But by far the most important Soviet influence on Grierson during this period was Sergei Eisenstein's *Battleship Potemkin* (1926). This film had originally been intended to be the first in a series of films planned to commemorate the 1905 Revolution, in which Tzarism was partially replaced by democratic institutions.[110] On 19 March 1925, Eisenstein was appointed director of the film, and, on 21 December, *Battleship Potemkin* was given its première at the Bolshoi Theatre.[111] However, the Soviet authorities at Goskino were initially hostile to the film, and relegated it to second rank exhibition theatres only. It was only after the intervention of the poet Vladimir Mayakovsky that the film was given a foreign première, which eventually took place in Berlin, on 29 April 1926.[112] Although hampered by German censorship, *Potemkin* was successful in Germany, where it ran for over a year in Berlin alone. German intellectuals such as Ernst Toller, Max Rheinhardt, Asta Nielsen, and Egon Erwin Kisch praised *Potemkin* highly, whilst Douglas Fairbanks described his viewing of the film in Berlin as 'the most intense and profoundest experience of my life.'[113]

Fairbanks, who was then under contract to Famous Players Lasky, went on to Moscow in July 1926, where he negotiated with Goskino for a print of *Potemkin*.[114] When the print eventually arrived in America, Grierson, and Jack Cohen – the film critic of the *New York Sun* – were engaged to edit the film's titles. At that time little was known of the Russian cinema in America, and, therefore, it was not surprising that Famous Players Lasky assigned the task of preparing the film's titles to one of the few people working for them who knew anything about the Russian cinema, i.e., Grierson. Along with Cohen, Grierson prepared the English titles for *Potemkin*, and in the process came to know the film 'foot by foot and cut by cut.'[115]

Grierson was influenced by *Potemkin*, particularly with respect to three crucial aspects of the film. The first of these was the film's command of montage and visual orchestration. Grierson claimed that Eisenstein was 'the best visual composer of the day',[116] and, in an article published in *Motion Picture News* entitled 'Putting Punch in a Picture', he attempted an analysis of *Potemkin* in terms of its manipulation of dramatic tempo and visual composition. He concluded that *Potemkin*, by its use of intrinsically cinematic technique, had significantly advanced knowledge of tempo, montage, and composition in the cinema.[117] He described the montage sequences in the Odessa Steps sequence of *Potemkin* in terms of their contrast, association, mass, tempo, and movement, and this was a significant achievement given that, by 1926, no substantial analysis of Eisenstein's methods in *Potemkin* had yet been undertaken in the West. When he wrote that Eisenstein could 'explode several details into an idea,'[118] he also revealed an intuitive understanding of a fundamental aspect of Eisenstein's methodology: his conception of montage as the juxtaposition of two elements, in a dialectic which resulted in the production of a third:

> montage as a collision. A view that from the collision of two given factors arises a concept.[119]

> The foundation for this philosophy is a dynamic conception of things. Being as a constant evolution from the interaction of two contradictory opposites. Synthesis arising from the opposition between thesis and antithesis.[120]

The classic example of this form of dialectical montage was the sequence of shots of marble lions (a lion sleeping, a lion waking, and a lion rearing up), which – when juxtaposed – gave the impression of a single lion rearing up in fury at the massacre which had taken place on the Odessa Steps.[121] Although Grierson did not refer directly to this classic sequence, his frequent references to Eisenstein's use of 'symbolic counterpoint' in *Potemkin*, shows that he had a good understanding of the underlying principles of dialectical montage.[122]

A second aspect of *Potemkin* which influenced Grierson, was the amount of naturalist representation in the film. The film celebrated the mutiny of sailors aboard the *Potemkin*, on the Black Sea in 1905. To this end, a considerable amount of research into press and documentary records took place, and the entire film was shot on location in Odessa and Sevastapol, aboard the *Twelve Apostles*: the ship used as the *Potemkin* in the film. Few professional actors were employed in the film, and most of the cast were recruited from the streets of Odessa.[123]

Grierson believed that the cinema possessed an intrinsic capacity for naturalist representation, and argued that the best films were those which realized that capacity, whilst the worst were those which subordinated it to theatricality and artificiality. This was the basis of the distinction which he drew between the 'unhealthy studio mania' of the German cinema, and the healthy open-air cinema of the Soviet and American cinemas.[124] Grierson also argued that no actor or studio setting could recreate the existential intricacy of 'real' people or 'real' land-scapes. He believed that that existential complexity could only be represented through shooting on location, and by using amateur actors whenever possible, in order to represent 'the poetry which exists in the natural.'[125] It was because of this belief in the inability of the actor to recreate 'real people', that Grierson argued that the actor should attempt to represent a 'mythological', rather than psychological human reality.[126] He believed that such a simple and universalist acting style could operate in harmony with naturalist representation.

A third important feature of *Potemkin* which influenced Grierson, was the film's social comment. Grierson argued that Eisenstein, and the other Soviet film-makers, had 'made society on the move the subject matter of art,'[127] and he contrasted this with the lack of social comment in the American cinema.

But although Grierson was strongly influenced by certain aspects of *Potemkin*, he was also critical of other aspects. He felt that in countering the individualistic obsession of the American cinema, *Potemkin* displayed an equivalent obsession with collective realities, and also minimised the importance of individual realities.[128] He disliked the film's overt politicism, and felt that 'the Bolshevik ideal' had blinded the Russians to personal themes.[129] He argued that the type of film represented by *Potemkin* could not be successful in the 'individualistic culture of America,'[130] and criticized Eisenstein's obsession with the 'mass in war', rather than with 'the mass in peace'.[131] Finally, Grierson did not believe that Eisenstein had constructed a model which could usefully dramatize peace-time social relations,[132] and he also believed that *Potemkin* was too 'formalist' to be accessible to a mass audience.[133]

It is clear, therefore, that although *Potemkin* undoubtedly had a major influence on Grierson, he held strong reservations about the film, from as early as 1926. It was not the case, as previous critics have claimed, that he was overwhelmed by the film.

Grierson's account of *Potemkin*, and the Soviet cinema, was also distorted by the same idealist world-view which distorted his understanding of the American cinema and the yellow press. This idealist world-view led him to interpret the Soviet films in terms of the immutable ethical themes, which he thought they contained. For example, in 1929, when he had left America, he described Dovzhenko's *Earth* (1929) as 'Not necessarily socialist. . . outside the realm of politics. . . simple, timeless.'[134] He also described the representation of peasant communities in *Earth* in the following terms: ' There is not an element of them all that those who know the villages – here or anywhere – will not recognise as a simple and ancient truth is recognised: with a somewhat strangling recollection of beauty.'[135] *Earth* did have a mystical and pantheistic dimension, and, consequently, was strongly criticized within the Soviet Union. Outside the Soviet Union, that same dimension was interpreted, mistakenly, as the film's central message:

> Without, that same passionate love of man and all nature was mis-understood, and applauded, as a sign of indifference towards the contemporary struggle or the standards of the artist's socialist homeland, a sign that he was not 'engagé'. Nothing could have been more false. This artist was the most 'engagé' of all the talents in all Soviet art.[136]

In fact, *Earth* was committed quite openly to the socialist struggle. The plot of the film covered the murder of a village chairman, who had attempted to modernize and collectivize the agricultural production of the village.[137] The film was produced against the background of the campaign against the kulaks, which began in May 1928, as part of Stalin's policy of the collectivization of agriculture. By 1930, half of Soviet agricultural production came from collective farms, yet substantial resistance to collectivization still remained.[138] It was this problem which Dovzhenko addressed in *Earth*, within a format which portrayed the death of a village chairman as a sacrifice essential for social renewal: 'Pantheism? No. Nature worship? Not at all. Sound Marxist dialectics: the union of opposites.'[139]

Grierson was one of the foreign critics who misunderstood *Earth*. His idealist world-view led him to attribute qualities to this and other Soviet films, which the Soviet film-makers themselves would have rejected. This places the value of Grierson's account of the early Soviet cinema in question. However, there is no such dispute over the value of his persistence in promoting Soviet films in the West, even though his claim to have 'set the fashion for its [*Potemkin*'s] reception by the English speaking critics,'[140] was exaggerated. Grierson supported the Soviet films in the face of powerful and hostile political forces, which usually regarded them as intrinsically subversive. He also criticized those who, like Douglas Fairbanks, gave in to this political pressure. After bringing *Potemkin* to America in 1926, Fairbanks found it expedient to distance himself from the film.[141] Grierson also played a pioneering part when he analysed the formal and methodological structures of *Potemkin*, and he was instrumental in integrating the ideas and methods of the Soviet cinema into the independent film sector in England during the 1930s. Despite his limited understanding of the Soviet cinema, he played a significant part in promoting and supporting it in the West.

The other major influence on Grierson's ideas on cinema during this period was Robert Flaherty. Flaherty (1884-1951), began his adult career as an explorer. Between 1910 and 1921 he led four expeditions into the Hudson Bay area of Canada, in order to map unexplored territory. From

1915 Flaherty adopted the practice of filming the native Eskimo inhabitants of the Hudson Bay area, and with that footage, he persuaded Revillon Frères, the French furriers, to sponsor the production of a film on Eskimo life.[142] That film, *Nanook of the North* (1922), represented events in the life of the Inuit Eskimos. The film was initially rejected by four distribution companies before being accepted for distribution by Pathé, after which, it was a critical and financial success worldwide.[143] Following this success Flaherty was commissioned to make a similar film of ethnic life, this time on a southern pacific island. The resulting film, *Moana* (1926), was commissioned by Famous Players Lasky, and distributed to a select circuit of art-house cinemas in America. However, mounting advertisement costs soon made this strategy untenable, and the film was re-released into general distribution under the new title of *Love Life of a South Sea Siren*. But despite these attempts to make the film more commercially viable, it was a box office failure in America, even though it became a critical and financial success in Europe.[144]

Grierson began working for Famous Players Lasky in 1925, around the time that Flaherty was commissioned to make *Moana*. He had been impressed by *Nanook of the North*, which he felt 'creates suspense, brings excitement and touches those satisfactions which western people can understand.'[145] Along with Walter Wanger and Jesse Lasky, he looked forward with anticipation to the release of *Moana*. Lasky had given Flaherty a *carte blanche* to 'Go anywhere you want in the world. Write your own ticket. All you have to do is bring us back another *Nanook*.'[146] Famous Players Lasky believed that they had discovered a successful formula in *Nanook* and wanted Flaherty to repeat the formula. However, *Moana* had none of *Nanook*'s inherent dramatic content, and its re-release under a title which stressed its non-existent erotic content, emphasized the producers' determination to promote it like the more dramatic *Nanook*.

Grierson's 1926 writings reveal that he was in agreement with Famous Players Lasky over *Moana*. Although he was critical of many aspects of the commercial cinema, his own success at the time was often due to his capacity to convince the film industry that he was a colleague, rather than a critic. As *Motion Picture News* had put it 'MPN is publishing the (Grierson) articles because we believe them to be of a constructive nature.'[147] Grierson believed that *Moana* had no practical or dramatic interest for the average viewer, and that its story was too slight.[148] He believed strongly that in any film, the story should be paramount.[149]

Grierson also argued that *Moana* had 'documentary value', but that this value was secondary to the film's value as a 'poetic statement of natural beauty'.[150] It has been argued that Grierson's use of the term 'documentary' in a 1926 newspaper review was the first time that the term had been used in English – by him or anyone else – to describe a film. However, Grierson did not use the term in the sense that it was later to be used by the documentary film movement. His usage was derived from the word 'documentaire', a term coined by French critics to distinguish serious travel and expedition films from travelogues.[151] The term was also derived from the English term 'document', meaning a body of factual information.[152] Both of these constructions differed significantly from the sense in which the term 'documentary' was used in the 1930s by the documentary film movement, i.e. to describe socially purposive actuality films.

Grierson believed that film possessed a capacity to record ordinary, everyday events and activities, and that human activity and practice was a distillation of generations of learning and experience. The camera, by focussing on, and isolating an individual activity or event, could reveal the inherent quality and complexity of that event:

> But its (the camera's) magic is even more than this. It also lies in the manner of its observation, in the strange innocence which, in a mind-tangled world, it sees things for what they are. . . The camera is, in a measure, both the discoverer of an unknown world, and the re-discoverer of a lost one.[153]

> Nothing in a word is so dramatically powerful for the camera as those characteristic gestures and rhythms of physical expression which long necessity has developed and time worn smooth.[154]

He argued that those 'characteristic gestures and rhythms of expression' were intrinsically dramatic, because they were the product of a struggle over necessity. He believed that the cinematic representation of those rhythms and gestures also captured that 'same struggle over necessity', and was, therefore, both naturalist and dramatic at one and the same time.[155]

An important point for Grierson was that the expressive activities which evolved through the struggle over necessity, and which the camera could record, were social rather than individual; because that struggle was a social, rather than an individual struggle. Although cinematic representation necessarily focussed on an individual activity of expression – as in the fishermen hauling in nets in Grierson's own 1929 film *Drifters* – that representation was essentially social, because the activity represented was 'characteristic' of the skill accumulated by a human community, in its struggle with necessity.[156] It is clear, therefore, that Grierson's conception of naturalism, and of dramatic significance, was essentially social, rather than individualistic in character, and that he was not concerned with individual recordings of events which had no social significance. If the cinematic representation of collective struggle was inherently dramatic, it could also be beautiful, given that dramatic and beautiful qualities often co-existed within the same aesthetic representation, and within the same material object or event. However, the beauty which Grierson saw in Flaherty's *Moana*, was not that of struggle over necessity, but that of 'natural beauty': 'an intense poetic feeling which, in this case, finds an outlet through nature worship.'[157] Although Grierson appreciated that kind of beauty, he believed it was of secondary value compared to the 'beauty of struggle over necessity', because the latter had a greater contemporary social significance.

On the other hand, the beauty which Grierson saw in *Nanook*, was that of social struggle. The narrative of *Nanook* emphasized struggle and hardship, unlike *Moana*, which emphasized peaceful and idyllic qualities. Writing in 1927, the critic Riccioto Canudo described *Nanook* as: 'a tragedy in which, from the beginning to the end, the protagonists remain the Elements pitted against Man with his Needs. It is, quite simply stated, a picture of the eternal struggle of human being.'[158] Grierson believed that such a story had considerable contemporary significance, because it reflected the daily struggle over necessity of the average person:

> Indeed, no matter how strange the setting and how strange the characters, the issue is a primitive issue found in all barbarian states where the struggle for life is constant and arduous: the masses of the western world can share it easily.[159]

So, in addition to its ability to record the social activities of expression which had evolved through struggle over necessity, the camera was also able to show the imperative of personal and collective improvement. Naturalist representation of 'typical' activities of expression contained an intrinsic ethical content, as well as an intrinsic dramatic and aesthetic content.

Given the above, it might seem that *Nanook* was closer to Grierson's ideas at the time than *Potemkin*. However, he had strong reservations about both of these films. He had argued that *Potemkin* did not provide a viable model of popular cinema, because it dwelt on issues of war and revolution 'the mass in war, not the mass in peace.'[160] Similarly, he argued that *Nanook* dwelt on issues which confronted primitive, rather than contemporary man, and that it was more important to investigate 'the jungles of Middlesborough and the Clyde, than the native customs of Tanganyika and Timbuctoo.'[161] Despite this, Flaherty and Eisenstein provided the two most important influences on Grierson's ideas on cinema during this period.[162]

Grierson's writings of the period reveal that, before he formulated his theory of documentary film in the early thirties, he had already formulated a theory of epic cinema. This theory was derived from his conception of the socializing and mediating role which cinema should have within democratic societies. In contrast to Walter Lippmann, who argued that any significant reliance on public opinion and mass communications to determine social policy would fail, Grierson argued that the cinema could play an essential mediating and socializing role. The cinema was: 'the only democratic institution which has ever appeared on a world scale. It is the internationale of sentiment and emotion.'[163] If cinema was to fulfil this role of socialization and mediation it would have to address the 'simple and fundamental dramatic needs of the world crowd'[164] rather than reflect the prejudices of film-makers. Film-makers must understand that 'this world crowd's demand of the cinema is profound, for all its seeming crudeness and simplicity. That way lies the true future of the cinema.'[165] He believed that public demand could be understood through an analysis of cinema box-office records, such as those which Famous Players Lasky had accumulated since the early twenties[166]:

> For years a complete account has been kept of box office records and audience reactions on each picture and every star. Till lately, the system of enquiry had been organized only in the United States, but it will no doubt be gradually extended to include other countries as well. Exhibitors all over the country are required to send in an account of the effect of each picture: whether it 'held up' or whether it 'let down', whether it started that word of mouth advertising which is the magic wand of all cinema miracle, or plainly 'flopped': what was said of the star, and whether, from the new evidence, that entity is waxing or waning, what seems to be expected of the star, what new faces have appealed. The exhibitor's own accounts are taken, and the public's reactions as they are gathered by posted questioners or eavesdroppers at the exits of a thousand and one theatres. Taken over a period of years, on pictures and actors of all sorts, and read against the history of box office fluctuations and rising and falling reputations, these voluminous records take on a certain reasonableness, and become something like a great sociological document. As a guide to certain matters of comparative psychology the evidence is almost unique.[167]

Grierson argued that it was more appropriate to ascertain public demand through these records, than through established liberal criticism, or the prejudices of film-makers:

> But listen to the critics. Hicks they call this world public, lowbrows, cripplewits, sex-seekers. The London *Times* vies with the American *Mercury*, *Harpers* with *Vanity Fair*, to encourage the movie producers to despise their public.[168]

> ... they (the film producers) were often not so much concerned

with making the cinema great as with serving their own private means.[169]

However, despite this prioritization of empirical analysis of box office records over the subjective preconceptions of critics, Grierson imposed his own subjective preconceptions on his study of public opinion:

> [the people want]. . . Elemental non-sophisticated themes, simple, lucid, and pungent themes developed with strength and dignity, elemental non-sophisticated themes of courage, love, sacrifice and achievement, caught in the roar and swing of great settings.[170]

This view of the public psyche was founded on his own subjective preconceptions, and he was convinced that a reading of the Famous Player Lasky box-office records would verify those preconceptions. He did not appear to believe that other readings could produce different, and equally valid, interpretations to his own. But the fact is that, rather than verifying a public demand for 'universal themes', an alternative reading of those records might discover a public demand for the kind of hokum and sentimentality which Grierson so disliked. For example, Cecil B. DeMille used the Famous Player Lasky records to develop a successful film formula based on high society costume dramas.[171] At another level, Grierson's own subjective interpretation of allegedly objective data, reflected the extent to which subjective abstraction informed and conditioned the supposedly objective and 'scientific' methods of American objectivist and positivist theory.[172]

Grierson's interpretation of the Famous Player Lasky records was also conditioned by his conception of the 'average mind.'[173] Although he rejected the more extreme ideas of Lippmann and Merriam, he was influenced by their view that the average citizen was unable to form rational judgements on public events.[174] But, in contrast to Lippmann and Merriam, Grierson believed that social information could be summarized in order to emphasize its most important elements. Because the 'average mind' was 'incurably simple and unsophisticated,'[175] and because it responded to emotion rather than reason, it could only respond to a communications medium which embodied those characteristics.[176] The communications medium which most embodied those characteristics was cinema:

> It is an ideal world for capturing the imaginations of common people. It is visual, it is silent, it is non-intellectual, it can capture the vivid simplicities of romance and adventure as no medium could ever do before. It can idealise, it can mystify.[177]

However, Grierson believed that, before the American cinema could perform such an important sociological function, it would have to be reformed. He believed that this could be accomplished by achieving higher levels of technical competence in the craft of film-making, and by the representation of 'big themes', i.e., universal truths, and important social realities. He argued that the film *Variety* (1925) contained superficial themes, but was successful because of its technical competence; whilst *The Vanishing American* (1925) contained a 'magnificent theme', but was diminished by its sentimentality and poor technique.[178] *Ben Hur* (1924) contained both superficial themes and poor technique; whilst *The Big Parade* (1925) contained 'a clear, simple, universal and dignified theme, and a powerful treatment (technique).'[179] *The Vanishing American* was based on the 'average foundation' of a Zane Gray western story, which Paramount had developed into a 'great story' of the decline of the Red Indians, 'That was noble stuff. There was something of the wilderness of space and the infinity of time written on it, that took one's breath away.'[180] However, Grierson felt that this film had been diminished by the film-maker's insistence on reducing the story into the background for a banal love affair, 'The story ... became like any other story of gentle, gentle heroines, and nasty, nasty villains.'[181] Grierson blamed this on Hollywood's tendency to trivialize important issues. Nevertheless, he was careful not to lay the blame for *The Vanishing American* on the film's producers, who were among his main contacts in Hollywood:

> I don't believe the weakness of *The Vanishing American* was Hollywood's fault. Paramount bought a second-rate story and failed in a brave attempt to turn it into a first-rate story. The element of hokum was there to dog the picture from the start.[182]

This example of disingenuous backtracking illustrates Grierson's willingness to compromise with authority, when necessary. The rest of his writing over this period makes it clear that he did believe that Hollywood was to blame for the poor quality of many American films. Indeed, his criticism of *The Vanishing American* exemplified one of his biggest criticisms of Hollywood: that, in Hollywood films, the social environment was reduced to a backdrop for 'boy-meets-girl scenarios.'[183] This led, in his view, to the trivialization of social representation.

But Grierson also believed that the American cinema contained qualities which could constitute the foundation of a more significant 'epic cinema', and that the intrinsic naturalism of Hollywood westerns and comedies provided an appropriate basis for more sophisticated representations of the social environment.[184] In this respect, he believed that the American cinema was more socially significant than either the German and Russian cinemas.

Grierson believed that a socially relevant epic cinema could be constructed from a synthesis of American naturalist and dramatic method, German technical competence, and Russian knowledge of montage and social representation. This epic cinema would employ 'fundamental and universal themes',[185] an effective populist dramaturgy, and naturalist and collective representations which enabled the spectator to suspend his or her disbelief in the un-reality of the fictional diegesis.[186] Grierson's epic cinema would avoid formalism, over-sophistication, and psychologism, and would emphasize unsophisticated themes, and external social and concrete realities.[187] The function of the film star would also be different in epic cinema. Instead of fulfilling the normal function of sustaining banal stereotypes, the star would fulfil a 'mythological function,'[188] by representing elementary themes and ideas. In addition, the star would also fulfil a sociological function by acting as a role model with which the audience could identify.[189] Another important new function of the star in epic cinema, would be to inject 'human significance' into a story drawn from the contemporary social environment, in order to achieve an improved balance between individual and social representation.[190]

Grierson believed that representation of the social environment should have priority over representations of personal psychology, and that films should represent the inter-relation of the individual and the social. Previous attempts at this type of representation had failed because the social environment had been reduced to a backdrop for 'boy-meets-girl scenarios':

> The scene may be new but it is only included in the sense that it provides a back-drop for the same old story. *Men of Steel* does not mean that the story of steel and the heroes of steel thunder their way across the screen: not a bit of it. *Men of Steel* merely means that another professional hero has melodramatised his way to another professional heroine, with Pittsburgh views in the distance.[191]

But Grierson felt that this habitual under-representation of the social could be rectified:

> I am merely suggesting a change of focus from the point at which people emphasise story sequences and think up environments for them, to the point at which people emphasise the cinematic power that may be taken from environment and think up a story to give human significance to it. I feel that the cart has been put before the horse in cinema, and that the true source of cinema drama (the world of movement and spontaneous behaviour) is not being drawn on as much as it should be.[192]

This model of a populist, naturalist and socially-oriented cinema, which avoided formalism, psychologism and overt political comment, did not correspond to any films being made during the 1920s, including *Battle-ship Potemkin* and *Nanook of the North*. One of the films most often quoted by Grierson as an example of epic cinema was James Cruze's *The Covered Wagon* (1923), a western about the wagon trains which took settlers into the American West during the mid-nineteenth-century. However, although *The Covered Wagon* corresponded more closely to Grierson's model of epic cinema than either *Potemkin* or *Nanook*, it still lacked technical proficiency, and was also, like *Nanook*, set in the pre-industrial past.[193]

Grierson defined films such as *The Covered Wagon* (Cruze, 1923), *The Iron Horse* (John Ford, 1924), and *The Big Parade* (King Vidor, 1925), as epics of 'quality', and he distinguished them from films such as *Ben Hur* (Fred Niblo, 1925), and *The Ten Commandments* (Cecil B. DeMille, 1923), which he defined as epics of 'quantity'.[194] Although *Ben Hur* was a much more expensive film to make than *The Covered Wagon*, Grierson felt that it lacked 'hugeness', and merely consisted of 'a sequence of second-hand gestures and second-hand episodes. . . it was a quantity film.'[195] He also revealed his lifelong concern with religious questions when he objected to DeMille's religious epics, on the grounds that 'the preposterous array of nightgowns wigs and false beards was a travesty of every reality the gospel could possibly intend.'[196]

It is clear, therefore, that no films of the 1924–7 period corresponded exactly to Grierson's conception of epic cinema, and, in fact, the films which he liked most over the longer 1924–39 period were not those most frequently credited with influencing him, ie., *Potemkin*, *Nanook*, and *Berlin* (Ruttmann, 1926).

Three films which did correspond closely to Grierson's model of epic cinema, and which also influenced the later documentary film movement, were: *Storm Over Asia* (Vsevolod Pudovkin, 1928), *Turksib* (Victor Turin, 1929) and *Earth* (Alexander Dovzhenko, 1930).[197] All of these films were made after Grierson had left America for England. However, they must be discussed here because they bear the closest resemblance of any films of the 1924–34 period to Grierson's theory of epic cinema.

Writing in 1930, Grierson described *Earth* as 'one of the greatest films ever made.'[198] *Storm Over Asia* was based on an episode in the Russian Civil War of 1920, when an English army of occupation in Mongolia captured a partisan fighter. Filming took place in Verkhne-Udinske, the capital of the Buriat-Mongolian Republic, and the film used large quantities of documentary footage.[199] The use of naturalism within a social and political context in these two films made a strong impression on Grierson.[200]

However, it was Turin's *Turksib* which made the greatest impression on him. *Turksib* was produced on a low budget for Vostok-Kino, a production company established in 1928 to make films for the eastern republics of the Soviet Union.[201] It was an account of the construction of the Turkistan-Siberian railroad, and represented each stage of that construction, from beginning to final completion. *Turksib* corresponded more closely to Grierson's model of epic cinema than any other film of the 1924-34 period. It was naturalist, dramatic and popular commercially. Above all, it represented the inter-relation of individuals within an important contemporary social institution. The narrative and pictorial content of the film were also organized around a central thematic theme of man's struggle over nature: 'The theme was handled with astonishingly skilful editing, the audience being worked up to an intense emotional crisis by the sheer brilliance of technique. Individual scenes of strong dramatic value abounded in every part.'[202] Writing in 1930, Turin has also commented on *Turksib*:

> From the very outset it is necessary to approach the work of filming *Turksib* not as one would approach a culture film, even in the broadest interpretation which can be given this term, but as a film without actors, demanding no less attention than the making of any story film. If we do it this way we may be sure that our film on the building of the Turkistan-Siberian railroad will not only be useful and cultural, but entertaining and emotional as well.[203]

Turin's intentions, as reported by Valentin Turkin,[204] corresponded closely to Grierson's. *Turksib* was also, in many respects, the precursor of the documentary films which Grierson produced between 1929 and 1939. He believed that it was 'the most influential model of the time for the documentary men outside Russia,'[205]:

> There is, I believe, only Turin and *Turksib* which for all its patches of really bad articulation is the single job which takes us into the future. *Turksib* is an affair of economics, which is the only sort of affair worth one's time and patience.[206]

Although Grierson was strongly influenced by Eisenstein's montage and Flaherty's naturalism, neither of these two film-makers provided the model for either his theory of epic cinema or his theory of documentary cinema. No film produced by Grierson during the 1930s, except Basil Wright's *Song of Ceylon* (1933-4), conformed to the model established by Flaherty, and no film, except possibly Grierson's own *Drifters* (1929), conformed to the model established by Eisenstein. In contrast, Turin's *Turksib* not only provided a model for both the theory of epic cinema, and the theory of documentary cinema, but also provided a bridge between the two theories.

The influence of *Turksib* on Grierson has been underrated, just as the influence of *Potemkin* has been overrated. Writing in 1931 – less than two years after *Potemkin* had received its British première at the Film

Society, on 10 November 1929, Grierson did not even include Eisenstein's film in a list of films in 'the grand tradition of Russian cinema', even though *Storm Over Asia, Earth* and *Turksib* were included.[207]

Grierson also realized that the transformation of popular cinema into epic cinema which he envisaged, could not come about unless the existing institutions of cinema were reformed. He believed that mainstream cinema was characterized by a 'pestiferous individualism', which contributed towards the production of 'stereotyped films'.[208] He also believed that most Hollywood personnel were only interested in personal opportunism.[209] In order to combat this he proposed the creation of a new film academy, which would play a role in the construction of a co-operative film culture, and would conduct its activities within an ideal and spirit of public service. In the *Chicago Evening Post* articles on modern art, he had argued that academic disciplines should be applied to artistic production, and, similarly, when writing on the cinema, he also argued that a 'university of cinema in Hollywood' should be founded: 'in which directors and cameramen and the various experts of the industry could formulate the terms of their work.'[210] Grierson hoped that, by this means, objective academic discipline might regulate the subjective opportunism of Hollywood.

By the term 'university of cinema' Grierson meant a curriculum of seminars, lectures and training sessions, which would be available to the film-making community at Hollywood. He proposed the establishment of a 'cinematic institute', which would protect and develop the interests of the industry as a whole, and he also proposed the inauguration of a journal or monograph which would publish the transactions of that society. This conception of a cinematic society differed from that represented by existing craft based organizations, such as the Society of Motion Picture Engineers; and from that represented by self-congratulatory organizations such as the Academy of Motion Picture Arts and Sciences. Grierson's idea of a cinematic society was more comprehensive. It embodied all branches of the industry, and envisioned a significantly more critical and pedagogic institution than existed at the time. Similarly, his conception of a society monograph, or journal, also differed from existing trade journals, such as *Motion Picture News* and *The Exhibitors Herald*, in that it would fulfil a more critical function than that carried out by those journals.[211]

In addition to the new cinematic institute and the new journal, Grierson also proposed that regular exhibitions of paintings should be held at Hollywood, in order to develop a greater awareness of pictorial composition amongst film-makers. He also proposed that poetry readings and literature classes should be held, in order to develop a greater awareness of 'the poetic', and of linguistic usage.[212]

These proposals for the reconstruction of the American cinema were based around a demand for a co-operative, critical, socially purposive body, which would be grounded in an ideal of public service.[213] This demand was partly derived from the 'scientific' models of social engineering which Grierson encountered at Chicago University, and partly from Walter Lippmann's criticism of existing institutional practices, but it was also derived from a knowledge of the reorganization of the cinema in Soviet Russia, the extent of which was considerable. The cinema and photography industries had been nationalized in 1919 by Lenin, and had been placed under the control of the People's Commissariat of Education, also known as Narkompros.[214] Narkompros was led by two of the most influential Bolsheviks: Anatoly Lunacharsky, the Commissar for Education, and Nadezhda Krupskaya, Lenin's wife.[215] Krupskaya was in charge of the film sub-section of Narkompros, Kinopodotel,[216] and this organization later became the State Film Organization, Goskino. In addition to this, there was also a State Film School, with faculties of Camera, Scenario Writing, Direction, and Film Theory;[217] and various influential cultural groupings, such as The Left Front of the Arts (with journals *Lef* and *Novy Lef*), Proletkult, and the All Union Association of Proletarian Writers.[218]

Although Grierson did not have a complete knowledge of these organizations and institutions, he had sufficient to understand the extent to which the Soviet State had reconstructed its film industry. He was impressed by the high priority given to film in Russia, and by the involvement of top-ranking political figures in cinema affairs. The contrast with the American situation was stark, and although he disagreed with Soviet State control of the Russian film industry, he believed that the Russians had successfully demonstrated the potential which film had as an instrument of social engineering and reform. The Russian example also had a considerable influence on his later ideas on the function of a state funded documentary film movement.

Grierson's Rockefeller Fellowship expired on 26 April 1927, and on 31 January 1927 he sailed from New York to London, having spent twenty-seven months in America. The American visit had been formative, and significant in terms of his future involvement in the cinema. He had arrived in America in order to carry out sociological research into immigration movements, but had left convinced in the belief that the establishment of a socially purposive cinema was an essential prerequisite for the continuation of democracy. Over the next few years, between 1927 and 1934, he attempted to establish a State-sponsored documentary film movement in Britain.

4 John Grierson, the Empire Marketing Board Film Unit, and the documentary film movement 1927–33

By 1927 Grierson had developed a theory of socially purposive film-making, based on the premiss that sectors of the commercial film industry could be persuaded to undertake such production. However, that theory had been developed without reference to the practical difficulties involved in such an undertaking. Between 1927 and 1933, he was given the opportunity to put his ideas into practice, not in the commercial industry, but in a government department. The outcome of this was the documentary film movement.

Grierson left America with a theory of epic feature film cinema, rather than a theory of documentary cinema. But he also left convinced of the inherent tendency of commercial cinema to trivialize important social issues. On the basis of this conviction he concluded that there was greater potential for quality film production through a penetration of the newsreel and actuality markets, which were 'ripe for a takeover.'[1] It was this perception of the practical opportunities presented by the newsreel market which led Grierson to abandon his plans for making epic films, and to adopt a strategy of documentary film production. Nevertheless, the central themes and ideas in the theory of epic cinema reappeared in, and influenced, the theory of documentary cinema, and any attempt to understand the latter without reference to the former would be misconceived.

Whilst in America, Grierson had followed debates on the question of state publicity and propaganda through the pages of *The Times*. It was there that he first learned about the Empire Marketing Board,[2] which, by 1927, had become the largest government publicity organization in Britain.[3] In *The Times* he had read and been influenced by articles by the English poet Robert Nichols, on commercial constraints on the growth of a socially useful cinema.[4] On his return to England, Grierson contacted Nichols, and persuaded him to write a letter of introduction to the Secretary of the Empire Marketing Board, Stephen Tallents. Tallents was impressed by Grierson:

I took to Grierson at first sight. He put his ideas as he has always done, with persuasive conviction. I did not fully grasp their purpose at that moment, but looking back, I can give a clearer account of them than I could have done at the end of that first meeting.[5]

But despite this good impression, Tallents was unable to employ Grierson as Films Officer at the EMB, because he had recently employed Walter Creighton, a friend of Rudyard Kipling and Stanley Baldwin, in that post. Consequently, Grierson remained unemployed, though he was commissioned to write a series of reports for the EMB Film Committee as compensation.[6]

Grierson was attracted to the EMB because it appeared to possess great potential, but, at the same time, he was completely unaware of its equivocal institutional basis and future.[7] The EMB was established as an inferior substitute for tariff reform and protectionist legislation, which successive Conservative and Conservative-dominated coalition governments had been prevented from implementing.[8] After the First World War, many prominent spokesmen had argued that Britain's economic reconstruction depended on the implementation of preferential tariffs, and on the resuscitation of Joseph Chamberlain's pre-war ideas on economic reconstruction within the British Empire.[9] Chamberlain had argued for free trade or imperial preference within the British Empire, and for the establishment of a tariff ring around the Empire. These ideas were picked up again in the 1920s by people such as Harold Macmillan, Robert Boothby, Lord Beaverbrook, Leo Amery, Philip Lloyd-Creame (later Cunliffe-Lister), and others.[10] The Conservative Party under Stanley Baldwin believed that a structure of protectionist legislation, combined with a system of imperial preferences, was the answer. The Party supported the findings of 1923 Imperial Conference which advised that a number of preferential tariffs to the value of 1,000,000 pounds should be established.[11]

Following the defeat of the Conservatives on the tariff reform issue in the 1923 General Election, the Labour Party gained power, and cancelled the preferential tariffs, which had been recommended by the Imperial Economic Conference. When the Conservatives were elected again in October 1924, after the fall of the minority Labour government, they found themselves pledged, unwillingly, against the introduction of protectionist measures, and, consequently, were unable to implement the tariffs recommended by the Imperial Economic Committee.[12] In order to circumvent this proscription, Philip Lloyd-Creame (later Cunliffe-Lister), then President of the Board of Trade, proposed that a direct grant be made to the Board of Trade or Colonial Office, for the purpose of improving facilities for the marketing of imperial produce.[13] Leo Amery, then Secretary of State for the Dominions and Colonies, reluctantly accepted this compromise, and a 1,000,000 pound Empire Marketing Fund was established, which was to be managed by an Empire Marketing Board.[14]

This solution enabled the Baldwin government to appease those who were demanding effective economic action in the Empire. However, from its very inception the EMB was regarded as an inferior and temporary substitute for tariff legislation. Although it received considerable acclaim from many quarters throughout its existence, it had no supporters, apart from Leo Amery, in positions of executive power, and was rendered irrelevant by the introduction of major tariff legislation in 1932 and 1933.[15]

When Grierson joined the EMB in 1927, he believed that he had entered an expanding institution which would enable him to put his ideas on socially useful film production into practice. But in fact he had joined an unstable and ultimately untenable institution which was eventually abolished in 1933.

The equivocal status of the EMB was reflected in its structure. As a departmental advisory committee, it was not accountable to Parliament, and could be abolished by the Secretary of State for the Dominions and Colonies.[16] Its terms of reference were that it should research and advertise Empire products. This involved research into improving the marketing of Empire goods, producing information on markets within the Empire, and publicizing Empire products in Britain. Finance was divided more or less equally between these three areas.' Although the Imperial Economic Committee, which reported again in 1926, had wanted 65 per cent of the EMB's budget spent on publicity, Amery had argued, successfully, that publicity was no substitute for efficient marketing and production.[18] This argument reflected the establishment view that the EMB itself was a poor substitute for tariffs.

The conflicting viewpoints on publicity expressed by the Imperial Economic Conference on the one hand, and by the Board of Trade on the other, were representative of two different and contradictory positions on the question of State publicity. The Imperial Economic Conference believed in the value of promoting a broad 'imperial ideology', whilst the Board of Trade and other government bodies believed that only concrete economic and legislative measures could improve economic performance. This sceptical attitude to the question of State publicity ensured that the EMB's publicity objectives were subordinated to its marketing and research objectives.

This subordination, seen within the context of the EMB's equivocal existence, further illustrates the extent to which Grierson's aspirations for a socially purposive film movement could never have been fully realized at the EMB. Nevertheless, there were some sympathetic individuals at the EMB who aided Grierson whenever possible. The most important of these was Stephen Tallents, who played a considerable role in the development of the documentary film movement.

During the First World War Tallents had worked with William Beveridge at the Ministry of Food on food rationing legislation and publicity.

The legislation broke new ground in that it was the first food rationing scheme ever implemented in Britain.[19] The politically sensitive nature of the Ministry's work meant that good public relations were a priority, and Tallents was influenced by the awareness of public relations methods shown by the Minister, Lord Rhondda, and by the unusual mixture of civil servants, business men, and publicists at the Ministry.[20] The Ministry's use of innovative public relations methods and non-Civil Service personnel influenced Tallents when he was appointed to the EMB in 1926. After leaving the Ministry of Food, he received a number of appointments before being appointed Secretary to the cabinet committee which was set up to deal with the General Strike.[21] He saw Baldwin's effective use of radio propaganda to defeat the strike at first hand,[22] and emerged from that experience as one of the leading government and Civil Service experts on publicity matters.[23]

Stephen Tallents (centre, with wine glass)

Tallents initially established two committees at the EMB: one for marketing and research, and the other for publicity production. The publicity committee consisted of twelve members, but its methods and policies were developed by Tallents, Huxley and three others: William Crawford, Frank MacDougall, and Frank Pick.[24] Tallents persuaded the committee that no suitable model for Empire publicity existed, and that they would have to devise appropriate publicity methods for their new purposes.[25] To facilitate this he employed personnel from industry and the media on temporary Civil Service contracts, until nearly 70 per cent of the EMB's staff were drawn from outside the Civil Service.[26] This arrangement differed radically from the composition of other government departments, and illustrated the extent to which Tallents was prepared to break new ground in order to pursue a suitable publicity strategy. The personnel whom Tallents employed also differed from typical civil servants and advertising people, in that they possessed a wider range of opinions than was the norm. This was true of Tallents himself, who possessed an extensive knowledge of the arts, and a 'catholicity of interests.'[27]

Although it is true to a degree that Tallents was the main driving force and inspiration behind the innovative publicity methods for which the EMB later became renowned, he also surrounded himself with individuals who believed similarly in the need to develop new strategies of State publicity production. In addition, many of his ideas were derived from his experience of State public relations and publicity methods at the Ministry of Food, and from contemporary debates on the need for an effective government information service. Tallents' achievement lay, therefore, not in the origination of embryonic publicity ideas, but in the establishment of a channel through which ideas already in circulation could find expression.

The most important of these ideas, and one fundamental to the publicity ideology of the EMB, was a belief in the value of generalized, as opposed to narrowly targeted, publicity. The intention was to construct a broad discourse of imperialist ideology which would cement the Empire together, and challenge the growing influence of socialist ideology:

> What we wanted to sell was the idea of the Empire as a co-operative venture between living persons interested in each other's work, and in each other's welfare. Our task was, not to glorify the power of the Empire but to make it live as a society for mutual help, a picture of vivid human interest, as well as of practical promise.[28]

This preference for a generalized publicity policy was partly influenced by a requirement to avoid publicizing the particular products of particular companies. In a period when State control of industry was unfashionable, such an operation would have been open to the charge of government interference in commercial activity by aiding one producer at the expense of others. However, although this was a significant factor in shaping the EMB's policy of generalized publicity production, even more important were contemporary currents of thought on the need to construct a broad ideological discourse for purposes of national and imperial unity. These were reinforced by the sentiments expressed in the Balfour Declaration of 1926, which defined relations between Great Britain and the Dominions as that between 'autonomous communities. . . united by a common allegiance. . . and freely associated.'[29] The EMB believed that the best way of establishing a common allegiance through publicity was by shaping a common consciousness through a broad-based publicity policy.

The Publicity Committee believed that existing commercial advertising methods and agencies would be unsuitable for realizing these objectives, because of the predominant belief in the advertising industry that only narrowly targeted, short term publicity, could achieve concrete results.[30] Tallents believed that the EMB must produce its own publicity, and also commission work which it thought appropriate. This, inevitably, antagonized some sectors of the commercial advertising industry, who also disagreed with the EMB's position on generalized publicity: 'Advertising in the commercial sense, advertising to gain and hold markets, must be in the highest degree specific.'[31]

Despite this, the idea of broad-based publicity did have a historical legacy within British publicity production. Middle-class opinion had often been hostile to commercial advertising because it contradicted liberal principles concerning objectivity and impartiality. As a response to this hostility, some advertisers brought out publicity which was less overtly biased, and was aimed at improving the general image of the manufacturer concerned.[32] The appearance of this form of advertising was also influenced by industrial over-production and market saturation, which forced advertisers and producers to consolidate existing markets, rather than to penetrate new ones. This obliged advertisers to develop a strategy and methods which were designed to establish a relationship of greater trust and identity between producer and consumer, rather than to sell a particular product.[33]

This type of advertising, which became known as 'prestige advertising', was more broad-based and less biased than narrowly targeted advertising.[34] It was produced almost exclusively by the corporate sector, because it needed a producer who was sufficiently large to set aside capital which would have no short term return on investment. Most prestige publicity was produced in the form of printed material, but, from 1903 onwards, some short advertising films were also made, such as, *The Story of a Piece of Slate* (1904) and *The Manchester Ship Canal* (1912).

These early traditions of broad-based publicity production were reinforced during the First World War, when organizations such as the Foreign Office News Department and the War Propaganda Bureau, produced broadly targeted, covertly propagandist, publicity. Officials at the Foreign Office News Department believed that the object of publicity was not to hammer home a particular point of view, but to establish 'a relationship of mutual trust and confidence.'[35] That relationship partly depended upon persuading the addressee that the publicity material he or she encountered was objective, rather than biased. This propaganda strategy found its most lasting expression in the official war films of the period, and particularly in *The Battle of the Somme* (1916).[36] However, this strategy entailed a degree of risk for the authorities in that, in order to appear unbiased, a certain quantity of 'negative' material had to be represented. But it was felt that these risks would be outweighed by the benefits gained from fostering a closer identity between the public and the war effort.[37]

Some critics[38] have argued that the publicity innovations of the EMB were derived exclusively from American thinking on public relations, yet it is obvious that there was a clear continuity between the British traditions of broad-based publicity production mentioned above, and the policies of the EMB. Although American ideas on publicity and public relations did influence the EMB, many of those ideas complemented, and were integrated into, existing British traditions of generalized publicity production at the EMB. The EMB was neither an exclusive source of original thinking, nor was it predominantly influenced by American ideas. It integrated American ideas into a continuing British tradition, and produced a synthesis: one manifestation of which was the documentary film movement.

The EMB's policy of creating a relationship of identity between publicist and spectator, through the mass production of generalized publicity, inevitably led them to consider the question of film production. Their consideration of this medium was given impetus by the findings of the Imperial Conference of 1926, which stated that films should be made from a

> general cultural and social point of view as well as with reference to the development of trade, and to its potential value as a means of giving the people of the various parts of the Empire a more vivid realisation of one another's lives and surroundings.[39]

The Imperial Conference found the issue important enough to be referred to its standing General Economic Sub-Committee, which in turn stated that:

> Cinema was not merely a means of entertainment, but in addition, a powerful instrument of education in the widest sense of that term, and, even when it is not used avowedly for purposes of instruction, advertisement or propaganda, it exercises indirectly a great

influence in shaping the ideas of the very large numbers to whom it appeals. Its potentialities in this respect are almost unlimited.[40]

In some parts of the Empire films have been produced, illustrative of the conditions and resources of those countries or of the activities of government departments. . . . It would, in the opinion of the sub-committee, be very advantageous if the production and exhibition of films of this nature could be continued and increased.[41]

These views on the social and cultural potential of film were very similar to those of Grierson, and they reveal the extent to which he, the documentary film movement, and the EMB Publicity Committee were part of a wider movement of concern over the social and educational role of film.

On the publication of the report of the Imperial Conference, Leo Amery, then Secretary of State for the Dominions, came under pressure to implement some form of imperial film production. Consequently, when Rudyard Kipling, arch-imperialist, Conservative and cousin of the Prime Minister (Stanley Baldwin), approached Stephen Tallents with proposals for making a film, Amery encouraged Tallents to accept the proposals.[42]

In August of 1926, Tallents spent an afternoon in the country with Kipling, during the course of which Kipling offered to lend his name to the production of a propaganda film, on the condition that Walter Creighton, who had shared his involvement in the organization of the 1924 British Empire Exhibition at Wembley, should be allowed to direct the film. Creighton came to see Tallents in November 1926, and the two of them then spent the weekend with Kipling working on a scenario. Later that month, Tallents obtained Amery's authority to convene an EMB conference for the purpose of examining the Creighton-Kipling project.[43]

At the first meeting of this Film Conference, on 1 February 1927, the Creighton-Kipling scenario was accepted, largely on the basis of Kipling's status and reputation: 'The collaboration of Mister Kipling, would, it was felt, prove of the greatest value to the film as a commercial asset.'[44] However, in accepting the Kipling-Creighton proposals, the Conference was also forced to appoint Creighton, who knew nothing about film-making, as the EMB Film Officer.

A few weeks after committing himself to appoint Creighton, Tallents met Grierson for the first time, and was immediately impressed by the latter's knowledge of film. However, he was unable to appoint Grierson as Film Officer, and so commissioned him instead to write a series of reports on film production in Europe.[46]

Grierson's first report took the form of a long memorandum entitled 'Notes for English Producers'.[47] It was divided into two parts. The first part, entitled 'Cinema and the Public – An Account of Audience Reactions and of the Conditions of Popular Appeal in the Cinema', duplicated many of the ideas he had expressed in his American writings, and particularly · in *Better Popular Pictures* (1926).[48] However, the second part, entitled 'English Cinema Production and the Naturalistic Tradition', contained his first clearly articulated definition of the form, content, and purpose of documentary film. Any attempt to understand the development of Grierson's ideas, without reference to this important document, is likely to misinterpret his theory of documentary film.

In Part I of the memo, Grierson argued that the unlimited potential for cinematic experiment was constrained by public demand, 'The public is the final arbiter of form in matters cinematic.'[49] This implied a need for film producers to understand public demand, and Grierson argued that the British cinema was unsuccessful in this respect. He again argued that Famous Players Lasky had made a contribution towards an understanding of 'the deeper principles of popular appeal'[50] and that their box-office records constituted 'a sociological document ... on matters of comparative psychology.'[51] Although he admitted that Famous Players Lasky's actions were determined by self-interest rather than altruism, he went on to argue that the quest for commercial appeal was necessarily determined by the imperative of appealing to an existing, and valid, public demand.[52] This equation between profit maximization and public demand was naive, but it does reveal the extent to which Grierson remained optimistic about the possibility of using cinema as a positive instrument of social purpose.

Grierson also argued that an effective, socially purposive cinema must engage and resolve the dreams and ambitions of the public, and must provide models for social action.[53] This provision depended upon a positive representation of contemporary social realities. Representations which were either negative or unfamiliar, could not fulfil the instrumental intentions of a socially purposive cinema, because the public would be unable to identify with them. This was why certain genres of film, such as history films, fantasy films, excessively psychological films, and realist films, were only moderately successful. Grierson believed that 'objective realist' films should avoid excessive negative representations,[54] that historical and fantasy films should be rooted in everyday experience to some extent, and that films dealing with psychological interiority should show 'the mental processes which determine events,'[55] rather than dwell on the mental processes for their own sake.

As in the 1926 writings, Grierson's arguments in this document reveal an insistence that film should deal, in practical ways, with issues of choice and action in the social environment. In the 1927 memorandum he went on to argue that the central instrumental function of film was to represent the interdependence of individual and social relations. Such a representation would, he believed, contribute towards the continuity of those relations. This function could be achieved by transforming genres such as the western, in which a morality of individual dilemmas was played out, into a more socially useful format, in which individual values could be linked to social and national values. A western which dealt with an individual's struggle against adversity, could be made into a film dealing with an individual's struggle to build social institutions, such as the Pony Express, for example.[56]

Although Grierson's arguments here constituted a 'realist' theory of cinema, in the sense that he advocated the representation of contemporary social realities, his arguments did not amount to any form of 'critical' realism. The films which he wanted made would neither give an objective account of contemporary reality, nor cultivate the critical faculties of the spectator. Instead, they would seek to guide the spectator into an understanding, cum acceptance, of the status quo.

Grierson's model of epic cinema bore little relation to the limited budget and resources available to the EMB, and in Part II of the 1927 memorandum, entitled 'English Cinema Production and the Naturalistic Tradition', he was driven by necessity to define a film practice more appropriate to those resources.

Grierson had expressed a preference for films shot on location, as opposed to those shot in the studio, from as early as 1925. This preference stemmed, primarily, from his conviction that actuality footage was intrinsically superior to studio footage, because it revealed a greater quantity of information about the empirical world, and about the interdependence of social and individual relations. But it also stemmed from his convictions concerning the nature of film, and human nature. Grierson's conception of 'human nature', as expressed in the 1927 memorandum, consisted of a belief that the 'popular mind' was disposed towards representations of optimistic adventure and images of the social world.[57] At the same time, his conception of the nature of film consisted of a belief that the specificity of film lay in its ability to represent natural and social phenomena in visually dramatic terms.[58] This conjunction of a human disposition towards social and natural representations, and film's ability to satisfy that disposition by creating such representations, led Grierson to argue that the naturalist tradition of location filming was both intrinsically popular, and essentially cinematic.[59]

Despite this intrinsic ability of film to satisfy an essential human need through representations of the interconnected world of personal and social relations, Grierson argued that, in commercial cinema, such representations were usually subordinated to trivialized tales of individual dilemmas. But in the Soviet cinema, on the other hand, representations of individual issues were subordinated to representations of collective issues. Grierson argued that a synthesis of individual and social representation was needed, and he believed that the EMB could achieve such a synthesis, by using the moribund genre of the travelogue and actuality film.[60]

Grierson postulated two different categories of naturalist film production . The first category would consist of films seven to nine reels in length, which would correspond to his earlier model of epic cinema. The second category would consist of films of one to four reels in length, which would have simple plots, no film stars or studio locations, and would represent both primitive cultures and modern industrial society.[61]

Grierson argued that these films would have to be superior to, and different from, existing actuality film genres:

> But if these pictures are to avoid the fate of industrial commercial and so-called educational pictures of the past and if they are to be really effective for educational and propaganda purposes they will have to be made on entirely original lines. They have gone frequently about the business of regarding some scene or other without the first regard to the value of tempo, rhythm and composition: indeed without realizing that, even where a story is absent, intensely exciting effects can be gained by exploiting movement in masses in a dramatic way.[62]

The processes of cinematic construction would be fully realized in those films, in which the visual aspects of prosaic subject matter 'could be orchestrated into cinematic sequence of enormous vitality.'[63] Grierson cited examples of such orchestration from Eisenstein's *Battleship Potemkin*. Although he did not feel that this film provided a suitable model for documentary film production, he did believe that it could provide examples of dramatic editing which would be essential to the development of an effective documentary film practice. Because this documentary practice would not use the normal points of appeal used by the commercial feature film (stars, production values, etc.), it would have to rely on a sophisticated use of montage and visual composition: 'there is every reason to believe that industrial and commercial films require an even greater consideration of visual effects than the average dramatic film. They have indeed little else on which to subsist.'[64]

Grierson went on to argue that western governments would be unlikely to provide the funds and resources necessary to make feature length naturalist films, and he recommended that the EMB should undertake production of six shorter films: 'a series of short glorified news-reelers,'[65] which would be produced by a small team of film-makers employed directly by the EMB. Grierson believed that this could 'mark a new phase in cinema production,'[66] and he argued that, in order for these films to achieve propaganda objectives, they would have to succeed first as films, rather than merely as propaganda. The secret of their success lay not in their subject matter, but in their 'cinematic treatment'.

This first definition of the 'Griersonian' documentary film contained both formalist and naturalist elements. Both were essential to Grierson's definition, but it is clear that the former had priority over the latter. Contrary to conventional wisdom, Grierson's first definition of the documentary film was primarily formalist, with actuality footage having a relatively low priority.

Grierson's memorandum was well received by Tallents and the EMB Film Committee, and was widely circulated outside the EMB. Leo Amery thought it 'very interesting indeed,'[67] and so did the author John Buchan, who had been in charge of the Department of Information during the First World War, and who praised Grierson's theory of an epic-idealist theory of uplift.[68] However, despite this response, Grierson was unable to put his ideas into practice because he was only employed to write reports, and not to make films. Between April and July 1927 he travelled through France and Germany in order to report on specialized film production practices in those countries,[69] and his conclusions were set out in a second report, entitled *Further Notes on Cinema Production*, which was dated 28 July 1927.

Whilst the first report had considered questions of production, this one was primarily concerned with questions of distribution, exhibition and finance. In it, Grierson argued that the commercial cinema's drive towards profits maximization led to the creation of a superficial, sub-standard mass cinema, and to the formation of a mass audience which was conditioned to consume inferior films.[70] This construction of a superficial mass cinema also suppressed the development of minority genres, such as the documentary and educational film, whilst the formation of a standardized mass audience suppressed the development of minority audiences for those minority genres. In opposition to many critics of the day, who argued that the British cinema could produce more sophisticated films than the American cinema, Grierson asserted that the British film industry could never produce quality films of specialized interest, because it was driven by the same profit maximization imperatives as the American film industry: 'The producers and exhibitors with any sense of the future are promising much, but they are steering their course as well as they can, after the crowded galleons of Paramount, Metro, Universal, Fox and PDC. And this is inevitable.'[71] Grierson concluded from this that any attempt by the EMB to use mainstream channels for either production or distribution would result in the production of trivial films, and he gave as an example of this the case of the British Instructional company, who: 'made some very good nature films, but who could not make a profit theatrically and had to set up a department for non-commercial showings, and apply for institutional sponsorship.'[72] Grierson believed that a primary objective for the EMB was the development of a specialized distribution and exhibition system, and the organization of a 'new cinema public' for films of specialized interest. He believed that a paying public, which would correspond to the public of 'the more intelligent literary reviews,'[73] would support an independent cinema theatre, or cinema circuit, and an independent film production unit. In Paris he was particularly impressed by the example of the Vieux Colombier Cinema, which was managed by Jean Tedesco.[74] The Vieux Colombier possessed its own film laboratory, film technicians and editing facilities, and the films shown there were, according to Grierson, neither 'popular' nor 'highbrow', but 'quality films', shown to an 'influential audience'.[75] 50 per cent of the films shown were documentaries shot in the French colonies, but Grierson felt that many of these were 'semi-amateur efforts' of low technical and educational value.[76]

Grierson felt that an isolated independent cinema such as the Vieux Colombier was an unsuitable model for a British system of specialized film production, because one cinema could not provide the finance necessary to sustain an independent production unit in Britain. He also felt that even a small chain of independent producer-exhibitors would not survive economically, and concluded that the only solution would be the formation of an international organization, which could command large enough prices from distributors to enable some measure of independent production to take place.[77]

Since such an organization did not exist, and was not likely to exist in the foreseeable future, Grierson concluded that EMB film production could not rely on a paying public, and would have to be sponsored by State institutions or by corporate bodies. In America he was impressed by the examples of the Eastman Foundation, which had sponsored fifty films on educational subjects, and the American Department of Agriculture, which had set up non-theatrical distribution, production and exhibition systems.[78]

This second report for the EMB revealed that Grierson had shifted conclusively from a belief that socially purposive films, and documentaries in particular, could be made by the commercial cinema. The report also revealed that he dismissed the possibility of making documentary films without some degree of financial sponsorship, and that he saw the State, or corporate sponsorship, as providing the only practicable basis upon which to construct documentary film production. Taken together, these two reports set out Grierson's initial conception of a comprehensive documentary film system, incorporating production, distribution, exhibition and finance.

Shortly before Grierson's second report appeared in July 1927, Walter Creighton left for America, in order to study film-making methods there. This gave Grierson the opportunity to expand his activities at the EMB, and his first acts were to organize a programme of screenings at the Imperial Institute, and to compile an index of films which he felt were of value as Empire propaganda. In March 1928 he presented proposals for a programme of EMB film production to the EMB Film Committee. These proposals were accepted by the Committee and set out in a confidential Film Committee memorandum of 1 March 1928.[79] This memorandum has been attributed to Grierson,[80] but in fact it was a Film Committee memo, which incorporated Grierson's proposals more or less verbatim.

The memorandum, entitled 'The Empire Marketing Board and the Cinema', submitted proposals for improving and updating the film index, establishing a film library and cinema at the Imperial Institute, establishing new distribution and exhibition channels, and initiating film production at the EMB.[81] As an initial production strategy, the Film Committee, heavily prompted by Grierson, proposed the production of two three-reel films: one on the pedigree cattle trade, and one on the herring fisheries. Negotiations with a commercial film company, New Era Films Ltd, had already commenced, and a provisional agreement had been reached whereby New Era would provide technical assistance, studio facilities, and a distribution contract.[82] However, control over production, and ownership of the negatives, would remain with the EMB. The Film Committee proposed that Walter Creighton should direct the film on pedigree cattle, and that Grierson, 'who has long experience at sea,'[83] should direct the film on herring fishing.

In 1928, Gervas Huxley, the Secretary of the EMB Publicity Committee, returned from a tour of the Dominions with the Colonial and Dominions Secretary Leo Amery, to discover that Grierson, who had been appointed in his absence, dominated EMB publicity plans, and exercised a significant influence over Tallents: 'John Grierson [was] a thirty year old Scot with the air of a tough little terrier, under whose dynamic spell Tallents had so completely fallen that it seemed that films should form the most valuable single medium for the attainment of the Board's objects.'[84] When Huxley had left on his trip the EMB film production policy was based on the production of a single feature length film: Creighton's *One Family*. The extent of Grierson's influence at the EMB was revealed by his success in persuading the organization to adopt a completely different policy, based on the establishment of a production and distribution system for short documentary films. The proposals put forward by the Film Committee in their memorandum of 1 March, corresponded almost entirely to the ideas expressed by Grierson in his two reports for the EMB, and this reveals the considerable influence which he wielded there.

Although the Film Committee's dual production programme of the herring film and *One Family* (the film on pedigree cattle had been dropped) was sanctioned by the EMB, it was opposed by the Treasury. It was not until a meeting at Leo Amery's rooms at the Dominions Office on 27 April, at which Amery, Walter Elliot and Tallents managed to persuade two sceptical Treasury officials that the EMB's film production proposals were viable, that consent was finally granted.[85] However, this confrontation with the Treasury was only the first of many in a process of attrition which eventually led to the abolition of the EMB Film Unit in 1933.

DRIFTERS

When assent was finally granted to the EMB's film production proposals Grierson was officially employed as Assistant Films Officer, and a production contract was negotiated with New Era. Grierson had been eager to direct a film for some time, and had become increasingly disillusioned by Civil Service and EMB bureaucracy. When clearance to begin production was finally granted he responded with enthusiasm, and by the late spring of 1928, had already visited several possible sites for location shooting.[86] Shooting began during the summer of 1928, and was completed towards the end of November. In December, Grierson began to edit the 10,000 feet of rushes. He was assisted in this by Margaret Taylor, who later became his wife. The editing was finally completed in the summer of 1929,[87] after which Grierson showed the completed film to the EMB Film Committee, who insisted that some of the more spectacular montage sequences should be removed. Grierson reluctantly agreed, and when the altered film was shown once more to the Film Committee, it was approved. However, Grierson later secretly reinserted the edited sequences, and the reconstituted film was cut into a negative at the Olympic Kine Laboratories at Acton.[88]

Drifters was a silent four-reel film, of 3,631 feet, and fifty-eight minutes. It was produced by New Era for the EMB, and was distributed by Associated British Film Distributors. Grierson was the director, editor, writer, and scriptwriter, and the cameraman was Basil Emmott (and sometimes Grierson), of New Era. Shooting on location took place at Lerwick, Hanna Voe and Noss Head in the Shetland Islands, at the Plymouth Marine Biological Research Station, and on the trawlers *Maid of Thule* and *Renovelle*, on the North Sea.[89] A set of the interior of a fishing boat was also built at the fish-market in Lerwick, and was designed by the sculptor John Skeaping, with whom Grierson had taught whilst at Armstrong College in 1923.[90] *Drifters* was first exhibited at the 33rd meeting of the Film Society at the Tivoli Palace on the Strand, on Sunday 10 November 1929, where it appeared on the same billing as Eisenstein's *Battleship Potemkin* (1925) and Walt Disney's *The Barn Dance* (1929).[91] It received its first commercial screening on 9 December 1929 at the Stoll Picture House in London.

Grierson (right) with Basil Emmott, filming *Drifters*

The plot of *Drifters* is simple and uncomplicated. The film opens with shots of a fishing village, Hanna Voe, and of men walking towards their ships. This is followed by sequences showing trawlers preparing to put out to sea, and these sequences are interspersed with sequences showing gannets, puffins, kittiwakes, and cormorants – all filmed at Noss Head. The trawlers are then seen out at sea (on the *Maid of Thule*, around Lerwick), and then fishing nets are cast, and the trawlers are seen drifting through the night (on the *Renovelle*, around Lowestoft). This is followed by shots of fishermen seen below deck (filmed on the interior set at Lerwick), and this is then followed by shots of dog fish, conger eels, and herring, shown swimming freely or trapped in nets (shot at the Marine Biological Research Station at Plymouth). The film then shows the nets being drawn in during a storm (shot on the *Renovelle*, near

Lowestoft), after which the trawler sails back into port, where its cargo is gutted and barrelled (shot at Lerwick fish market). The final sequences of the film show trains and ships taking the cargo to national and international markets.

The immediate origins of *Drifters* can be found in the model of documentary film which Grierson elaborated in the second part of his 1927 memorandum: 'English Cinema Production and the Naturalistic Tradition'.[92] In that model he posited two different types of 'naturalistic film': the feature length epic, and the one-to-four-reel documentary. According to Grierson, the latter category would consist of socially purposive films whose primary purpose was to represent the inter-dependence of social and individual relations. These films would possess simple narrative structures, which would be organized around dramatic rhetorical devices of 'achievement through struggle', and orchestrated through a sophisticated articulation of cinematic techniques and devices. No professional actors or studio locations would be used.

There is a clear correspondence between this model and *Drifters*. Like the model, *Drifters* has a simple narrative structure: boats go to sea, fish, and return their catch to harbour. The centre of the film consists of an account of a struggle over nature, and montage is used to impart dramatic and lyrical significance upon this core material. Finally, as in the 1927 model, the final sequence of the film represents an interdependent structure of individual and social relations. There is, therefore, no doubt that *Drifters* was directly derived from the 'glorified newsreel'[93] which Grierson outlined on pages 20-1 of the 1927 memorandum. This point needs to be emphasized because previous interpretations of the film have often been unaware of the existence of the memorandum, and this has resulted in misconceptions as to the origins, content and significance of the film.[94]

Other misconceptions have been created by a lack of awareness of the influence of idealist thought on Grierson. The term 'documentary' is normally applied to a detailed empirical description of events and circumstances, but *Drifters*, although a documentary film, presents only a generalized and impressionistic account of the events and circum-stances which it represents. This lack of detailed description was com-mented on by many contemporary reviewers, who also argued that *Drifters* did not provide an adequate account of the herring fishing industry.[95] This criticism was summed up by the American critic, Harry Allan Potamkin, writing in *Close Up*, in 1930:

> This was a film intended to show labour. If Mr Grierson thought to extend it to inferences beyond the facts of toil, to the total economy of exploitation, his attempts at inter-reference between sea and market, fish and broker, were certainly too inadequate. He was

more concerned with the representation of fish than with the representation of a labour process.[96]

Potamkin's criticism was correct: *Drifters* did prioritize the represent-ation of fish over the representation of human labour, but Grierson explicitly stated that he was not interested in verisimilitude or critical analysis, but in symbolic generalization:

> The popular success of the film depends, I believe, on bringing the weight of the impersonal background (of the sea and the wind, of the gulls, the underwater and the boats) and giving it all the mystery, movement and size we know how to. . . . The fishing detail and the human detail should fit into this background and should not be allowed to take charge.[97]

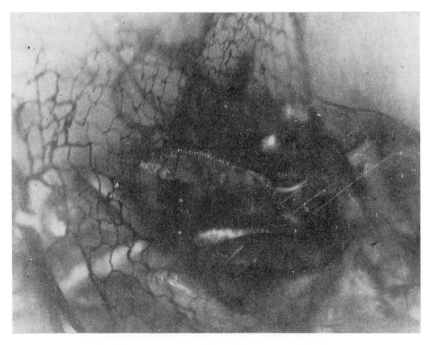

'The mysteries of the underwater', *Drifters*

Here, Grierson stated that naturalistic representation was subordinated to symbolic expression in *Drifters*. This assertion is borne out by a close study of the film itself. Many sequences are dominated by images of natural forces and phenomena, which have no immediate function within the linear development of the narrative. Take, for example, the following sequence from reel one:

men walking towards boats (long shot) / waves breaking on shore (close up) / birds (close up) / violent waves (close up) / birds (close up) / sky (close up) / birds (close up).[98]

This montage of sequences disrupts the linear development of the narrative and establishes a connotational axis which expresses the immutability and inherent mystery of natural elements. Although these sequences are followed by a sequence representing the fishing fleet – thus showing the interdependence of the natural and human worlds – it is significant that three out of the four reels of *Drifters* begin with representations of natural elements.[99]

This predominance of impressionistic representations of natural elements was also reflected in the film's titles. For example: ' The log line tells the miles. Far to seaward swim the herring shoals. The skipper keeps a lookout for appearances, while down below is the singleness of the sea.'[100] In a silent film the principal function of titles (language) is to counteract the propensity for visual images to generate a plurality of readings, by articulating meaning in a more precise way. Such articulation is necessary in order to facilitate narrative development. The third title in the sequence mentioned above: ' The skipper keeps a look out', is a descriptive phrase which fulfils this narrative function. However, even this title was sandwiched between two symbolic titles: 'appearances' and 'the singleness of the sea'.

An analysis of the initial draft titles for *Drifters* reveals an even greater predominance of generalized symbolic references. Initially, the title sequences quoted above were meant to be as follows: ' The logline ticks out miles. Thirty or forty or fifty miles in the singleness of the sea. Somewhere beneath, the craning of water eyes of the shoals.'[101] This initial version was even less descriptive than the final version, and the choice of final version reflected the way in which the imperatives of narrative development forced Grierson to modify his original project of complete symbolic generalization. However, that project still shaped the majority of the titles and sequences in *Drifters*.

The choice of musical accompaniment for *Drifters* also reflected Grierson's prioritization of symbolic generalization. All the accompaniments suggested in the draft scenarios were by nineteenth-century romantic composers, including Mendelssohn, Wagner, Rimsky Korsakov, Liszt, and Fauré,[102] and the music played at the premiere was Mendelssohn's *Fingal's Cave Overture*.[103] This romantic music accentuated the dramatic and lyrical effects which Grierson was trying to achieve. For example, the title ' The Storm Gathers' was to be accompanied by Wagner's *Flying Dutchman Overture*, and the title ' The Sound of the Sea' by Mendelssohn's *A Midsummer Night's Dream*.[104]

The subordination of naturalistic verisimilitude to symbolic expression in *Drifters* was a product of the influence of idealist thought, and, of the idealist distinction between the real and the phenomenal, in particular. This distinction, which Grierson often referred to in his writings, has never been fully understood by previous critics. For example, Stuart Hood interpreted it by relating it to a definition of 'the real' in the Oxford English Dictionary: 'having an existence in fact and not merely in appearance.'[105] Hood went on to argue that 'it is difficult to see what he (Grierson) means by 'more real in the philosophic sense',[106] and interpreted Grierson's distinction between the real and the phenomenal in terms of 'the passage from the plain (or fancy) descriptions of natural material to arrangements, rearrangements, and creative shapings of it.'[107] Hood was correct up to a point here, and credit must be given to him for grasping the importance of this distinction between the real and the phenomenal within Grierson's ideas. However, a full explanation of Grierson's use of this distinction can only emerge from a study of its origins in philosophical idealism.

Writing shortly after *Drifters* was made, Grierson explained the reason for the subordination of naturalistic verisimilitude to symbolic expression in the film, in terms of the greater value of 'the real' over 'the actual': 'In documentary we deal with the actual, and in that sense with the real. But the *really real*, if I may use that phrase, is something deeper than that. The only reality which counts in the end is the interpretation which is profound.'[108] Here, Grierson explicitly argued that the intrinsic empirical naturalism of the documentary representation must be organized in order to express general truths, which exist at a level of abstraction beyond the empirical. The raw material of documentary representation is meaningless in itself, and can only become significant when invested with interpretative intention and achievement. Grierson claimed that Shakespearian blank verse was an 'artificial form of utterance... (but)... is as near reality – philosophic reality – as material utterance can reach.'[109] He went on to claim that many other modes of aesthetic expression were 'artificial', yet able to infer 'the real', because the real consisted of general truths and abstract mental structures , which could not be empirically represented.[110]

Grierson's use of this distinction between the real and the empirical originated from his encounter with philosophical idealism at Glasgow University.[111] He was particularly influenced by the writings of F. H. Bradley, in which a distinction was drawn between the empirical world, and an underlying reality,[112] and by Kant's distinction between the empirical world and a 'noumenal' reality of synthetic *a priori* categories, which existed at a level of abstraction beyond the empirical.[113]

Grierson frequently referred to this distinction between the real and the empirical in his university writings during the 1920s,[114] and in his

American writings on modern art.[115] He also referred to it in his 1926 writings on cinema,[116] and throughout the 1927-33 period. For example:

> (The camera)... stirs the mind to most necessary wonder; it does it itself by picking out from the chaos of daily fact and daily happening, moments of size and strength and beauty, giving promise of that higher articulation in which the chaos of daily event is beauty itself.[117]

Grierson referred to this distinction, using numerous references to idealist philosophers such as Kant and Plato, throughout his life, and even towards the end of his life, he continued to describe film-making in terms of abstracting structures from empirical detail.[118]

This prioritization of essence over appearance explains the priority given to symbolic expression in *Drifters*. Grierson spoke about 'exalting' each sequence in *Drifters*, and about 'glorifying the herring' and 'attaching splendour' to it.[119] This approach led him to make extensive use of metaphor and allegory, as in the sequence where a whale was used as 'a ponderous symbol for all that tumbled and laboured on that wild morning.'[120] But of all the symbolic rhetorical devices used in *Drifters*, the most important was that of dramatic structure, and, in particular, the dramatic theme of the individual's struggle against nature. Grierson believed that this dramatic device was an ideal means through which to express general and abstract truths.[121] In the representation of the fishermens' struggle against nature, the reality expressed was that of humanity's struggle against nature, whilst, in the representation of the whale, the reality expressed was that of the immensity of natural forces. In both cases Grierson gave the particular representation a general, metaphysical significance.

A similar process of transformation occurred in the final reel of *Drifters*, in which Grierson used montage to express the interdependence of sea fishing and the market place. Sequences representing the trawler at sea were intercut with sequences representing activities of the market place, in order to illustrate the interdependence of one to the other. The reality which Grierson wished to express in these sequences was that of the inter-relation of social practices within a social totality, but he also wished to express the reality of the way in which 'simple heroic labour' was transformed into a market commodity.[122] However, Grierson's account of this transformation, in *Drifters*, contained few specific references to the means by which labour was degraded by market forces, nor did it contain any significant criticism of that process. This lack of detail, and of critical content, has provided a basis for many criticisms of *Drifters*. Yet, in an article published in 1930, entitled 'Silver Scales, but not the Scales of Justice',[123] Grierson showed that he was critical of exploitative practices within the herring industry. In the article,

'simple heroic labour' and its transformation into a market commodity,
Drifters

he criticized the actions of middle-men and owners in reducing fish catches, in order to raise prices and safeguard profits, and went on to argue that this led to economic hardship in the fishing villages.

No such critical points were made in *Drifters*, partly because Grierson was restrained from making them through his position as a civil servant, and partly because his purpose in the film was to express a reality which transcended particular issues of economic exploitation or social hardship. Like most examples of idealist aesthetics, *Drifters* operated at a level of generality which removed it from concrete historical reference, and situated it within a supra-historical world. *Drifters* also illustrates the dual progressive/conservative nature of idealism. The progressive aspect can be seen in the film's critique of capitalist relations of production, whilst the conservative aspect can be seen in the representation of those same relations as part of an inter-dependent social totality. This ambivalence within the film is characteristic of the progressive and conservative influence which idealism had on Grierson's ideas, and on the development of the documentary film movement. In addition to the influence of philosophical idealism, another major influence on *Drifters* was contemporary film theory, and contemporary modernist cultural movements.

According to Arnold Toynbee, the 'post-modern' period began in the last two decades of the nineteenth century, when classical liberal beliefs in progress, science and reason came under question.[124] This questioning of previously sacrosanct beliefs was caused, to a large extent, by the failure of western capitalist society to deal satisfactorily with poverty and inequality.[125] The failure to resolve these problems cast doubt on the ideologies which had served to legitimate capitalism since the early nineteenth century. One consequence of this was that artists and intellectuals turned increasingly to irrationalist ideologies, which were often derived from oriental sources, and which emphasized subjective, visionary realities.[126] For example, Nietzsche condemned bourgeois rationalism, whilst Bergson believed in a subjective logic which was fundamentally different from the conventional logic of space–time naturalism.[127] The concepts of 'dream' and of 'myth' also became important for artists and intellectuals, and were considered to be viable means of ordering reality into a coherent and meaningful whole.[128] T. S. Eliot argued that myth provided a means of 'controlling, of ordering, of giving a shape and a significance to the immense paradox of futility and anarchy which is contemporary history.'[129] In his *The Interpretation of Dreams* (1899), Freud also described a kind of dream logic which operated largely without reference to the conventional causal assumptions of rationalist and empiricist ideology.

Whilst these developments were taking place in the arts, parallel developments were also taking place in the natural sciences, and, between 1895 and 1915, the conception of the physical world, and of the individual's ability to comprehend it, was brought into question.[130] In 1900 Max Planck's quantum theory represented the physical world as a complex interdependent structure of energy, and Werner Heisenberg developed his theory of the 'Uncertainty Principle', which asserted that scientific enquiry was not objective, but always affected the object under observation.[131] In 1915, Einstein developed his model of a non-Euclidean four-dimensional space–time continuum, in which space and time, observer and observed, were inter-connected and inter-dependent.[132] These developments emphasized the subjective and provisional nature of scientific method, and the limitations of deductive reason.

As the mechanistic propositions of newtonian physics, and the putative methodological premises of positivism, came under question, cultural discourses such as naturalism, which was derived from objectivist and mechanistic assumptions, also came under scrutiny.[133] Naturalist methodological assumptions emphasized that objective knowledge could only emerge from empirical observation of nature. However, new scientific theories increasingly emphasized the impossibility of objective observation. Consequently, naturalism as a cultural practice came under question, as artists explored how aesthetic representations were constructed out of material structures of organized symbols and codes. Art objects were produced, whose internal organization of aesthetic codes and symbols were structured according to imperatives other than those of naturalistic representation, and this led to an increasing engagement with formal experimentation.[134] In Cubist painting, for example, the three-dimensional euclidean space of perspective painting was transformed into a multi-dimensional spatial *gestalt*;[135] whilst in literature, the illusionism of the nineteenth-century novel was disrupted by the use of linguistic and literary devices, designed to emphasize the use of language as an instrument of signification, rather than of mimesis.[136]

Grierson had been familiar with the characteristic formal and conventionalist[137] concerns of modernist cultural theories since his university days. In his philosophy classes he had read Bergson, Nietzsche and other irrationalist philosophers,[138] and in an American periodical called *The Dial*, which was his 'principal guide' to modernist aesthetics,[139] he read James Joyce, T. S. Eliot, Andre Derain, Ezra Pound, Carl Sandburg, and Wyndham Lewis. Some of these writers influenced him directly in the making of *Drifters*. He was particularly influenced by Joyce, by Eliot's *The Waste Land*, and by Sandberg, whose *Slabs of the Sunburnt West* influenced the use of montage in *Drifters*.[140] Grierson also became familiar with contemporary painting through *The Dial*, which, between 1920 and 1924, published reviews and illustrations of work by Gontchorova, Rodchenko, Picasso, Matisse, Gauguin, Chagal, Kokoschka and Reinhardt. He also wrote on post-impressionist painters, and on Russian and German avant-garde cinema,[141] and became familiar with the formalist film theories of Arnheim, Balazs, Lindsay, and others.

It is clear, therefore, that Grierson was aware of modernist aesthetics, and, in particular, of the modernist emphasis on form. That emphasis was also a central feature of early film theory, which was largely based on the belief that film was an instrument of creative signification, rather than of mimetic reproduction. Vachel Lindsay, the first American to publish a theory of film, and whom Grierson cited as having influenced him,[142] argued that film was a poetic and aesthetic means of expression. Similarly, the French critics Louis Delluc and Riciotto Canudo compared film to music and poetry, and attempted to isolate its specific formal properties.[143] Bela Balazs, one of the first major film theorists, who also had a considerable influence on Grierson, argued that film could express a poetic reality which existed beneath the rational.[144]

This emphasis on film as an aesthetic structure, rather than as an instrument of mimetic illusionism, can also be found in the writings of another theorist who influenced Grierson: Rudolph Arnheim, from the *gestalt* school of psychology. The German words 'gestalt' and 'gestalten' mean 'structure' and 'process of making',[145] and the basis of *gestalt* psychology was the thesis that psychological phenomena were articulated wholes, or *gestalts*, which were structured and organized by the individual subject.[146] The *gestalt* psychologists believed that the individual subject constructed psychological *gestalts* by abstracting a coherent world of objects and events from the multiplicity of sense data. They also believed that this process was intrinsically creative.[147] Rudolph Arnheim described this process as the 'primary transformation' of sense data into a coherent *gestalt*, and he described the process whereby the artist abstracted general features from particular *gestalt* fields, and then embodied them within works of art, as 'secondary transformation': 'The artist uses his categories of shape and colour to capture something universally significant in the particular.'[148]

Arnheim argued that primary transformation, in which the apparatus of perception organized a world of objects and events, was fundamentally different from secondary transformation, in which the artist organized a diegetic world of objects and events through a use of material properties, and non-material codes, conventions, and symbols.[149] The function of primary transformation was also different from that of secondary transformation. The function of primary transformation was to organize particular groupings of sense data into particular *gestalt* fields, whilst that of secondary transformation was to organise general features of particular *gestalt* fields into a *gestalt* of general, and aesthetic, significance. Although perception was itself a creative process, its essentially pragmatic and utilitarian purpose was different in kind from the primarily aesthetic purpose of secondary transformation. In addition, according to Arnheim, the aesthetic purpose of secondary transformation was mainly realized through the use of 'general' and 'typical' representations.[150]

Arnheim disapproved of naturalist representation, which, he believed, obscured the difference between primary and secondary transformation, and argued that film should demonstrate its reality as a signifying structure by re-focussing attention from the object represented to the characteristics and conventions of the medium. However, he also believed that a continuous cross-reference should take place between the object represented and the conventions of representation which enabled the object to be represented. This was so that the viewing subject would be aware of both object and representation, and of their separate ontological identities. This ruled out both naturalism and excessive formalism, both of which disrupted and obscured the dialectical relation between object and representation.[151] Arnheim also argued that the total ensemble of cinematic techniques and characteristics should be used to represent this dialectic between the object signified, and the means of signification.[152]

There are many correspondences between Arnheim's and Grierson's ideas. The emphasis on totality in *gestalt* corresponded to the emphasis on totality which Grierson derived from idealist aesthetics. This correspondence was not surprising, given that *gestalt* was also partly derived from a German neo-kantian perspective.[153] Similarly, the emphasis which Arnheim placed on creative articulation, rather than on photographic reproduction, also corresponded to an emphasis which Grierson derived from idealist thought and modernist aesthetics. Grierson also identified with Arnheim's attempt to develop an account of the specific aesthetic properties of film,[154] and with his view that excessive formalism obscured and distorted the film's representation of the external world.[155]

However, Grierson differed sharply with Arnheim over the latter's emphasis on the importance of using all the cinematic techniques and characteristics of film. This view could not be reconciled with any sort of documentary practice, and Grierson accused Arnheim of failing to distinguish between different genres of film and of failing to appreciate the potential of documentary.[156] Grierson also criticized Arnheim for failing to take issue with questions concerning the social purpose of film, and he claimed that Arnheim had done this in order to avoid confronting Marxist theory.[157]

Arnheim was one of the leading avant-garde film theorists of the period, and his prioritization of symbolic expression over naturalism certainly influenced Grierson. But Arnheim's emphasis on formal properties must be distinguished from the emphasis put on formalism by theorists such as Victor Shklovsky, Boris Eichenbaum, and Roman

Jakobson. Like Arnheim, Shklovsky argued that the techniques of art should stretch out the process of perception and make it difficult; but, unlike Arnheim, Shklovsky went on to argue that the disruption of conventional representation should be an end in itself.[158] Shklovsky's notion of 'making strange' (*ostranenie*) was echoed by other Russian formalists, such as Boris Eichenbaum, Osip Brik, and Boris Tomasevsky, who gathered around the Opayez Society between 1916 and 1927,[159] and it was further refined into the notion of 'foregrounding', by a second wave of literary formalism which took place in Prague during the late twenties and early thirties. This aesthetic of 'making strange' and 'foregrounding' often led to excessive formalist abstractionism, and some literary theorists, such as Jan Mukurovsky, began to argue that the totally foregrounded work of art would virtually eliminate its object of reference in the external world, and would have little social value.[160]

Grierson's position on formalism and naturalism was much closer to that of Mukurovsky, Balazs and Arnheim, than it was to that of Shklovsky, Brik, or Tomasevsky. He was temperamentally and philosophically opposed to 'over-aestheticization' and 'art for art's sake',[161] and was also opposed to excessive formalism, which, he believed, could 'land you in abstract sequences which are anything but purposive in their total effect.'[162] He was particularly critical of the 'excessive formalism' of some German expressionist films, and of the Russian Kino Eye films of Dziga Vertov, which he found to be 'merely observational' and 'lacking in interpretative power'.[163] His criticism of Vertov's *Man With a Movie Camera* (1929), was essentially the same as his criticism of other avantgarde films of the period, such as Cavalcanti's *Rien que les heures* (1926), and Ruttmann's *Berlin* (1926-7). He believed that the formalism in these films had become an end in itself, and that their ability to interpret reality had been abrogated.[164]

A degree of uncertainty has always existed regarding the influence of 1920s avant-garde film theory on Grierson. Most critics have been content to refer to the influence of Eisenstein, yet it is clear that *Drifters* cannot be accounted for by reference to Eisenstein's theories alone. *Drifters* was influenced by the use of montage in *Battleship Potemkin*, but in other respects Grierson's film was quite different from Eisenstein's. Yet few critics have discussed the influence of Arnheim on *Drifters*, and fewer still have mentioned the influence of Balazs. The lack of attention paid to the influence of Balazs is unfortunate, and probably stems from his absorption within Stalinist ideology during the 1930s.[165] Before this, however, Balazs was a theorist of major importance, and a scrutiny of his writings during the 1920s reveals that his ideas were closer to Grierson's at the time, than Eisenstein's were. Grierson had been familiar with Balazs' ideas since the early twenties,[166] and his first contact with them was through the pages of *The Dial*, in which Balazs was the only major European film theorist to contribute between 1920 and 1924.[167]

Like Arnheim, Balazs was opposed to excessive formalism, and argued that there must be a dialectic between form and content. In his 1930 book *Der Geist des Films*,[168] he argued that film could transcend naturalism by developing specifically cinematic means of restructuring actuality footage. According to Balazs, this process of restructuring should be apparent to the spectator, so that he or she could perceive the film as an articulated artifact, rather than as a 'window on the world'. But Balazs also argued that this attempt at foregrounding the structure of the film should not lead to excessive formalism.[169] His opposition to formalism was partly determined by the notion that form should function as a means to an end, rather than as an end in itself, and partly by the Marxist notion that formalism was 'a degenerative phenomenon of bourgeois art.'[170] Balazs was writing within a discourse of socialist realist aesthetics, a discourse within which the term 'formalist' had mainly negative connotations after 1928.[171] Like Arnheim, he believed that film should use every means available to 'extract truth from the empirical fog of reality,'[172] and, also like Arnheim, he was critical of the limitations imposed by working within a documentary format.

Although there were many parallels between Balazs' ideas in *Der Geist des Films* and Grierson's ideas, Balazs' book still expressed the standard avant-garde criticism of documentary. However, Balazs' earlier writings, and in particular his *Der Sichtbare Mensch oder Der Kultur des Films* (1924), were much more sympathetic towards documentary.[173] Although an English translation of this book did not appear till 1930, extracts from it had been published in *The Dial*, and Grierson was well aware of the ideas expressed in it before he made *Drifters* in 1929-30.

In the 1924 book, Balazs argued that film could express a poetic reality which existed beyond the rational, and that the visual representation of physical gesture and activity could express general truths which language could not:

> The gestures of visual man are not intended to convey the concepts which can be expressed in words, but such inner experience, such non-rational emotion which would still remain inexpressed when everything that can be told in words, has been told. Such emotions lie in the deepest levels of the soul and cannot be approached by words which are mere reflections of concepts. . . What appears on the face, and in physical expression, is a spiritual experience which is rendered immediately visible without the intermediary of words.[174]

This was a primarily visual and non-cognitive aesthetic, which, in emphasizing the importance of empirical observation, also emphasized the importance of documentary as a viable form of film practice. There was a considerable resemblance between Balazs' belief that 'The artist could represent. . . the soul's bodily incarnation in terms of gesture or feature,'[175] and Grierson's belief that documentary could represent 'the characteristic gestures and features which time has worn smooth.'[176] Both of these quotations reveal the same emphasis on the ability of the naturalist image to signify more abstract realities, and their close correspondence indicates the extent to which Grierson was familiar with Balazs' ideas.

The preceding quotes from Balazs reveal many parallels with idealist aesthetics. This is not surprising, given that Balazs came to Marxism from a neo-hegelian tradition. Writing in 1976, J. Dudley Andrew argued that a contradiction existed between the emphasis which Balazs put on documentary representation, and his assertion that use should be made of the full ensemble of filmic devices. Andrew argued that this contradiction characterized most formative film theory during the 1920s.[177] However, this contradiction can be explained, and shown not to be a contradiction, by reference to the neo-idealist tradition from which most formative film theory emerged.

Both Balazs and Grierson believed that formative methodology (montage etc.) could be used to interpret empirical data in order to express more abstract realities. However, although abstract reality was of greater value than empirical reality, the existence of the latter was a necessary pre-condition for the expression of the former. The abstract articulation of empirical material involved a dialectic relationship, hierarchically structured, within which formative methodology and actuality footage co-existed, and did not contradict each other. This explains the co-existence of both in Balazs' and Grierson's writings. Balazs placed greater emphasis on naturalist representation than any other major film theorist, including Arnheim and Eisenstein.[178] Consequently, it was his theories, rather than those of Eisenstein or Arnheim, which approximated most clearly to what Grierson was trying to achieve in *Drifters*.

Although Grierson's writings after 1930 suggest that the main model for the documentary film movement was the socially purposive cinema of Turin and Pudovkin, he also stated that the main model for *Drifters* was not socially purposive, but 'imagist':

> The imagist or more definitely poetic approach might have taken our consideration of documentary a step further, but no great imagist film has arrived to give character to the advance. By imagism I mean the telling of story or illumination of theme by images, as poetry is story or theme told by images: I mean the addition of poetic reference to the 'mass' and 'march' of the symphonic form.

Drifters was one small contribution in that direction, but only a small one. . . . Looking back at the film now, I would not stress the tempo effects which it built (for both *Potemkin* and *Berlin* came before it), nor even the rhythm effects (though I believe they outdid the technical example of *Potemkin* in that direction). What seemed possible of development in the film was the integration of imagery with the movement.[179]

Drifters can best be understood, not as a socially purposive film, but as an 'imagist' film, which was influenced by the formalist imperatives of avant-garde film theory, and by the philosophical idealist distinction between the real and the phenomenal. In comparison to other contemporary models, it corresponded closely to Dovzhenko's *Earth* (1930), Flaherty's *Nanook of the North* (1920); and to the naturalist/formalist aesthetic which Balazs had expounded in *Der Sichtbare Mensch oder Der Kultur des Films* (1924), and in *Der Geist des Films* (1930).

The expansion and decline of the EMB Film Unit, 1930-33.

The critical and commercial success of *Drifters* enabled Grierson to put his plans for documentary film production at the EMB into practice.[180] On 28 April 1930, the EMB Film Committee submitted proposals for the creation of an EMB film unit, which would be supervised by Grierson, and would receive additional help from New Era Films.[181]

Grierson's first two employees were Basil Wright – who began work for Grierson in December 1929 – and John Taylor. They were soon joined in the attic rooms of New Era, at 179 Wardour Street, by the New Era cameraman, J. D. Davidson. Grierson's proposals to the Film Committee in April 1930 were designed to acquire official recognition for this group, and to facilitate its expansion. This initial trio were soon joined by Arthur Elton, who had read English and Psychology at Cambridge, and had written film criticism for *Granta*. These four were later joined by J. N. G. Davidson, who had edited *Granta* at Cambridge; Edgar Anstey, who had previously worked as a Junior Scientific Assistant in the Department of Industrial and Scientific Research; Paul Rotha, the author of *The Film Till Now* (1930); Marion Grierson, Grierson's youngest sister; Evelyn Spice, who was a friend of Marion Grierson; Margaret Taylor, John Taylor's sister; and Jonah Jones, Chick Fowle, and Fred Gamage, who were trainee cameramen or office assistants. This group were later joined by Stuart Legg and Harry Watt.[182] In order to disguise this expansion from the Treasury, a strategy was developed whereby all those mentioned above were employed by New Era, rather than the EMB, and were then posted out on long term contracts to the EMB Film Unit. Grierson was the only member of the documentary movement, at this stage, who was directly employed by the State.[183]

During its first year of existence, the EMB Film Unit assembled films out of existing footage. These were either short 'poster' films, or single-reel films displayed at the Imperial Institute cinema.[184] The poster films were thirty-foot loops projected on continuous daylight projectors at EMB exhibitions, railway stations or shop windows. They were nearly all made by Basil Wright and Paul Rotha, and used various 'trick titles, abstract effects and models.'[185] Single-reel films, such as *Conquest* (1930), *Lumber* (1930), *South African Fruit* (1930), *Canadian Apples* (1930), and *Sheep Dipping* (1930), were made entirely from existing stock footage, and no new film was shot in their making. Grierson believed that the editing and re-editing of film provided the best possible training for his young film-makers. It was also the least expensive form of film production.[186]

Once film production at the Film Unit was underway, Grierson began an intensive campaign to publicize the work of his film-makers. He had begun to write film criticism in England in June 1929, and from then till 1933, he contributed to many periodicals and journals, including, the *Clarion*; the *New Clarion*; *Everyman*; *New Britain*; *Sight and Sound*; *Artwork*; *Cinema Quarterly*; and others.[187] He also maintained close contacts with many critics and journalists who were sympathetic to the documentary movement: including W. A. J. Lawrence of *The Times*, Ritchie Calder of the *Daily Herald*, Caroline Lejeune of the *Observer*, Cedric Belfrage of the *Daily Express*, William Jeffrey of the *Glasgow Herald*, Ernest Dyer of the *Newcastle Chronicle*, Charles Davy of the *Yorkshire Post*, and Robert Herring of the *Manchester Guardian*.[188] In addition to these contacts, Grierson also sought as many invitations to speak before audiences as he could physically accommodate. He encouraged his film-makers to do likewise, and, for example, Paul Rotha has recollected speaking in more than twenty-five cities during his four month long period of employment at the EMB Film Unit, from January to May 1931.[189] Grierson first met his friend, and future biographer, H. Forsyth Hardy in 1930, when Hardy was working as a reporter on the *Scotsman*. This meeting established a relationship whereby Grierson arranged for Hardy to see each documentary film as soon as it was made, so that Hardy could then give it a favourable review in the *Scotsman*.[190]

One of the film unit's most successful entrepreneurial coups was the film display which it assembled for the 1930 Imperial Conference. The film display was a great success, and the Conference, which was already convinced about the need for more films about the Empire, recommended that the EMB should act as a centre for the production of instructional films.[191] The Conference also recommended that the terms of reference of the EMB should be widened, in order to enable it to produce publicity for trade throughout the Empire; rather than just publicity for the consumption of Empire goods in Britain.[192] Following this, the film unit was given another major boost when a Special Committee, which had been established by the Secretary of State for the Colonies and Dominions, Leo Amery, to advise on liaison between the EMB and the Department of Overseas Trade, recommended that the activities of the EMB Film Unit should be expanded.[193]

In the summer of 1931, Grierson and Tallents managed to obtain an increase in the budget of the Film Unit, on the basis of the Imperial Conference's supportive recommendations, and this enabled the production of more sophisticated films to be undertaken.[194] However, these new films had not progressed far beyond the scriptwriting stage when they were temporarily shelved as a consequence of the employment of Robert Flaherty. Flaherty had contacted Grierson from Germany after a contract to make a film in Russia had collapsed. Grierson then approached Tallents with a request for Flaherty to be employed at the EMB, and Tallents managed to persuade the Treasury to employ Flaherty at an 'undisclosed fee'. A sum of £2,500, an enormous sum by film unit standards, was then made available to Flaherty in order to finance the production of a film for the EMB.[195] The employment of a film-maker of such high status as Flaherty was a considerable achievement for Grierson, and for the documentary movement. However, Flaherty's appointment was almost certainly a consequence of the support given to the film unit by the Imperial Conference the previous year. Had that support not been forthcoming, Tallents and Grierson would certainly have failed to secure Flaherty's appointment.

Grierson was well aware that Flaherty's working methods, which involved considerable quantities of location shooting, could easily over-run the budget which had been set for the film. His apprehensions were soon confirmed when Flaherty went quickly over budget, and when the rushes were shown at the EMB he insisted that film unit staff, and not Flaherty, should edit them. Basil Wright and Arthur Elton were then sent out to shoot additional footage, and Edgar Anstey edited this, and Flaherty's footage, under Grierson's supervision, at Grierson's home in Southwark.[196] The resulting film, *Industrial Britain* (1931), was a roman-tic celebration of industrial craftsmanship, and contained some of the best industrial photography of any film of that period. Along with *Drifters*, it was the most successful film to be made at the EMB, and was also the first significant example of Grierson's method of group film-making.[197]

In the autumn of 1931, work on the films which had been delayed by the Flaherty film, began once again. The resulting films were: *The Country Comes to Town* (Wright, 1931), *O'er Hill and Dale* (Wright, 1931), *Lumber* (Wright, 1931), *Upstream* (Elton, 1931), and *Shadow on the*

Still from *Industrial Britain*

Mountain (Elton, 1931). These films, together with *Industrial Britain*, were sold to Ideal Films, a renter-producer company formed in 1926, and owned by the Gaumont British Picture Corporation.[198] This group of films, which became known as the Imperial Six, was a significant advance on the poster films and editing exercises of 1930. They were two-reel films, of around thirty minutes duration, which used freshly shot film, in addition to library footage. However, despite this improvement, the only film of this group to have had any lasting appeal, was *Industrial Britain*, and this was primarily because of Flaherty's camerawork, and not because of the editing carried out by the documentary film makers. By 1931, none of Grierson's protegés had acquired sufficient experience in the craft of film-making to make films of lasting quality. In addition to dominating the film unit as leader and producer, Grierson was also the unit's outstanding film-maker, and if he had directed the Imperial Six – with professional help from within the film industry – those films would have been better than they actually were. The only two films of real quality which emerged from the EMB Film Unit were *Drifters*, and *Industrial Britain*, and, in both cases, these films were edited by Grierson, and photographed by established professional photographers.

Grierson's strategy in making the Imperial Six was influenced by his belief in the necessity of building a movement up from scratch. However, this strategy also led to a situation where the overall quality of EMB film production was relatively low, because insufficient professional expertise was drafted in from the commercial film industry.[199] It also led, in addition, to a situation where Grierson was able to completely dominate the young individuals under his control. This was commented on by several critics at the time. Caroline Lejeune of *Observer*, one of the most enthusiastic early admirers of the documentary movement, accused Grierson of moulding his protegés into inferior copies of himself, and of creating a 'rather tiresome tradition'[200] which threatened the advance of British avant-garde film-making. The relative success of *Industrial Britain* and *Drifters*, both of which were made with outside help, and the relative failure of the other EMB films, which were not, tends to support Lejeune's argument. Although there were practical difficulties involved in attracting professional expertise to the film unit, the main difficulty lay in Grierson's disinclination to allow his authority to be undermined by fellow professionals, whose ideas might differ from his own.

Despite the expansion of production which followed from the support of the Imperial Conference, and from the continuous lobbying carried out by Tallents and Grierson, the early summer of 1931 marked the summit of the EMB's expansion. In December 1931 the Film Committee was informed that its funding would be reduced, and that, thereafter, the film unit would have to be maintained at 'mere subsistence level', with all production work kept to a minimum, and priority given to completing existing productions. The purchase of a badly needed sound synchronization system was, therefore, postponed indefinitely.[201] Following this, the film unit vote was cut again in April 1932, and only £2,950 was set aside for production expenses during the 1932-3 period. This was only 450 pounds more than had been set aside for the production of one film by Flaherty the previous year.[202] Finally, in December 1932 the total film unit budget was cut from £10,000 to £6,000, and a complete embargo was placed on new production work.[203]

This inadequate level of finance and resources effectively undermined Grierson's vision of establishing a socially purposive cinema sponsored by the State, and led him to explore alternative means of sponsorship and finance. In February 1931, he travelled to North America on behalf of the EMB, in order to study specialized, non-theatrical film-making there. He was particularly impressed by the American Bureau of Mines Film Unit, and by its sponsorship arrangements whereby the Bureau put production proposals to corporate sponsors, and then controlled all aspects of resulting production. Grierson learned that the Bureau of Mines Film Unit had negotiated a contract with Paramount Pictures to produce and distribute 400 short films. These films, which would all be theatrically distributed, would represent various aspects of American industry, and would constitute 'the very largest propaganda scheme on foot anywhere.'[204]

The American Bureau of Mines Film Unit provided Grierson with a model of non-governmental corporate sponsorship which left significant editorial control over production with the film-makers. But, in 1931, just before the economic crisis of that year broke, Grierson still believed that effective, socially purposive film production could best be pursued within government departments, or public institutions. Because of this, it was the Canadian Motion Picture Bureau, and not the American Bureau of Mines, which became his preferred model for the future development of the documentary film movement.

The Canadian Motion Picture Bureau (CMPB) was established as a branch of the Canadian Department of Trade and Commerce in 1917. It had a wide remit to produce both cultural and trade propaganda, and enjoyed complete editorial control over its production and distribution activities. According to its Director, Frank Badgley, who presented a written report to the EMB Film Committee in August 1928 it was the largest organization of its kind in the world.[205]

The relative autonomy of editorial control and freedom from financial and political pressure which the CMPB enjoyed, made it an appropriate model on which Grierson could base his strategy of documentary film production. He was almost as enthusiastic about the organization of educational film-making in Soviet Russia, and argued that Sovkino, Goskino, Narkompros and Kinopodotel[206] had made Soviet cinema 'a manipulator of ideologies and an integral part of the educational life of the country.'[207] However, he believed that the control which the Soviet state exercised over Soviet cinema, would place excessive constraints upon film-makers, and be unacceptable in the West.

When the EMB Film Unit's production budget was slashed in 1931, Grierson realised that State support on the Canadian scale would no longer be obtainable. He therefore turned back to the system of non-governmental corporate sponsorship practised by the American Bureau of Mines Film Unit. A sponsored contract with His Master's Voice Gramophone Company resulted in Arthur Elton's *Voice of the World* (1932), which was the first industrially-sponsored documentary to be made by the documentary film movement. Stuart Legg then made *The New Generation* (1932) for the Chesterfield Education Authority, and Basil Wright made *Song of Ceylon* (1933) for the Ceylon Tea Board. A number of minor films were also made for various government departments, including the Ministry of Agriculture and Fisheries, the Scottish Department of Agriculture, the Post Office, the Air Ministry, the Admiralty, the Department of Overseas Trade, and the Telephone Advisory Service.[208]

It is clear from the above that the documentary movement did not succeed in attracting as many outside sponsors as it would have liked. However, the Film Unit's attempts to attract outside sponsors were hampered by its lack of a sound-synchronization system. The sound film had arrived in 1927, when American films such as *The Singing Fool* (1927) and *Broadway Melody* (1927) appeared, using the new Western Electric sound-synchronization system. Public demand for sound films soon led to a radical reorganization of the film industry, and to the introduction of new production and exhibition practices. Small producers, unable to meet the costs of the new technology, went bankrupt, not only because of public demand for the new sound films, but also because the supply of silent films was reduced progressively after 1927.[209] These circumstances made it difficult for the EMB Film Unit, all of whose films were silent, to obtain theatrical distribution.

In addition to the lack of a sound-synchronization system, the Film Unit's inability to obtain theatrical distribution and attract commercial sponsors, was also the result of the appearance of the 'double feature' programme, and the lack of legislative protection given to the short film industry in the Cinematograph Films Act of 1927. In the 1927 memorandum which Grierson wrote for the EMB Film Committee, he argued that the second-rate feature films which appeared in the same programme as top box-office films, could be replaced by four-reeler documentaries, of the *Drifters* type.[210] However, the appearance of the sound film undermined Grierson's expectations, because renters then had a large number of silent films on their hands, which they could neither afford to scrap, nor tender on a competitive basis. As a consequence, the practice of placing a silent film on the same programme as a sound film appeared. This undermined Grierson's hopes for getting theatrical distribution for his documentary films, which were squeezed out of the market by four-to-eight reeler silent films.[211]

Grierson's expectations were also undermined by the lack of legislative protection given to short films in the Cinematograph Films Act of 1927. The most important provision in the Act was the establishment of a minimum quota for British film production. This had been made in order to counteract American dominance of the British film industry. However, the Act only provided quota protection for films of over 3,000 feet in length, and the short films industry suffered as a consequence. Between 1929 and 1935, the footage of short films made in Britain dropped from 170,000 feet, to 68,000 feet.[212] This context of recession in the short films industry, together with the appearance of the double feature programme, and lack of suitable sound equipment, made it virtually impossible for the documentary film movement to succeed in obtaining commercial distribution and external sponsorship. In the few cases when the Film Unit did succeed in overcoming these obstacles, its lack of bargaining power meant that sponsors could dictate the terms which suited them. This was the case with the Imperial Six, where an inappropriate commentary was added to the films, despite Grierson's objections.[213]

These obstacles to theatrical distribution and external sponsorship led the EMB Film Unit to concentrate increasingly on non-theatrical distribution, and it was in this field that the documentary movement achieved its greatest success prior to 1934. By 1932, an estimated 1,500,000 people, mainly schoolchildren, had seen EMB films at the Imperial Institute Cinema.[214] In addition, 294 schools, and seventy-three other organisations also used EMB films, making the film unit the largest supplier of educational films in Britain.[215] Although some of these statistics may have been exaggerated by Grierson and Tallents, they nevertheless represented a considerable achievement for an organisation only one year old in 1932.

Grierson's vision of a socially purposive cinema, working within the State, was undermined by the context within which the Film Unit found itself. Despite the support of influential sympathizers, the position of the EMB and the EMB Film Unit became increasingly untenable, until, in September 1933, both were abolished. However, Stephen Tallents was able to obtain an appointment as Public Relations Officer at the Post Office, and, as a condition of that appointment, he insisted that the EMB Film Unit should be transferred to the Post Office. The Post Office eventually agreed to this, and, as a result, the documentary film movement survived the collapse of the EMB. However, despite this reprieve, the new GPO Film Unit continued to encounter the same problems which had hindered the expansion of the EMB Film Unit up till 1933. The next chapter of this book will investigate how those problems continued to affect the documentary movement up till 1939, and how the movement coped with an adverse political environment.

5 The General Post Office Film Unit 1933–9

Despite the conviction behind their campaign to save the EMB, Grierson and Tallents' priority was to ensure that the skills necessary for effective government publicity were preserved.[1] William Crawford, who had worked at the EMB between 1926 and 1931, was a member of the Post Office Telephone Advancement Committee, and he helped persuade the Post Office to appoint Tallents, arguing that Tallents was the leading expert in public sector publicity.[2] The Post Office suffered from a poor public image during this period, and Tallents' appointment was eagerly sought. This in turn made it easier for him to persuade the Post-Master General, Sir Kingsley Wood, that Grierson and the Film Unit should also be employed at the Post Office.[3]

At the Post Office, Grierson and the Film Unit found themselves in an auspicious environment. Prior to the transfer, the Post Office had commissioned two films from the EMB Film Unit: *Telephone Workers* (1932), and *The Coming of the Dial* (1932). These were routine instructional films which advertised a new telephone exchange system then being introduced by the Post Office.[4] In addition to these commissions, Sir Kingsley Wood also argued that 'it was of great importance to the continuity of Post Office publicity policy that the EMB Film Unit and Film Library should be preserved.'[5] However, despite this supportive environment, the documentary movement remained subject to the same pressures and constraints which had afflicted it between 1927 and 1933.

Shortly after transfer the Film Unit moved to larger premises in Soho Square, Central London, and also acquired an old art studio for sound recording purposes at Blackheath, in south-east London. The Post Office had provided the Film Unit with a sound recording system, but had been forced to purchase a cheap, and inferior, British Visatone system. As a consequence of this, many of the documentary movement's films, including the classic *Night Mail* (1936), suffered from inferior sound quality.[6]

Soon after the aquisition of sound, the professionalism and technical competence of the Film Unit was enhanced by the appointment of Alberto Cavalcanti, who joined the unit in 1934. Cavalcanti was a Brazilian who had gone to France in the early twenties to study architecture. Whilst in Paris he became involved with a group of French avant-garde film-makers, including Jean Renoir, René Clair, and Jean Vigo, and made two experimental films: *Rien que les heures* (1926-7) and *En rade* (1927), both of which achieved critical acclaim. The main concern of the French avant-garde during the twenties was to explore the possibilities of film form and reject conventional 'filmed theatre'.[7] Cavalcanti was influenced by this approach, and, in 1934, came to London, where he was put in contact with Grierson by Jimmy Rogers, who had been his cameraman on both *Rien que les heures* and *En rade*.

Alberto Cavalcanti

Grierson was familiar with Cavalcanti's work because both these films had been screened at the London Film Society, and he immediately offered him a temporary contract.[8] At the time, Cavalcanti was probably using the documentary movement as a stepping-stone into the feature film industry, although he was later to deny this.[9] He eventually stayed with the GPO Film Unit throughout the thirties, and played a significant role in the production of the documentary movement's best films. His knowledge of film technique also complemented Grierson's knowledge of philosophy and aesthetics, and the combination of these two influences was largely responsible for shaping the development of the documentary movement from 1934 to 1938.[10]

Basil Wright

Much of the GPO Film Unit's early production consisted of routine two-reelers on aspects of Post Office services. Scope for artistic licence was necessarily limited, although Grierson and Cavalcanti took the opportunity to explore technical and aesthetic problems whenever possible. These films included *Cable Ship* (1933), which dealt with the Post Office's work in repairing submarine telephone cables; *Six-thirty Collection* (1934), on the collection, sorting, and despatch of mail at a

London post office; *Weather Forecast* (1934), on the collection and com-munication of information on weather systems; *Under the City* (1934), on the maintenance of telephone cables in London; and *Droitwich* (1934), on the erection of the tallest radio station mast in Britain. These films were shot on location, on small budgets, and are of interest in that they contained some of Cavalcanti's first experiments with symbolic sound.[11]

In addition to these films, two significant films which had been begun during the EMB period were also made. These were: *Song of Ceylon* (1934) and *BBC Voice of Britain* (1934), which were commissioned by the Ceylon Tea Board and the BBC respectively. When Grierson realised that the creation of an extensive production unit at the EMB was unlikely he attempted to obtain commissions from outside bodies. In 1932, Gervas Huxley, who had been the Secretary of the EMB Film Committee, and was at that time Public Relations Officer for the Ceylon Tea Propaganda Board, commissioned Grierson to make a set of four films on tea production. Grierson appointed Basil Wright and John Taylor to make the films, and, when Wright and Taylor returned from Ceylon with the footage, he instructed Wright to merge the four short films into one long one.[12] He also hired the composer Walter Leigh, and the photographer and pianist Lionel Wendt, to work on the music score and script respectively, alongside Wright.

The final version of *Song of Ceylon* retained the four part construction of the original commission. In part one, 'The Buddha', Wright used associational editing devices which orchestrated sound and image formalistically, to convey a sense of timeless tradition. In part two: 'The Virgin Island', images of modern industry and commerce predominated, whilst in part three: 'The Voices of Commerce', a contrast was made between traditional ways of life and the intrusion of a modern commercial culture. This contrast was emphasized by the use of contrasting montage devices, such as images of natives using elephants to knock down trees and a voice-over commentary which gave details of market prices. In part four: 'The Apparel of a God', the film returned to religious themes, and closed with shots of palm foliage similar to those with which it began. This gave the film an abstract quality, hinting at timelessness and completeness.

Song of Ceylon is a formalist and modernist documentary, rather than a piece of naturalistic reporting. Like *Drifters*, it also uses symbolic expression to represent contradiction and inter-connection. For example, sequences in part three of *Song of Ceylon*, in which images of traditional and modern life are contrasted, are similar to the final sequences of *Drifters*, in which the labour of fishermen is contrasted with – and connected to – an industrial and commercial infrastructure. But whereas *Drifters* ends with images of a modern industrial world, *Song of Ceylon* ends with themes of traditional ritual and experience.

Contrasting images of ancient and modern in *Song of Ceylon*

One of the most interesting aspects of *Song of Ceylon* is its use of sound. The narration was spoken by Wendt, using the text of a seventeenth-century travel book about Ceylon.[13] The archaic prose, and the disembodied details of trade prices, contrasted with the film's visuals, and represented the documentary movement's first significant experiments with the use of non-synchronized sound. Although not as historically significant as *Drifters*, or some later documentary films, *Song of Ceylon* remains one of the most technically and aesthetically accomplished films to be made by the documentary movement, and was awarded the *Prix du Gouvernement Belge* at the Brussels Film Festival of 1935.[14]

The other major production begun during the EMB period, and carried over into the GPO, *BBC Voice of Britain*, was less successful. In 1932, the BBC commissioned the EMB Film Unit to make a publicity film. The resulting film was the longest and most expensive film to be made by the Film Unit, and was designed to appeal to a more popular market than *Song of Ceylon* or *Drifters*, by including sequences on some of the BBC's light entertainment programmes. It was another example of Grierson's collaborative approach to film-making, and included contributions from Cavalcanti, Stuart Legg, Harry Watt, Evelyn Spice, and Grierson. However, the film was not a success, and failed at the box-office. It was also strongly criticized by several critics, including Graham Greene.[15]

During the period in which these films were in production Britain was experiencing a major economic recession, and, as a response, the government established a number of select committees to investigate ways of reducing 'wasteful government expenditure'. The transfer of the Film Unit to the Post Office had initially been sanctioned by the Treasury for a period of six months only.[16] When that probationary period came to an end the Film Unit was investigated by a Select Committee, which published a highly critical report on 2 July 1934.[17] Some of the arguments contained in that report, by civil servants and representatives from the film trade, reveal the extent of opposition to the documentary movement which existed at the time.

The trade representatives who gave evidence to the Select Committee believed that the government ought to put the resources of the GPO Film Unit into the private sector, rather than allow the Film Unit to compete with existing commercial interests. This was particularly strongly felt by the Gaumont British Corporation, which was then trying to gain control of the short films market. The trade was represented on the committee by Mary Field, a maker of educational films and director of Gaumont British Instructional Ltd. She was supported by Neville Kearney, the head of the film industry branch of the Federation of British Industry, and by R. S. Lambert, a director of the British Film Institute. The British Film Institute had been established in 1933, after the publication of a report by the Commission on Educational and Cultural Films entitled *The Film in National Life*. The Institute regarded the documentary movement as an obstacle to its attempts to become a centre for publicly-funded activities within the film industry, and wished to take over many of the functions then being carried out by the movement.

At one level the arguments of the British Film Institute made sense, and it would have been more appropriate for it to become a centre for publicly funded film activities, than a Film Unit housed in the Post Office. In addition, the GPO Film Unit had never been given official consent for many of its activities, and the British Film Institute was fully justified in complaining that these unsanctioned activities obstructed its own development. However, it is important to understand the nature of the Institute during this period, and its relation to the corporate sector. The Institute was politically to the right of the documentary movement, and involved with Conservative groupings.[18] If it had taken over the role of the GPO Film Unit, it would merely have commissioned conventional publicity films, from GBPC and similar. In this respect it would have functioned in a way common during the inter-war period, as a quango which channelled public finance and resources into the corporate sector. Because Gaumont British had the best resources, in terms of distribution and exhibition, it would have been the main beneficiary. Government public relations film-making would then have developed in a standard way, but this only serves to illustrate the fact that Grierson and the documentary movement were not typical public relations publicists. They were political activists, who used public relations in order to promote social reform. Of course, such a role was never, and could never, be officially sanctioned, but this does not mean that more significant films would have been made had the Film Unit relinquished its role in favour of the British Film Institute. In fact the opposite would have been the case.

Despite this, the Select Committee had little real alternative but to agree with the arguments put by the film trade. It instructed the Film Unit to cease using one permanent contractor, and to put out contracts to tender in the normal way. The Committee also reasserted objections that the existence of a government Film Unit constituted unfair competition with the trade, and unacceptable government interference in commercial activity.[19] The committee went on to argue that the existence of a Film Unit based in the Post Office which made films for other government departments, was an anachronism, and that, in future, Post Office film-making should be confined to the promotion of Post Office services only.[20] Finally, the Select Committee instructed the Post Office to supervise the Film Unit closely, and to report back on the changes which had been recommended by 31 March 1936.

These recommendations posed a considerable threat to the Film Unit, and their implementation would have radically reduced the film-makers' control over production, and curtailed the growth of the documentary movement by proscribing films commissioned by other public bodies. It was, therefore, imperative that Grierson and Tallents devised a means of limiting the impact of those recommendations. During the negotiations with the Treasury which followed, the Post Office succeeded in extracting an agreement whereby the Film Unit would remain in 'direct artistic control' of GPO film production.[21] The Treasury interpreted that agreement as meaning that Grierson would be employed as the 'creative staff', and that all production work would be carried out by commercial contractors. However, at a meeting of the Post Office Film Unit Committee in November 1934, at which proposals for implementing the Post Office's agreement with the Treasury were considered, Grierson proposed that – in addition to himself – Arthur Elton, Basil Wright and Stuart Legg should also be employed as 'creative staff'.[22] He also proposed that a minimum of thirty people should be employed by a single contractor – New Era – to work on long-term contracts for the GPO Film Unit. Grierson's objective was to stretch the Treasury agreement to its limit. The Post Office Film Committee and Public Relations Department, both of which supported Grierson's general aims, accepted the proposals, and managed to override the objections of the Treasury, which was unhappy about the Post Office's interpretation of the Select Committee's instructions.[23] Nevertheless, the Treasury still instructed the Post Office to keep the Film Unit under 'constant review', and to report back by 1936.[24]

The Post Office's willingness to defy the spirit, if not the letter, of the Select Committee and Treasury's instructions, revealed the extent of support which Grierson and the Film Unit enjoyed at the Post Office. However, despite this help, the Film Unit remained vulnerable to criticism from both the Treasury and the commercial film trade. When Grierson selected New Era as Post Office contractor, and filled it with his protegés, the Treasury again criticized the untenable distinction between 'creative' and 'non-creative' staff, and instructed that none of the directorial staff should be directly employed.[25]

Once again, this threatened Grierson's hopes for the documentary movement. However, he was somehow able to pull off one of his most successful coups, by convincing the Treasury that the irrational distinction between creative and non-creative personnel could be resolved by the employment of all the contractor's staff at the Post Office.[26] This achievement enabled a more rational administrative structure to become established at the Film Unit, which in turn enabled the Post Office to ward off criticism more effectively.

However, despite the success of Grierson's tactics in this case, other tactics were far less successful. The ploy of pretending that the Film

Unit's films were made by a commercial contractor had been used successfully in 1928, but, by 1934, the Treasury was familiar with this ruse.[27] The continued use of this strategy as late as 1935 was bound to be counter-productive, as was Grierson's decision to allow Arthur Elton to begin making a film for the Ministry of Labour, *Workers and Jobs* (1935), only weeks after the Treasury had reminded the Post Office that the Film Unit was not allowed to make films for outside bodies.[28]

Grierson (left) with Arthur Elton

By the end of 1935, Grierson had become pessimistic about the Film Unit's chances of surviving the 1936 Committee of Enquiry review as a significant production force.[29] Stephen Tallents left the GPO to take up an appointment at the BBC in 1935, and his departure meant that the film-makers were deprived of his protective offices. Tallents' successor, Ernest Crutchley, was a more traditional type of civil servant, and

Grierson realised that he would insist on the introduction of more orthodox practices at the Film Unit.[30] The restrictions which had been
imposed on production by the Treasury and the Select Committee, led
the film-makers to believe that further progress at the Post Office was
unlikely, and, at Grierson's instigation, many left to join or found other
organizations. Edgar Anstey established the Shell Film Unit, and also
produced the British edition of *The March of Time* newsreel. Donald
Taylor, Paul Rotha and Stuart Legg established the Strand Film Unit, and
Basil Wright established the Realist Film Unit.[31] Finally, Grierson himself
announced his intention to resign before the Committee of Enquiry was
set up,[32] and he eventually left in June 1937.[33]

The first Film Unit to be established by the documentary movement
was the Shell Film Unit, which was established by Edgar Anstey in 1934,
but which had its origins in contacts made prior to that by Paul Rotha.
When Rotha left the EMB Film Unit in 1932 he contacted Jack Beddington, then in charge of publicity for Shell-Mex and BP. Beddington had
financed several publicity ventures prior to meeting Rotha, and had
employed artists such as Paul Nash, John Piper, Graham Sutherland, and
John Betjeman.[34] He responded favourably to Rotha's ideas, and offered
the latter a contract, to be sponsored jointly by Shell and Imperial
Airways. However, Rotha was not allowed to take the contract as an
individual, and was forced to become attached to Bruce Woolf's British
Instructional Films. He made several films with BIF including: *Contact*
(1933), *Roadworks* (1933), *Rising Tide* (1933), *Shipyard* (1934-5), and *The
Face of Britain* (1934). *The Face of Britain* was shot whilst he travelled to
and from Barrow-in-Furness during the making of *Shipyard*. He was
reading J. B. Priestley's *English Journey* (1933), at the time, and was able
to compare his own experiences of the depressed areas with those of
Priestley. This had a considerable impact on him, and was influential in
placing him to the left of many of the other film-makers within the
documentary movement.[35]

Grierson was first introduced to Jack Beddington by Rotha at a private
screening of *Contact*, and following this Beddington asked Grierson to
write a report on how Shell could improve its use of film publicity. The
Shell Film Unit eventually emerged from this report. However, the Unit
did not produce many significant films, either because of the restrictions
placed on such production by corporate private sponsorship, or because
of the inclinations of the film-makers who worked there. Most of the films
produced were routine instructional films such as J. B. Holmes' *How to
Cook* (1937), and the unit was not as important as either the GPO or
Realist Film Units.

The first independent film unit to be established was the Strand Film
Unit, which was established in 1935.[36] Grierson believed that a small
group of public relations officers, many of whom had once been

connected with the EMB, could form the basis of an industrial sponsorship system. This group included Gervas Huxley of the Ceylon Tea Board, and Frank Pick of London Transport. To these should be added Jack Beddington of Shell and BP, Snowden Gamble of Imperial Airways; Col Medlicott of Anglo-Iranian Oil; S. C. Leslie and A. P. Ryan of the Gas Industry; Tommie Tallents – Stephen Tallents' younger brother – of the Orient Shipping Line; Niven McNichol of the Scottish Office; and Alexander Walcough of the oil industry.

In order to begin production at Strand, Grierson diverted two films which had been commissioned by the Ministry of Labour: *On the Road to Work* (1936), and *Stand by for Work* (1936). The former was significant in that it contained instances of direct speech recorded on location: a difficult enterprise, given the bulky nature of the Film Unit's sound equipment. Paul Rotha spent three years at Strand as producer, and only played a part in the actual production of two films: *The Future is in the Air* (1937), and *Today We Live* (1937). The latter was the most significant film to emerge from the Strand Film Unit, and is a good example of the quality documentary which Grierson hoped it would be possible to make from corporate or semi-public sponsorship. During the Depression, the National Council for Social Service initiated community projects amongst unemployed miners, whilst the Land Settlement Association transported miners to rural settlements run on a co-operative, non-profit-making basis.[37] Both bodies asked the Strand Unit to make films, and money was raised from the Carnegie United Kingdom trust.

Today We Live contained some moving accounts of the effects of unemployment on miners, and used direct dialogue, with miners speaking into camera. It also included a famous sequence, shown many times since, of miners scavenging for coal on a slag tip. The film ends with the implication that social reform was necessary, but this is muted to some extent by the emphasis which is placed on the good work being done by the National Council for Social Service. This encapsulated the dilemma for a film-maker like Rotha, who wanted to make social comments, whilst being forced to remain within the restrictions imposed by private sponsorship. *The Times* described the film as 'not propaganda but a film with a purpose', and compared it favourably with the 'agonising pictures painted by those serious novelists who have looked on unemployment and despaired.'[38] In other words, compared to passages in Priestley's *English Journey*, or Orwell's *The Road to Wigan Pier* (1937), *Today We Live* contained a certain amount of 'uplift', which *The Times* found constructive. The question is, whether films such as *Today We Live* merely served as a 'safety valve' for social discontent, or whether the critical material which they contained contributed to a process of reform. This question, which recurs throughout debates on the documentary movement, is an important one, and will be dealt with in detail later.

Alexander Shaw, Stanley Hawes, Jack Holmes, John Taylor, Ruby Grierson, Ralph Bond, Donald Alexander, and George Noble all joined the Strand Film Unit at one time or another, but the only other significant films made at the unit were *Cover to Cover* (1936) and *Chapter and Verse* (1936), both commissioned by the National Book League. Both films contained interviews by T.S.Eliot, Somerset Maugham, John Masefield, Rebecca West, and Julian Huxley, in which these individuals talked unscripted into camera about literature. *Cover to Cover* was also the first film other than newsreels to be shown on BBC television, in 1936. Other sponsors of Strand films during the period were the Southern Railway: *The Way to the Sea* (1937), Imperial Airways: *The Future is in the Air* (1937), *Air Outpost* (1937) and *Watch and Ward in the Air* (1937) and Anglo-Iranian Oil: *Dawn of Iran* (1938). All of these were either corporate or semi-public bodies. Rotha left Strand after two years, and after this the Unit produced little of significance, making few of the socially-conscious films associated with Grierson.

In February 1937 the Realist Film Unit was established. This eventually became the most important of the documentary units outside the GPO, and produced some influential films. Realist was established by Basil Wright, and the initial production team consisted of Wright, Cavalcanti, John Taylor and, from time to time, Stuart Legg. Realist's most important early films were sponsored by the gas industry. This connection dated from when two successive Public Relations Officers within the gas industry: A. P. Ryan and S. C. Leslie, both Australians, had come to know Grierson. The gas industry eventually sponsored a number of significant films which commented on social issues. At the time, the Labour-controlled London County Council was installing electricity, rather than gas, in its council estates. The gas industry responded to this through appealing to the political views of the LCC, by sponsoring documentary films which emphasized the need for social reconstruction. The industry believed that the need to appeal to the LCC outweighed the risk of criticisms it might face from the right over 'political bias'. The industry was also trying to improve its image, and compete against the commercial threat posed by electricity, by associating itself with ideas of social reform and contemporary relevance. So, the interests of the documentary movement coincided with the political and economic priorities of a corporate public utility. However, if the Conservatives had been in power at County Hall, it is unlikely that the gas industry would have commissioned such films.[39]

Prior to these films, a film had been made for the Ministry of Labour which established the method to be followed in the gas films. This was *Workers and Jobs* (1935), which used location shooting and direct sound recording. It was shot in an unemployment exchange, and recorded the unscripted views of unemployed people in the exchange. This led on directly to the first film sponsored by the gas industry: *Housing Problems* (1935). In this film, the cine-verité techniques established by Elton in *Workers and Jobs* were further refined, although the bulky technology then available made this type of approach intrinsically difficult. Interviews for the film were shot on location, and although the slum tenants who were interviewed were given guidelines as to what to talk about, their actual speech remained largely unscripted.

But despite the social comment which it contained, *Housing Problems* represented the social problems it examined as fully resolvable, and the film ends with an over-optimistic vision of 'ideal' housing estates, which replace the slums. The final text is a contradictory document, in which criticism of poverty contrasts with the film's final message. Because of this, *Housing Problems* has become a paradigm case for those who argued that sponsorship compromised the critical faculties of the documentary film-makers. However, Grierson believed that a certain amount of critical material could be inserted into sponsored films. This was a strategy which all the film-makers employed, for example, Ralph Bond has said that *Today We Live* was supposed to be a film about how 'nice charitable people in the National Council for Social Services helped the unemployed by providing leisure facilities'. However, Bond was able to subvert this intention to a limited extent by inserting some critical comments about the lack of influence such activities had on dealing with the central issue of unemployment.[40]

Housing Problems was not a typical 'Griersonian' documentary, in that it did not combine montage and social reportage to the extent which Grierson believed was appropriate. However, Grierson always regarded it as a major production, and the same was true of the second film sponsored by the gas industry, *Enough to Eat* (1936). This was based on Sir John Boyd Orr's Social survey publication *Homes, Food, and Income* (1936), and dealt with the effects of poverty on diet and housing. *Enough to Eat* did not have the same degree of obligation to the activities of its sponsor as did *Housing Problems*, because the gas industry had no vested interest in restricting criticism of public health problems. On the contrary, such criticism actually appealed to the industry's main client, the LCC. Consequently, *Enough to Eat* was able to employ greater social comment than *Housing Problems*, and is perhaps a better example than the latter of the way in which sponsorship was used to promote the ideals of the film-makers.

The first two gas films to be started by Realist were *Children at School* (1937), and *The Smoke Menace* (1937). The former used a journalistic style, as in the previous gas films, whilst the latter used a style based on the American *March of Time* newsreel series. *March of Time* had a considerable influence on the documentary movement, with its strident narrative style and use of reconstructed dialogues between actors representing historical figures. It particularly influenced *Dawn of Iran* and *The Smoke Menace*, and had an influence on Grierson's ideas during the mid-to-late thirties.[41] Both *Children at School* and *The Smoke Menace* were able to make significant comments on the social conditions which they represented, and the Realist Film Unit later went on to make some of the most important films made by the documentary movement during the thirties.

After the formation of new production units, the next step in the consolidation of the documentary movement occurred with the establishment of Associated Realist Film Producers in 1935. ARFP was established in order to bring the various groups of film-makers together into a more cohesive collective. It set aside finance to keep each of its members in employment, and enabled Grierson to allocate contracts to Strand and Realist when it was becoming increasingly difficult to accept outside commissions at the GPO Film Unit. Later that year Grierson launched *World Film News*, a crusading monthly journal, under his overall editorship, which commissioned articles from prominent intellectuals, as well as from Grierson and the other documentary film-makers. Between 1936 and 1937 *World Film News* printed papers by writers as diverse as Bernard Shaw, Aldous Huxley, J. B. Priestley, Somerset Maugham, T. S. Eliot, Graham Greene, Alistair Cooke, Ivor Montague, and, of course, Grierson.

By 1937, the documentary movement consisted of four production units (the GPO Film Unit, Shell, Strand and Realist), an organizational body (Associated Realist Film Producers), and a journal (*World Film News*). ARFP was soon replaced, or taken over, by Film Centre, which was established by Grierson to co-ordinate sponsorship and allocate contracts to Realist and Strand. Film Centre's first major production programme was a series of seven films for the Films of Scotland Committee. This committee was established by the Scottish Development Council, which was financed by the government and other public bodies, and although the films were produced by different companies, Grierson made sure that a consistency of theme, treatment, and quality was maintained. However, none of these films were particularly influential.

As I have shown, constraints on film production at the GPO Film Unit led Grierson to look to corporate sponsorship as an alternative to State sponsorship. The documentary film-makers saw themselves first and foremost as a movement, and not as a group of individual artists. Their decision to strengthen the movement by establishing additional production units was, therefore, consistent with that perception. In terms of his vision of an effective, socially purposive documentary film movement, the GPO Film Unit was a disappointing failure, and Grierson saw no prospect of further improvement at the Post Office whilst he remained there. He was aware that his high profile leadership and unorthodox behaviour had aroused hostility in the Treasury and film trade, and he was also aware that the GPO Film Unit's best prospects for continued operation lay in adopting a profile more consistent with conventional Civil Service practice. His decision to leave the Post Office was partly based on the premiss that sympathetic civil servants within the Post Office would take the opportunity presented by his departure, to restructure the Film Unit in closer accordance with Civil Service norms, and thereby ensure its continuation.[42]

This premiss turned out to be well founded. The Public Relations Officer, Lt Col E. T. Crutchley, took the opportunity provided by Grierson's departure to divide up his old post of Film Officer into two more conventional ones: those of Production Supervisor, and Producer.[43] Grierson's successor as Head of Production at the Film Unit, Alberto Cavalcanti, found himself on the lowest rung of a Civil Service supervisory structure, in which all Film Unit production activities were closely scrutinized, and in which his own activities were restricted solely to matters concerning film production.

The remaining documentary film-makers at the Film Unit were initially apprehensive about this loss of control. However, it soon became clear that the new administrative structure would make them less vulnerable to external criticism, and would enable them to retain some measure of control over production decisions. Alberto Cavalcanti and Harry Watt have both commented on the degree of autonomy and stability which was created by the 1936 reorganization.[44]

The Post Office proposals for the reorganization of the Film Unit were accepted by the Treasury on 12 April 1937. However, the reprieve was only a temporary one as, only three months later, the Post Office received a communication from the House of Lords, which stated that 'in 1939 the whole case of the Film Unit should be reviewed to see whether there are still sufficient grounds for maintaining it as a State service.'[45]

As the 1930s moved towards international crisis, the Post Office argued strongly that the Film Unit should be retained, because it could play an important role if war were to break out.[46] The Treasury responded to this, in a way which reflected the dominant policy of appeasement, by arguing that there was 'no sign of an approaching international emergency,'[47] and therefore no reason for the continued existence of the Film Unit. The letter from which the above quotation was taken was written less than two months after Hitler and Mussolini signed the 'Pact of Steel', and less than two months before the declaration of war.[48] This indicates the establishment's lack of interest in, and opposition to, the kind of State film service represented by the documentary movement, even in late 1939. At the same time, preparations were going on to establish another kind of official film service if war were to break out, and this eventually led to the absorption of the GPO Film Unit into the

Ministry of Information in 1940. However, in the late thirties, the documentary movement was not favoured by the establishment. Despite the disapproval of the Treasury, the Post Office continued to argue the case for retaining the Film Unit throughout 1938 and 1939. One of the cornerstones of its case was the social and aesthetic qualities of the films which had been produced.

An experiment in dramatic construction, *Coal Face*

As already mentioned, much of the Film Unit's films consisted of routine two-reelers, such as *Cable Ship* (1933) and *Weather Forecast* (1934). Following the precedent set by the commercial distribution of the 'Imperial Six' group of films by the EMB, the intention was to distribute these films commercially in groups of six. The first such group was the 'Weather Forecast' group, which consisted of: *Weather Forecast, Granton Trawler, Six-thirty Collection* (1934), *Cable Ship, Spring on the Farm* (1933), and *Windmill in Barbados* (1933). This group was distributed by

Associated Talking Pictures in 1934, and was followed by the 'Post Haste' group, which consisted of: *Post Haste* (1934), *Coal Face* (1935), *Fishing on the Banks of Skye* (1936), *Pett and Pott* (1934), and *BBC Droitwitch* (1934). Other films included: Cavalcanti's *We Live in Two Worlds* (1937), *Four Barriers* (1937), *Message From Geneva* (1937), and *Line to Tschierva Hut* (1937); Harry Watt's *The Saving of Bill Blewitt* (1937), and *Big Money* (1938). None of these, apart from *Coal Face*, were particularly influential.

In addition to these films, the GPO Film Unit also made some films of lasting quality, such as *Song of Ceylon, Coal Face, Housing Problems, Night Mail* (1936) *North Sea* (1933) and *Spare Time* (1939). *Coal Face* (1935) was described in the Film Society programme of 27 October 1935 as 'an experiment in sound'.[49] W. H. Auden and Benjamin Britten were contracted to write the script and music score respectively, and Cavalcanti and Grierson were responsible for the orchestration of sound elements and general editing. The film foregrounded the use of music and sound in a non-naturalistic way, so that natural sounds, dialogue, speech, music, and choral singing were integrated into a dramatic unity. It also contained dramatic footage of mine work, accompanied by statistics on the harshness of conditions, and the high accident rate. It was a significant film for 1935, and a good example of the way in which sponsorship could be subverted to make films of social purpose. Because it had nothing to do with Post Office publicity it was issued under an experimental label, but it was, nevertheless, made at the Post Office, by a government Film Unit.

The collaboration of Britten and Auden in *Coal Face* was continued in a second, and probably the best known film made by the documentary movement, *Night Mail* (1936). Unlike *Coal Face*, which attracted little attention at the time, *Night Mail* received a great deal of critical attention, and was distributed successfully by ABFD. The plot is a simple one: the collection, sorting, and delivery of mail on a night train travelling from London to Scotland. The most significant sequences, created by Cavalcanti, Auden, and Britten, were those in which words and sounds were superimposed over images in a formalist way. As in *Coal Face*, words, music, and image were integrated into a totality. However, *Night Mail* is a film of particular sequences. The main body of the narrative is handled in a fairly pedestrian way, and the photography is not as impressive as in *Coal Face, Drifters, Song of Ceylon* or even *Housing Problems*.

As time moved on, Cavalcanti's influence on the GPO Film Unit increased, particularly after Grierson left to establish Film Centre in 1937. However, it would be a mistake to make too clear a distinction between Grierson's supposedly 'sociological' approach to film-making, and Cavalcanti's more 'aesthetic' approach. In fact, Grierson believed that the aesthetic and sociological functions of the documentary film went hand

Formalist superimposition of word, sound, and image in *Night Mail*

in hand, and that aesthetic experimentation was an important part of the work of the Film Unit. Prior to leaving the GPO Film Unit he had employed Len Lye, Norman McLaren, and Humphrey Jennings – all of whom made films which give the lie to the myth that he was only interested in sociological film-making. For example, Lye made *Colour Box* (1935), *Rainbow Dance* (1936), and *Trade Tattoo* (1937), all of which involved painting directly on to celluloid. Norman McLaren also used animation techniques in *Love on the Wing* (1937), and Cavalcanti indulged in whimsical experiments such as *Pett and Pott* (1934), and *The Fairy of the Phone* (1936). Although Grierson regarded these films as minor films, which they were, he encouraged and supported aesthetic experiment at the GPO Film Unit. There is some evidence that Grierson became strongly influenced by the didactic style of *March of Time* during the late thirties, and Paul Rotha has claimed that this had an undue influence on his ideas.[50] There is some truth in this, but even so, Grierson's ideas on film-making remained remarkably consistent throughout his life, and, at the centre of those ideas, there was a clearly articulated conception of the integration of the sociological and aesthetic functions of film-making.[51]

After 1937 it became more difficult for the GPO film-makers to make films for outside bodies, or to make films which were not evidently related to the specific needs of Post Office publicity. Nevertheless, the film-makers did have some room to manoeuvre, and some important films were made after this date. The most significant development in film-making at the GPO Film Unit after Grierson left was the development of the naturalistic drama documentary. Two films were particularly important in embodying this new style, both made by Harry Watt, with help from Cavalcanti. These were, *The Saving of Bill Blewitt* (1937), and *North Sea* (1938). The former used 'real people', who acted roles in a scripted film, and spoken dialogue replaced the usual voice-of-god narration. This film led on to the far more important *North Sea*, a film which influenced the development of British cinema during the war years, and afterwards.

North Sea is significant because it represents the first successful attempt by a section of the documentary movement to integrate documentary techniques and methods into a format derived from the feature film. Unlike in most documentary films, there is no voice-over commentary. Instead, a fictional diegesis carries the narrative, and individual characterization is employed, as in a feature film. The advantage of this approach is that working-class people are able to speak and act within the narrative, rather than be interpreted by professional actors, who would almost certainly come from a middle-class background. This gives the film an added realism. However, the characters in *North Sea* do not speak for themselves, but instead speak words and ideas scripted by the film's director, Harry Watt. This results in an unsatisfactory and superficial representation of working-class experience, because Watt is clearly unable to identify with his characters sufficiently to do them justice. In addition, *North Sea* places the captain figure in the narrative in a privileged position. In the film, a storm threatens the safety of the trawler, and Watt vests all significance and authority in the captain figure, whilst the rest of the crew obey his will like willing 'heroic' automatons. This may have reflected something of the reality of a captain's absolute authority on one of these ships, but it remains disturbing that Watt should have represented the ordinary crewmen as he did. It is interesting, given that no member of the documentary movement came from a working-class background, that Watt should invest the centre of his film in the captain, and should treat the crew so superficially. In *North Sea*, a middle-class or lower-middle-class sensibility is stamped across the working-class culture the film portrays. This was a common fault in many of the films which came out of the

The crew in need of strong leadership in *North Sea*

The captain exerts his authority over the crew in *North Sea*

documentary movement, but the naturalistic style employed in *North Sea* emphasizes this. *North Sea* also lacked the characteristic Griersonian concern for montage. The main aim of the film was to integrate documentary naturalism into the 'seamless' fictional realism of the commercial cinema. It is no surprise, therefore, that Grierson had his doubts about the film, given that his aesthetic was such a deeply modernist one.

Nevertheless, Cavalcanti and Watt had little alternative but to evolve a more popular style at the GPO Film Unit. The situation there showed no sign of improving, and they believed that the Film Unit would eventually be closed down. The only alternative, they thought, was to move into the commercial cinema, and *North Sea* was made with this in mind. Cavalcanti has since disputed this[52], but the evidence suggests that both he and Watt were trying to evolve a style which would be more acceptable to commercial film producers, and indeed Watt has since admitted that.[53] However, it is difficult to see where Watt and Cavalcanti would have been able to make films like *North Sea* in the commercial film industry in the late thirties. Had it not been for the war, *North Sea* might well have become a one-off, as Watt himself has admitted:

> Although *North Sea* was a slight commercial success, it had basically no effect or influence on the commercial film-makers of the time, and after making it, Cavalcanti and I were having great difficulty in finding other similar dramatic stories under the necessary sponsorship of the Post Office. It is very possible that, if war had not come, the British documentary movement might have drifted back into the more instructional commentary type of film.[54]

Instead, *North Sea* provided a model for many British war-time films, and initiated a whole tradition of British realist cinema. It was an extremely significant film, even if not a particularly good one, and even though its representation of labour relations verged towards the authoritarian.

The final important film to be made at the GPO Film Unit was Humphrey Jennings' *Spare Time* (1939), which consists of a compilation of sequences on aspects of working-class leisure activities. Some aspects of the film, such as the 'kazoo band' sequence, in which Jennings represented a kazoo band somewhat ambivalently – and not in the heroic Griersonian style – were regarded as insulting to working-class culture by Grierson and other documentary film-makers. This reaction was hardly surprising, given that the documentary movement had struggled for some time to represent working-class experience in a positive light. However, their criticism of *Spare Time* was misdirected, and Jennings' film ranks with the best in the documentary movement. Jennings' sympathetic representation of working-class culture is carried out with intelligence and sensitivity, and still retains a considerable impact today.

The documentary photography, and somewhat oblique commentary manages to avoid the simplistic representation of working-class culture which characterizes many of the films made by the documentary film movement.

The Post Office was able to use these achievements to back up its case for the continued existence of the Film Unit. One of the films it quoted most often was *North Sea* which was the GPO Film Unit's most commercially successful film.[55] The Post Office argued that:

> the GPO Film Unit has now a high and well established reputation as a producer of documentary films. None of its products has been a palpable failure, and many of these have been strikingly successful. *North Sea* in particular has earned over £4,000 in rentals (a sum believed to be a record for documentary films) and has been generally acclaimed by the press as setting a new standard in this field, despite the fact that its release coincided with the release in this country of the far more costly film *The River*, produced under the auspices of the American Government and heralded with a remarkable amount of publicity.[56]

The Post Office used the establishment of the Ministry of Information in August 1939 to argue that the GPO Film Unit should be considered as a government Film Unit, rather than just a Post Office Film Unit, and also argued that it should be transferred to the Ministry of Information on the outbreak of war.[57] This is, in fact, what happened, and the GPO Film Unit was saved from closure in 1939 by the outbreak of the Second World War, when it became part of the Ministry of Information, and was renamed the Crown Film Unit. This new environment, within a central government department, enabled the documentary movement to develop and expand, and to make some of its most influential documentaries, including: *Target For Tonight* (1941), *Fires Were Started* (1943) and *Western Approaches* (1944). However, neither the move to the Ministry of Information, nor the Second World War, was sufficient to secure the future of the State-sponsored documentary film movement. On 9 October 1939, the film-makers received a letter from the Treasury informing them that the Film Unit would be abolished within six months of the end of the war.[58]

From 1927 onwards, Grierson had wanted, first and foremost, to establish the documentary film movement securely within a central department of State. However, this did not come about until late 1939, and even when it did, at the Ministry of Information, it was made plain to the film-makers that their position was only a temporary one, and that the Film Unit would be abolished when the war ended. In terms of Grierson's initial hopes for a socially purposive, State-funded documentary film movement, which would carry out educational and propaganda work in close contact with political legislators, and at the same time contribute towards a process of social reform – the history of the State-funded documentary movement between the wars must be counted as one of comparative failure.

Of course, the documentary movement did expand during the nineteen-thirties, but the pursuance of corporate sponsorship outside the State, or other public bodies, was always a secondary alternative for Grierson. The documentary movement's strategy was founded on the belief that, whilst making routine films, they would also be able to make the occasional film of social purpose. But this was not achieved to a significant enough extent. Grierson himself had already accepted this by the late thirties, and, in 1939, he left Britain for Canada, where he was appointed as first Film Commissioner for the National Film Board of Canada. It was in Canada that he was at last able to establish the sort of documentary film movement which he had been unable to establish in Britain.

6 Public relations, propaganda and documentary film 1900–39

The history of the EMB and GPO Film Units reveals a history of ambivalence, indifference, and sometimes hostility, on the part of certain groups within the establishment and film trade. Although the movement did expand during this period, and had influential supporters, it was always subject to pressures which restricted its development. In terms of Grierson's original vision of a State Film Unit, the history of the documentary film movement between the wars was one of failure.

In order to understand some of the reasons for this, it will first be necessary to relate the documentary movement to a more comprehensive picture of government propaganda in Britain during the inter-war period. When this is done it is apparent that the same attitudes which influenced the development of the documentary movement, also influenced attempts to develop an extensive State propaganda service from as early as 1914. However, the origins of those attitudes lay further back than 1914, and before looking at the development of government propaganda during the inter-war period, it will first be necessary to understand the historical changes which brought modern forms of corporate public relations and government propaganda into being. As a consequence of those changes, governments and corporate institutions were forced to initiate public relations and propaganda strategies, in order to defend their interests, and to manage public opinion. But this need to placate public opinion also implied a diffusion of privileged information into civil society, and this was frequently resented. The documentary film movement was associated with these developments, and, in order to understand the movement's evolution, it will first be necessary to relate it to this context of the evolution of modern traditions of public relations and propaganda, and to the attempts by corporate institutions and government to limit the possible reformist consequences of those traditions. It was precisely this kind of damage control exercise which caused the the British State to restrict the expansion of an extensive, semi-autonomous, government propaganda service during the inter-war period.

The origins of corporate public relations practices can be found in developments which occurred in world capitalism after 1870. The four main characteristics of those developments were: (a) the development of industries around new scientific knowledge; (b) the development of mass production methodologies and technologies; (c) the exploitation of the mass domestic market; and (d) the growth of industrial combination.[1] Of these four factors, the most significant in relation to the development of corporate public relations was the expansion of corporate capitalism. Between 1897 and 1903 a considerable increase in the rate of corporate mergers took place in America. In 1897 there were only twelve national corporations in America, but, by 1903, there were 305.[2] During the same period corporate aggregate capital increased from 1,000,000,000 to 7,000,000,000 dollars,[3] and by 1901 the largest corporation, US Steel, had boardroom control of 158 smaller companies.[4]

However, this degree of corporate expansion soon led to the formation of anti-monopoly pressure groups. Opposition to corporate expansion came from small-scale urban capitalists, agrarian capitalists, the older American middle class and aristocracy, the old and new lower-middle classes, and some sections of the working classes. By the turn of the century, anti-monopoly protest posed a significant threat to the expansion of corporate capitalism in America, and the corporations responded in a number of ways. One such way involved a manipulation of the local and national press: a strategy which dated from the expansion of the railways in the 1840s, when railroad owners were first granted charters of incorporation.[5] The industrial practices followed by the railroads aroused considerable criticism, and were responsible for the appearance of the first anti-trust legislation measures: the Inter-State Commerce Commission of 1886, and the Sherman Anti-Trust Act of 1890. Although these legislative interventions were rendered ineffective by Supreme Court judgments, they served to increase public awareness and criticism of the railroad companies.[6] The railroads responded to this criticism by employing press agents to write favourable press reports, and by bribing politicians, journalists and editors.[7] Public criticism was dealt with relatively effectively by these means until 1900, after which, the emergence of an influential anti-monopoly movement forced the railroads, and other corporations, to evolve new policies.

These policies first emerged in a coal mining dispute of 1906, when the Pennsylvanian anthracite coal industry hired a Public Relations Consultant called Lee.[8] He immediately implemented a strategy which consisted of drawing selected journalists into a consensus over the activities of the corporation, and of releasing more information into the public domain.[9] The new policy was a success, and, as a consequence, Lee was appointed as Public Relations Consultant by the Pennsylvanian Railroad Company in order to defuse criticism over a serious railway accident. The company's standard policy had been to keep journalists from the scene of the accident. However, Lee's strategy, which involved subtle manipulation of the press and public opinion, brought the company its best ever press. The hand picked journalists who collaborated with Lee did so because the arrangement between Lee and themselves was mutually beneficial: they obtained privileged information, whilst the corporation was able to structure that information in its own interests. A consensus was established which served the interests of both parties.

In 1906, Standard Oil, US Steel, and the American Telegraphy and Telephone Company established modern public relations departments, and, by 1908, most American public utilities used modern public relations methods.[10] The public relations industry grew rapidly after 1900, and continued to expand throughout the inter-war period, until it became integrated into top management and national politics. One of the most influential public relations figures, E. L. Bernays, served on the US Committee on Public Relations at the Paris Peace Conference of 1918, and also established the first independent public relations agency in America in 1919.[11] Another influential figure was Walter Lippmann, a journalist whose book *Public Opinion* (1922) had a significant influence on the documentary film movement.

Of the various factors which influenced the development of corporate public relations, the principal one was the expansion of corporate capitalism and the social reaction to that expansion. The impetus to instigate public relations practices originated, primarily, from the requirement of corporate institutions to defend themselves against exterior constraints, and the principal objective of public relations methodology was to create a relationship of identity and consensus between the corporation and exterior groups. This allowed the corporation to manipulate the media, but it also implied a certain diffusion of executive control, through the release of potentially damaging information into the public domain.

The historical forces which led to the development of public relations in America, also led to a similar development in Britain. However, the growth of monopoly capitalism in Britain occurred at a much more protracted pace than in America, and, as a consequence, very little anti-monopoly criticism appeared until mergers occurred on a significant scale during the inter-war period.[12] When this expansion occurred it led to expressions of concern over the implications of unrestricted corporate expansion.[13] However, this concern remained limited, and the terms of debate concerning corporate expansion revolved around the question of 'State interference in the economy', rather than around issues of corporate malpractice. In general, it was the few existing examples of government and municipal monopoly, such as the Post Office and the London County Council, which attracted most criticism.[14] So, whereas in

America, anti-monopoly criticism was influenced by a demand for the State to act as an instrument of control over the corporate sector, in Britain, it was primarily influenced by a demand for a reduction of State intervention.

Although the expansion of corporate capitalism was the most important influence on the development of corporate public relations, two other factors also had a significant influence. These were: (1) the use of public relations as an extension of the rationalization of internal company relations, and (2) its use as a particular publicity strategy in periods of market saturation. It was the latter of these factors which had the greatest influence on British traditions of public relations publicity prior to 1914.

During The Great Depression of the 1880s, market saturation led to the implementation of techniques designed to consolidate existing markets, rather than penetrate new ones. The principal objective of these techniques was to develop a relationship of trust and identity between producers and existing consumers.[15] This strategy led to the development of so called 'prestige advertising', which was a precursor of later public relations publicity. This advertising used pictorial and linguistic devices to project the brand name and ethos of a manufacturer, in contrast to earlier advertising, which advertised a particular product. It appeared less manipulative than earlier advertising, and succeeded in making the advertising industry more respectable.[16] Because it required a significant financial outlay, and because returns on investment were neither immediate nor certain, it was mainly produced in the corporate sector.

Although corporate prestige advertising appeared mainly in poster form, it also appeared in the form of short films. These films were important because they were the first to be used as vehicles for corporate public relations publicity, and because they pre-dated those made by the documentary movement by almost twenty years. Like prestige posters, they were almost all made by corporate companies. They were primarily descriptive, and expressed little if any social comment on the industrial processes which they represented. They included films such as *Bootmaking* (1906); *The Story of a Piece of Slate* (1904); *Life on the Oxo Cattle Ranch* (1911); and *The Manchester Ship Canal* (1912).[17] These films were good examples of prestige publicity in that they attempted to improve relations between producer and consumer by using the pictorial devices of the medium to enhance the prestige of their sponsors. They did not appear in significant numbers until 1904, and by 1906 had been overtaken in popularity by the feature-length fiction film.[18] Despite this, they continued to act as the major vehicle for corporate publicity up to and beyond the First World War,[19] and can be seen as precursors of the documentary movement.

These films were amongst the most interesting examples of pre-war corporate publicity in Britain. However, conditions in Britain before 1914 were not conducive to the expansion of corporate public relations. The principal motivating factors of intensive corporate expansion, and public reaction to that expansion, did not exist. However, after 1914 the need to manage public opinion became a central concern of the British political establishment, and pre-war traditions of corporate publicity became integrated into the State propaganda service which emerged during the First World War.

During the war Britain embarked upon a major programme of propaganda production, and, by 1918, possessed one of the most extensive propaganda services in the world. However, that service did not come into being without first having to overcome considerable factional in-fighting, and, throughout the war period, opinion was unevenly divided between those who were apprehensive about the expansion of State propaganda, and those who believed that an extensive government propaganda service could bring about social unity. These conflicting attitudes on the positive and negative implications of State propaganda became entrenched during the war period.

When war broke out in August 1914 the establishment believed that it could be prosecuted without modifying the central principles of *laissez-faire* liberalism: free trade, a currency on the Gold Standard, and a non-interventionist State.[20] However, it soon became apparent that these principles would have to be significantly modified if the war was to be won, and, consequently, the State was forced to assume control over extensive areas of the economy and civil society. These controls accumulated during the course of the war, and eventually led to a radical transformation of the role of the State within society.[21]

This transformation of political and economic relations also influenced practices and institutions of information manipulation in Britain, and, from 1914 onwards, a political culture developed which was prepared to use the mass media in order to aid the war effort. However, that culture did not become established without first having to overcome opposition from influential groups within the establishment, who were apprehensive about the idea of an extensive State propaganda service. Those groups believed that public opinion could be managed through censorship, rather than through publicity campaigns. This attitude was most common within groups near the centre of the State apparatus, for example, in the Treasury, the Home Office, the War Cabinet, and the various military departments.[22] They believed that wartime government was the prerogative of political, industrial and military elites, and were apprehensive about the use of propaganda campaigns which might incite the public. These attitudes were firmly rooted in an Edwardian perception of the world, in which the public and media could still be excluded from the upper levels of decision-making. However, by 1914, the collective involvement of different social groups and classes in the war effort meant that restrictions on the dissemination of significant social information were no longer feasible.

Such restrictive attitudes were irreconcilable with the social reality which had evolved in conjunction with the 'rise of the working classes in political and economic importance.'[23] This new social reality dictated that there should be an increase in the dissemination of important social information, and, consequently, the State was forced to modify its policy of excessive censorship, and to develop relationships with the media and the public. This was illustrated when, following considerable criticism over excessive censorship, the authorities were forced to establish the Press Bureau in 1914, as a means of channelling selected information to the media.[24] There are obvious parallels here with the development of public relations in America. In both cases, the decision to increase information availability, and to develop a closer relationship with sections of the media, were primarily influenced by the fact that public opinion had become too powerful to ignore. Restrictive attitudes towards the use of mass communications were, therefore, bound to lose their dominant grip on propaganda policy in Britain as the war progressed. Nevertheless, they remained an influential factor in the development of British propaganda, both during the war, and throughout the inter-war period.

A more open approach to State propaganda during the war was found amongst bodies within the political establishment which had regular contact with the mass media. These organizations, the most important of which were the Foreign Office and the War Propaganda Bureau, believed in the necessity of involving selected organs of public opinion in the process of information manipulation: 'emphasis should be placed upon the personal contact between official and journalist in an attempt to form a relationship of mutual trust and confidence.'[25]

In addition to this belief in the need to extend the process of information manipulation, this approach to State propaganda was also characterized by a belief that the government origins of propaganda material should be disguised, and should appear to have originated from public figures and opinion leaders.[26] These strategies of indirect propaganda address depended for their success on the material they used appearing as objective as possible. Overtly propagandist material was excluded, and only material which gave the impression of an independent and objective 'report', was included. Although the WPB and the News Department shared the same approach to government propaganda policy, the latter operated within a Civil Service world, and was in touch with only a few 'quality journalists', whereas the WPB was in touch with a wider range of academic and public opinion.[27] Nevertheless, both organizations remained relatively remote from the main organs of mass opinion in society: the popular press, and cinema.

This was in contrast to other groups who became associated with government propaganda policy during the war, and who were connected with the mass media. These groups believed in the necessity of addressing the public directly through the use of overt mass propaganda campaigns. They became particularly associated with David Lloyd George, who was instrumental in bringing the press barons, Lords Northcliffe, Rothermere, and Beaverbrook into the government propaganda service.[28] The policies of these press lords represented a significant shift away from those of the Foreign Office and other organizations, and amounted to a shift from middle-class to mass cultural norms. This proved too much for many of the officials who had become established within the propaganda service before the arrival of the press lords, and, as a consequence, considerable hostility developed between these groups.

The advocates of mass publicity gained a significant influence in 1916 when Lloyd George was appointed Prime Minister of the new Coalition Government. He put the issue of propaganda on the agenda of the first meeting of the new War Cabinet, and insisted upon the establishment of a fully centralized mass propaganda service.[29] Following this the Department of Information was established, with a link to the Prime Minister through John Buchan (the novelist), who was appointed as Director on 9 February 1917.[30] However, the new Department failed to transform the existing propaganda service as Lloyd George had wished, and merely streamlined it, allowing the Foreign Office to retain effective control.[31]

The Department of Information's failure to initiate mass publicity campaigns and centralize government propaganda production, eventually led to its reorganization in 1918, when it became the Ministry of Information.[32] Under the Directorship of Lord Beaverbrook the new Ministry immediately implemented the policies which had been demanded by Lloyd George. However, Beaverbrook's appointment was resented by the old guard of civil servants and academics, and the staff of the Political Intelligence Department, who included Rex Leeper, Arnold Toynbee, and L. B. Namier, all threatened to resign 'rather than work under Beaverbrook or any other newspaper boss.'[33] This type of conflict went on throughout the war, and retarded attempts to reorganize and centralize the propaganda service. Even after February 1918, important government publicity bodies like the National War Aims Committee, the Political Intelligence Department and MI7, remained outside the control of the Ministry.[34] Despite this, the reorganization of February 1918 did reflect the continuing ascendancy of those in the propaganda service who advocated the use of direct mass propaganda campaigns.

Although the bulk of State propaganda produced during the war was in the form of printed material, a number of propaganda films were also made. However, the debate over government propaganda policy and strategy was particularly fierce over issues of film, because of the potential which it was assumed to have as an instrument of mass manipulation.[35] As a consequence, attempts to develop a centralized State film service during the war were often met with resistance, by those within the establishment who feared the possible social and political implications of such a development.

Establishment apprehension over the use of film was apparent from the beginning of the war. On the outbreak of hostilities the War Office had allowed cameramen to accompany the British Expeditionary Force into France. A decisive victory had been expected, but when the BEF was forced to retreat from Mons and Ypres in late 1914 all newsreel permits were withdrawn, and a blanket censorship was imposed.[36] This reaction reflected the military's mistrust of the media in general, but it also reflected their particular sensitivity about the 'Indiscriminate eye of the camera.'[37] This degree of censorship led to such resentment that the War Office was eventually forced to review its ban on cameramen, and it was agreed that only two cameramen would be allowed to film at the Front at any one time, and that those cameramen would be selected by both the film industry and the War Office. The first two cameramen chosen were E. C. Tong of Imperial Pictures and G. H. Mallins of British Gaumont, and they were replaced by only four others during the entire course of the war.[38] These limitations show the extent to which the establishment was prepared to go in order to control the use of film.

Another means of control was effected through an elaborate and convoluted system of censorship. Footage from the Front was sent to London for developing, printing and editing, and was then sent to the War Office for censorship, before being sent back to GHQ in France for final censoring. Eventually, the footage was sent back to Britain for distribution and exhibition, but this time-consuming process led to considerable delays in getting footage on to the screens, and the cinema was rarely able to equal the press's ability to comment on major events.[39]

The War Propaganda Bureau had formed its own Cinema Committee as early as 1915, but had found itself constrained by the refusal of the military authorities to provide the necessary facilities for front line photography. This situation was eased by the agreement of 15 May 1915, after which the Cinema Committee went on to make its first and most prestigious film: *Britain Prepared* (1915). This film, which opened on 29 December 1915 at the Empire Theatre, Leicester Square, was premiered by an influential audience, including the First Lord of the Admiralty, Lord Balfour. It was a popular and successful film,[40] and was responsible for breaking down some of the suspicion felt by the establishment towards State film production. Even so, that suspicion remained sufficient to retard the expansion of State film production during the war.

Despite this, films were produced, and, for the first three years of the war, they deployed the 'restrained' strategy of publicity production which dominated State propaganda production in general up till 1918. Technological and security factors prevented the filming of combat sequences, and support activities provided the main subject material in films such as *The Wonderful Organization of the Royal Army Medical Core* (1916) and *Marching Bluejackets* (1917).[41] These films were generally compiled from a selection of stock sequences, and possessed only a very basic editing repertoire. Although some – such as *The Wonderful Organization of the Royal Army Medical Core* – used continuous linear narratives, and others such as *The Destruction of a Fokker* (1917) – used dramatic editing, the majority were extremely basic, and the titling they contained was low-key and descriptive, in contrast to the extremely jingoistic films then being made in Germany[42].

In the summer of 1916, a number of longer films of major military engagements were made, the first and most important of which was *The Battle of the Somme* (1916), which ran for one hour and seventeen minutes.[43] It consisted of a linear chronological narrative divided into five parts, which showed the preparations for and aftermath of the Battle of the Somme. This formula proved popular[44] and was repeated four more times in the following year with: *The Battle of the Ancre* (1917); *The German Retreat and the Battle of Arras* (1917); *The Great German Retreat and the Capture of Perrone* (1917); and *The Capture of Messines* (1917).

Apart from their length, chronological narrative structure, and (in some instances) dramatic footage, these films did not differ significantly from the earlier short films, and used a similar stock of filmic conventions. It has been argued that *The Battle of the Somme* in particular was 'realist' and 'fundamentally honest', because it showed footage of the dead, and was not overtly propagandist.[45] However, it must be remembered that this film was the product of a sophisticated propaganda strategy, the essence of which was that films should seem objective and 'true'. To this end, overtly propagandist material was excluded, and only material designed to manipulate the audience into believing it was watching a true record of events, was included. These films were not 'realist', in the sense of representing a wide-ranging account of conditions at the Front. Technological and security factors do not explain why there were no representations of broken bodies, rats, cess-pits etc. in them. In fact, such representations were not permissible within the frame of reference provided by the operative propaganda policy. *The Battle of the Somme* was designed to stimulate enthusiasm for the war effort, and this imperative conditioned its representation of reality. The footage of the dead which the film contained[46] could not have survived the extensive censorship system which existed at the time, if it had not been acceptable to that system.

Another characteristic which the British official films shared with Foreign Office propaganda policy, was a disinclination to use formats associated with mass culture. Although the official films were directed at a mass audience, they did not use cinematic forms derived from the commercial cinema and newsreel. This approach was criticized by those in the propaganda service who advocated the use of jingoistic propaganda films, and, when Lord Beaverbrook became Chairman of the War Office Cinematograph Committee in October 1916 he soon set about changing the style of State film production. By the end of the war, films such as *Our Empire's Fight for Freedom* (1918), in which the sentiments expressed were aggressively patriotic, were being made.[47] These jingoistic films quickly became popular, primarily because they used cinematic forms derived from the commercial cinema and newsreels.[48] Although *The Battle of the Somme* was a success, other films of its type declined in popularity as the war progressed, and a similar decline affected the official newsreel, the *War Office Topical Budget*, which was launched in May 1917. Despite exclusive access to footage shot at the Front, the *Topical Budget* was consistently less popular than the two commercial newsreels: Gaumont and Pathé.[49]

Although the State established an extensive propaganda service during the war, influential voices within the establishment remained apprehensive over the idea of a permanent State film service. This apprehension was frequently based on a concern that public information campaigns might generate a demand for reform. Sir Charles Higham expressed this concern when writing about the work of his Department of Enemy Propaganda in Germany: 'the policy was to appeal to the German petit-bourgeoisie to get them to rise against their masters... not aimed at labourers as this might create a Russian style revolution.'[50] This concern that propaganda campaigns might generate demands for reform, was behind much of the establishment's reluctance to use them.

That concern was evident throughout the 1919-39 period. After the Armistice, a general context of retrenchment prevailed, as the establishment attempted to contain widespread public demand for post-war reform and reconstruction. It was also a period in which attempts were made to re-establish pre-war political and economic relationships, and pre-war policies concerning the role of the State in society. During the immediate post-war period public demand for reform was submerged beneath a 'crescendo of demands for de-control' which stemmed from the corporate sector, and this resulted in the State giving up many of its war-time powers to corporate capitalism.[51] Although the State did expand its role in society during the inter-war period – mainly in order to finance and manage the social costs of reconstruction and welfare provision – this was done as much as possible in accordance with orthodox economic doctrines of balanced budgets and low levels of State intervention. From 1913 to 1934 the increase in public spending on welfare for the working class paralleled the amount of indirect taxation paid by working-class people over the same period. The amount of genuine redistribution was small, 91,000,000 pounds, or 2 per cent of the national income.[52]

The most characteristic aspect of government policy during the inter-war period was that of encouraging the growth of corporate capitalism. The Balfour Committee on Industry and Trade, which reported in 1929, concluded that the economy would benefit from 'amalgamation and consolidation'[53], and the Principal Supply Officer's Committee proposed that the Board of Trade should play an active role in encouraging corporate amalgamation.[54] Yet another means of promoting corporate expansion was through the Import Duties Advisory Committee, which granted applications for tariff increases on condition that the industries concerned initiated processes of industrial combination.[55] These processes of industrial combination continued, until, by 1935, the ratio of the corporate sector to the rest of the economy was equivalent to the American ratio.[56] These beliefs in the need to promote corporate expansion generally succeeded over concern about the dangers of monopolistic practices. All the committees which examined the question of monopoly power during the period, such as the Profiteering Committee, The Balfour Committee, and the Green Committee on Restraint of Trade, underplayed the dangers of monopoly, and emphasized the value of corporate expansion.[57] The general context was one of active intervention by the establishment in the expansion of monopoly capitalism.

This illustrates the difficulties faced by the documentary movement, as an organization committed to the idea of State intervention, within a period in which such intervention was inconsistent with prevailing economic and political ideologies. It also illustrates the difficulties which the movement faced as a result of its commitment to the idea of an extensive, semi-autonomous State propaganda service. Such a service was also inconsistent with those ideologies.

The dismantlement of State controls after 1918 led directly to the dismantlement of the State propaganda service. The Ministry of Information and Department of Enemy Propaganda were closed down on 31 December 1918, and what remained of war-time propaganda was transferred to the News Department of the Foreign Office.[58] The department had planned a publicity programme covering a wide range of topics, however, this broad remit soon came under criticism.[59] The Treasury instructed the News Department to abandon its planned production of cultural propaganda, on the grounds of unwarranted cost, and instructed it to concentrate solely on commercial and industrial propaganda. As a consequence, the News Department's budget for 1920-1 was cut from £100,000 to £80,000.[60]

This opposition between 'cultural' and 'commercial' propaganda represented two quite distinct approaches to the question of State publicity. On the one hand, the Foreign Office advocated the production of educational and cultural propaganda which would create a sense of British identity, which commercial and industrial material could then exploit. Whilst, on the other hand, the Treasury believed that State propaganda should be restricted to narrowly focussed commercial and industrial publicity. The Treasury objected to the production of wide-ranging State propaganda on the pragmatic grounds that such propaganda could bring no short-term, and few long-term benefits.[61]

The Treasury's arguments here must be seen against the context of the economic recession of 1920-2, which was one of the worst in British history,[62] and against the financial constraints imposed by the huge war debt. The recession led to demands for the return of 'classic remedies of deflation',[63] and, between 1920 and 1922, a policy of deflation was launched, backed by campaigns in the right-wing media. This culminated in the publication of the first two Geddes Reports on 10 February 1922.[64] These Reports recommended sharp cuts in government spending, and the abolition of some of the spending departments. The opposition to the existence of an extensive State propaganda service must, therefore, be seen against this context of deflationary recession.

Despite being forced to abandon its production of cultural publicity by the Treasury, the News Department still managed to include a cultural component in its regular programme. Its Press Section produced four categories of publicity material, one of which was a weekly article of 800-900 words on general subjects relating to commerce, industry, sport, science, and literature.[65] A cultural publicity component was also produced by the second major government propaganda department of the 1919-26 period: the Department of Overseas Trade. This department, which had been established in 1919, was charged with the task of reviving lost British export markets. However, although the DOT agreed with the News Department's views on the value of a broad publicity remit, its own terms of reference were even more limited than those of the News Department. Consequently, it was only able to include a cultural component in the work of its Exhibitions Division, which organized publicity for the annual British Industries Fair.

This situation contrasted sharply with that of private industry, where advertising and public relations were growth industries.[66] National expenditure on advertising rose from £31,000,000 in 1920, to £57,000,000 in 1928, after which it levelled out to reach £59,000,000 by 1938.[67] This expansion led to the introduction of new methods, one of the most important of which was market research, which was first introduced during the mid-twenties.[68] By 1924 the British public had been divided up into target groups, and statistical studies based on population census had been produced. In addition to market research, commercial advertising also absorbed ideas which stemmed from avant-garde artistic developments during the twenties. The pictorial ideas of Man Ray, Ernst, Picabia, and Picasso, all found their way into British commercial advertising during the period, as did American theories on public relations.

These developments showed up in stark contrast to the stagnation, and even contraction, which characterized government propaganda and public relations services during the period. Some cross-fertilization did occur, but this happened mainly after the founding of the EMB in 1926. Prior to 1926, the government propaganda service was in a poor condition. This was particularly true of government film-making, and, after 1918, establishment apprehension concerning an extensive State propaganda service was pursued particularly vigorously over the issue of government film-making,[69] with the result that the war-time film propaganda service was virtually eliminated.

In 1920 the News Department had proposed that a Foreign Office Film Unit be established, but the idea was dropped when it became clear that the proposal would be vetoed by the Treasury.[70] After this, the News Department's remit was restricted to that of encouraging individual film-makers to send their films abroad, and to sending suitable films to the occasional overseas festival.[71] But even this inadequate means of distribution declined during the twenties, as funds which had been made available for film propaganda were either diverted into other areas, or cut off altogether.

Between 1920 and 1927 the News Department's budget was cut steadily, from £80,000 in 1920, to only £17,000 in 1927. This coincided with a reorganization of the Department, which resulted in the promotion of press propaganda, at the expense of film propaganda.[72] This process was accelerated by the appointments in 1924 of Percy Koppell, as head of the News Department, and Austen Chamberlain, as Foreign Secretary. Koppell was more inclined towards press than film propaganda, whilst Chamberlain was generally indifferent to the question of government propaganda.[73] Given all these circumstances, it is not surprising that State film propaganda virtually expired between 1918 and 1929. The general context remained one in which the State was not prepared to use film, in any significant way, for purposes of social engineering and propaganda.

But although State film production declined during this period, the State continued to intervene in the film industry by making war-time film footage available to private companies. In 1920 the war films were sold to British Famous Pictures, who distributed them as a series of crude, jingoistic two-reelers.[74] A few years later, Gaumont British Instructional, part of the giant Gaumont British corporation, which had been closely involved with the government during the war, used war footage to produce *The Battle of Jutland* (1921), and *Armageddon* (1923). This policy of transferring State resources to the private sector was typical of the period.

In addition to intervention in the film industry through the sale of government assets, the State also intervened through the implementation of legislation. As with several other British industries, the film industry was dominated by American capital, to the extent that, by 1925, only 2 per cent of films shown on British screens were of British origin.[75] This imposed constraints on the British film industry's ability to expand and accumulate capital, and gave rise to demands for government action to rectify the situation. The result of those demands was the 1927 Cinematograph Films Act, which was passed under the auspices of the 1921 Safeguarding of Industries Act. The Act, which imposed restrictions upon American film activity in Britain, also made several of the practices through which American capital had become so dominant, illegal.[76]

The 1927 Films Act fulfilled a number of government objectives. It encouraged processes of combination then going on in the industry, it did something to stem the influence of American cultural norms, and it enabled the Conservative Government to implement politically controversial protectionist legislation. It represented the preferred form of State intervention in the film industry during the period: that of opening up markets for corporate capital through the use of legislation. This form of intervention was quite different from the direct State film production which marked the war period, and which later characterized the documentary film movement.

The history of the State-owned documentary film units fits into this history of British propaganda during the inter-war period, in many ways, and it is apparent that similar attitudes to those which constrained the development of the documentary movement also influenced the development of an extensive State propaganda service from as early as 1914. The development of propaganda and public relations practices, whether in corporate industries or in the State, primarily originated from the fact that public opinion had become too powerful to ignore. Strategies designed to establish a sense of identity and relationship, through the construction of an ideological consensus, had to be developed in response to this. But this brought with it an attendant loss or distribution of power, and the prospect of indirectly encouraging movements of social reform, and greater democratic participation in the affairs of the State. After 1918, the British State set out to re-establish the more hierarchical society which existed prior to 1914, and to recover the diffusion of political power which had occurred during the war. The existence of an extensive, semi-autonomous documentary film movement was incompatible with this.

The most characteristic aspect of government policy during the inter-war period, consisted of an attempt to shift away from the 'war socialism' of the 1914-18 period, in which the State exercised considerable inter-ventionist powers, to a State monopoly capitalist system, in which corporate market forces were the main regulators of society and the economy.[77] The ideologies of economic liberalism and corporate efficiency constructed a coherent picture of the social world, which was accepted by the majority of the British public.[78] One third of the working-class electorate who voted for the first time between the wars voted Conservative, and Ellen Wilkinson, the radical Labour MP for Jarrow, estimated that 30 per cent of the Jarrow working class voted Conserv-ative.[79] This was significant given that in 1934 Jarrow had the highest unemployment rate in the country.[80]

Despondency, despair, and poverty were undoubtedly influential contributory factors in such voting patterns, but perhaps the most important factor was the deeply engrained belief that economic prosperity could only emerge through freeing market forces from State intervention. The pace of economic reform was largely determined by the permanent officials of the Treasury, whom John Maynard Keynes described as being one of the main obstacles to reform:

> There has been nothing finer in its way than our nineteenth-century school of Treasury officials. Nothing better has ever been devised, if our object is to limit the functions of Government to the least possible and to make sure that expenditure, whether on social or economic or military or general administrative purposes, is the smallest and most economic that public opinion will put up with. But if that is not our object then nothing can be worse. The Civil Service is ruled today by the Treasury school, trained by tradition and experience and native skills to every form of intelligent obstruction.... We have experienced in the last twenty years since the war two occasions of terrific retrenchment and axing of constructive schemes. This has not only been a crushing discouragement for all who are capable of constructive projects, but it has inevitably led to the survival of those to whom negative measures are natural and sympathetic.[81]

This context of a sustained campaign to limit public expenditure and State intervention, was one of the principal causes of the failure of the documentary film movement between the wars. As temporary civil servants, or as mere contract workers, the documentary film-makers were continually subject to 'intelligent obstruction' from the Treasury, and Grierson was certainly one of those 'capable of constructive projects' who experienced 'crushing discouragement'. By advocating direct State intervention, in society in general, and in the film industry in particular,

Grierson and the documentary movement set themselves against the dominant policy and ideology of the period.

That opposition turned into direct obstruction when, in 1932, one of the two largest combines in the film industry, Gaumont British Picture Corporation, attempted to expand into the short films market already largely dominated by the State-owned EMB Film Unit. GBPC's intention was to establish a vertically integrated combine within the short films industry. However, this attempt was frustrated by the existence of the EMB Film Unit. In this instance, the existence of the documentary film movement not only contradicted government policy of encouraging corporate expansion in the film industry, but actually inhibited it. State legislation designed to expand the corporate sector was undermined by a State-owned production unit, the EMB Film Unit, whose activities constituted a barrier to corporate expansion within the market.

The existence of the documentary movement, as a government service which competed with the private sector, was the cause of much of the hostility directed at the movement by sectors of the film trade during the inter-war period. For example, the trade journal *Kinematograph Weekly*, though initially enthusiastic about the movement, soon changed its view when the movement was seen to threaten vested interests. Suddenly, the GPO Film Unit was believed to constitute 'unacceptable State interference in the film trade'.[82] A similar view was taken by the Film Producers Group of the Federation of British Industries, who argued that the policy of putting public expenditure (on the GPO Film Unit) into competition with private enterprise was: 'highly prejudicial to the interests of the taxpayer and to the development of an important and growing industry in which many millions of British capital have been invested.'[83] This view that State intervention contributed to recession by increasing existing levels of competition, reflected the orthodox economic thinking of the period. The orthodox view contended that government expenditure constituted a diversion of funds away from private enterprise, and only led to competition with private capital in an already saturated market.[84] According to this view, the correct policy in a recession was to reduce public expenditure and taxation. This view was held across Party lines. In 1922 the Conservative Chancellor, Stanley Baldwin, argued that government expenditure increased unemployment by competing with private capital,[85] and in 1924, the Labour Chancellor, Philip Snowden, argued that the function of the Treasury was to resist all demands for expenditure.[86]

These views were also held by successive Commons select committees on expenditure, which had ultimate control over the finance of the EMB and GPO Film Units. These committees consistently argued that the two State-owned film units competed with attempts by the film trade to exploit the short films market. Given this extensive conviction over the counter-productivity of State intervention in a commercial market such as film, and given government policy of encouraging corporate expansion in the film industry, it is hardly surprising that the documentary film movement failed to realize Grierson's hopes and expectations for it during the inter-war period. The economic and political power of the interests mobilized against the documentary movement always outweighed the limited support which the movement was able to mobilize in its own defence.

But opposition to the documentary movement must also be seen in relation to the larger context of establishment apprehension concerning the existence of a semi-autonomous government propaganda service. Governments and corporate institutions originally initiated propaganda strategies in order to manage volatile public opinion. But this brought with it an attendant diffusion of power into civil society, and the prospect of stimulating demands for reform through the creation of a semi-independent mass communication system. The inter-war period, in Britain, was one in which the establishment attempted to re-establish the more hierarchical society which had existed before the war. In addition, there was no mass public opposition to the dominant post-war policies of orthodox monetarist economics, which were based on doctrines of economic liberalism and corporate efficiency. There was, therefore, no need for the establishment to countenance the existence of a semi-autonomous propaganda service – such as the documentary film movement. The context was one in which the establishment tried to contain and diminish the democratic potential unleashed by the war, and to reconstruct the more stratified pre-war society. The existence of the documentary movement as a semi-autonomous 'civic education' service, with leftist leanings, was incompatible with this.

7   Documentary film and reform

The documentary movement also failed to establish itself securely within the State during the inter-war period, because it became associated, in the eyes of the establishment, with movements of social, political, and economic reform. Although doctrines of economic liberalism and corporate efficiency held majority support during the period, reformist movements which argued for increased State intervention and a more equitable distribution of social resources, also existed. The documentary movement was associated with this movement of reform, and suffered the disapproval of the establishment accordingly.

But although the documentary movement was associated with the reform movements of the inter-war period, it was not associated with groups which advocated a socialist transformation of society. On the left, the demand for socialism was articulated by the Communist Party, and by various groups on the Labour left, such as the Independent Labour Party and the Socialist League. These Labour Party groups advocated extensive nationalization, and a nationalization programme also appeared in one of the most important Labour Party documents of the 1930s, *For Socialism and Peace* (1934). However, Labour Party doctrine was in a transitional state during the 1930s, and the Labour left, represented by the ILP, the Socialist League, Stafford Cripps, G. D. H. Cole, Harold Laski, and others, was opposed by the right wing of the party, represented by the parliamentary leadership and the trade unions.[1]

Although Grierson and the documentary movement identified with this demand for social reconstruction through the agency of the State, they did not believe in a socialist transformation of society, nor in extensive nationalization. Writing in 1922, Grierson described democratic equality as 'impracticable',[2] and universal suffrage as 'an extreme thing.'[3] These views were partly derived from his influence by pragmatist and positivist ideas during the 1920s. These ideas, most notably expressed by Walter Lippmann, questioned the possibility of popular democratic government.[4] Writing in 1941, Grierson argued that he did 'not believe that socialism as we have thought of it will come at all ... given the conditions of modern technocracy, workers' self-management represents an unpractical and inefficient ... (ideal).'[5] He continued to question the practical validity of socialist ideals throughout his life, and this scepticism formed an integral part of his theory of documentary film.

So, although Grierson believed in the need for social reform, he did not believe in the need for a socialist reorganization of society. Similarly, although he believed that the State was the most important agent of reform, he did not believe that it should become too powerful. This belief was partly influenced by his criticism of the hegelian conception of the State,[6] and partly by the prevailing liberal view that an interventionist State could be used for sectarian, rather than national purposes. There was a general apprehension at the time that a strong State could turn into a fascist or communist dictatorship. Stanley Baldwin, then leader of the Conservative Party, even accused Franklin D. Roosevelt of turning America into a dictatorship through the implementation of the 'New Deal'.[7] Grierson supported the New Deal, but he shared contemporary apprehensions concerning the sectarian potential of an interventionist State.

Just as Grierson was opposed to excessive State control in general, he was also opposed to excessive State control of the film industry, in particular. He disapproved of the extent to which the State controlled the film industry in Soviet Russia, and did not believe that such a level of control would be acceptable in the west.[8] However, he did believe that some measure of State intervention was essential.

So, although Grierson and the documentary film movement can be identified with a demand for reform during the period, they cannot be closely identified with the socialist left. However, they can be much more closely identified with various movements of middle opinion during the inter-war period. These movements were diverse and heterogeneous, but this heterogeneity concealed a core of shared beliefs and values. In the first place, there was a belief in the essential soundness of established society; in the second place, there was a belief in the need for State regulation and intervention, and, in the third place, there was a rejection of the option of a socialist or fascist transformation of society.[9] These political and cultural parameters framed what some critics have described as a 'social democratic consensus', which developed in opposition to orthodox economic liberalism and marxism during the inter-war period,[10] and which became the most influential reform movement of the period.

Although the documentary film movement was related to this context of a minority social-democratic consensus, it was not related ideologically to what became the most historically important element within that consensus: keynesianism. Many of the influential ideas which became associated with middle opinion during this period were prompted and supported by David Lloyd George and his colleagues. These ideas were discussed at the Liberal Party Summer Schools, and eventually found expression in the Liberal 'Yellow Book' of 1928, entitled *Britain's Industrial Future*.[11] The most important contributor to this document, and to the Liberal Party election manifesto of 1929, was J. M. Keynes. Keynes favoured the free market, and believed that temporary State intervention could be introduced, when necessary, without disturbing the foundations of capitalism.[12] His ideas on stimulating investment and consumption appeared in his *General Theory of Employment, Interest and Money* (1936), which radically reassessed liberal economic theory, and which provided the main intellectual foundation for social-democratic reformism during the inter-war period.[13]

However, the political philosophy of Grierson and the documentary film movement cannot be equated with keynesianism. Grierson consistently argued for significant and permanent State intervention within the film industry and other social and educational institutions.[14] His ideas cannot, therefore, be equated with the temporary regulatory mechanisms advocated by Keynes. Neither can Grierson and the documentary movement be identified with the often overtly arrogant and patronizing remarks which Keynes sometimes directed at socialists and the public. For example, Keynes argued that, owing to its democratic character, the Labour Party could never exercise 'control over the ignorant',[15] and he described socialism as: 'a creed which, preferring the mud to the fish, exalts the boorish proletariat above the bourgeois and the intelligentsia who, with whatever faults, are the quality of life and surely carry the seeds of all advancement.'[16] Although Grierson and the documentary film-makers were influenced, sometimes at a sub-conscious level, by such views on the natural inferiority of the lower classes, it is inconceivable that they would have expressed themselves as Keynes did. On the contrary, Grierson and the other film-makers emphasized repeatedly that, in their opinion, the documentary movement's greatest achievement was its success in representing the intrinsic value of working-class life and experience.[17]

It is clear from the above that the documentary movement must be located to the left of keynesianism. However, one particular aspect of Keynes' thought was crucially important to Grierson's conception of a publicly-owned, socially purposive documentary film movement, and that was Keynes' notion of the 'public corporation'. Keynes strongly favoured the public corporation, as did Herbert Morrison, the Labour Party minister and Chairman of the London County Council, whose name has become most closely associated with it.[18] The public corporation was a semi-public, semi-independent enterprise, which was not subject to direct State control, but was managed by a board of governors drawn from various areas of public life. This board of governors were supposed to run their enterprise in the national interest, and not merely in accordance with the usual commercial goal of profit maximization. Public corporations became the preferred form of State intervention in industry after 1918, when they replaced the direct intervention which had been the norm during the First World War. They were introduced after 1918 whenever it was felt necessary to reorganize an industry on a national basis, as was the case with the Forestry Commission (1919), Imperial Airways (1924), the General Electric Board (1926), and the British Broadcasting Corporation (1926).[19]

The public corporation model was an important ingredient of middle opinion during the inter-war period, and one of the intellectual foundations of the 'middle way'. It represented a compromise between the two extremes of State control and unregulated capitalism, and played an important role in facilitating the emergence of a coherent political opposition to dominant conservatism. It was also the form of institutional structure which Grierson believed should be used for the documentary film movement. He argued that a State-owned documentary film movement would require a certain autonomy of operational control over matters relating to production and finance, and he believed that a public corporation, independent of direct State control, would guarantee that autonomy.[20] This belief in the need to ensure that the documentary movement remained independent of direct State control, was conditioned by the movement's experience of continuous interference by the Treasury during the inter-war period. But it was also conditioned by the examples set by two existing institutions, both of which provided a concrete precedent and criteria of application for a semi-autonomous, State-owned documentary film movement. These were, the Canadian Motion Picture Bureau, and the British Broadcasting Corporation. The latter, in particular, represented the kind of institutional structure which Grierson wanted most for the documentary film movement, and he argued that the failure to give documentary film the same institutional protection as that given to radio had resulted in: 'A powerful potential power for education and social purpose (being) turned over to commercial greed. Nothing I am sure damns so certainly the crazy way in which we are running the affairs of our generation.'[21]

However, despite Grierson's preference for the kind of institutional model represented by the BBC, there were fundamental differences between radio and documentary film which made the establishment of a documentary film-making institution based on the BBC highly unlikely, prior to 1939. In the first place, radio was a 'natural monopoly' which, at that time, had to be regulated on a national basis in order to manage the use of scarce radio wavebands. Documentary film, on the other hand, was not a natural monopoly, and did not require the same degree of regulation and control. In addition, documentary film production was already part of an existing commercial industry, whilst radio developed as a technology which had been under some measure of government control since 1904. There was, therefore, no government incentive to organize documentary on a national basis, within the protective frame-work of a public corporation. On the contrary, government policy was aimed at encouraging the growth of private corporations, as was evidenced by the consequences of the Cinematograph Films Act of 1927,[22] and by the support given by the Treasury to Gaumont British Picture Corporation's attempt to monopolize the short films industry in 1932-3.[23]

Contrary to Grierson's wishes, the documentary film movement never achieved the degree of security and independence which the institutional structure of a public corporation would have given it. The EMB was an executive commission under the political control of the Colonial and Dominions Secretary, and under the financial control of the Treasury. The EMB Film Unit was, therefore, under direct State control. Similarly, the Post Office, and the GPO Film Unit, were answerable to Parliament through the Postmaster General, and were also under the financial control of the Treasury. This was the actual institutional basis of the documentary film movement's relationship to the State during the inter-war period. However, Grierson's ideal relationship between the documentary movement and the State was that represented by a public corporation, as in the case of the BBC. It was this indirect form of relationship to the State which he referred to when he described himself as a 'government film man.'[24]

Grierson's political philosophy, particularly as reflected in his enthusiasm for the semi-independent public corporation, placed the documentary movement to the right of groups such as the Socialist League, who advocated extensive State ownership, and to the left of groups such as the keynesians, who advocated temporary State intervention in society and the economy. In terms of political philosophy, the documentary movement can be most closely associated with the ideas of individuals at the centre-left of the Labour Party, such as Douglas Jay and Herbert Morrison. However, that association cannot be too clearly defined, because of the extent to which the reformist ideologies of the period cut across traditional party boundaries. For example, in 1936, the Conservative radical Harold Macmillan attempted to establish a new Centre Party, under the leadership of the Labour MP, Herbert Morrison. Macmillan's aim, as set forth in his influential book *The Middle Way* (1938), was to 'obtain a fusion of all that is best in left and right.'[25]

The existence of this cross-party, centre progressive consensus, makes it difficult to identify the documentary movement with any particular political movement, or ideology. This difficulty is compounded by the fact that the documentary movement never associated itself directly with any party political activities. This was particularly true of Grierson, who always refused to make a party political commitment, even during his student days between 1918 and 1923, when the Red Clydeside movement had radicalized many of his contemporaries at Glasgow University.[26]

The documentary movement was associated with centre progressive politics in general, but it was also associated, in particular, with the emergence of a number of non-aligned pressure-groups after 1930. After the decline of political liberalism in the General Election of 1931, no significant political power base remained to promote centre progressive ideas. As a consequence of this, the promotion of those ideas passed into the hands of a number of pressure groups, which were constituted on a non-party basis. It is in this context of politically-marginalized, centre progressive pressure-groups, that Grierson and the documentary movement must be placed. These pressure-groups occupied a variety of ideological positions within the framework of centre progressive opinion, but they also had many significant features in common with each other, and with the documentary film movement. Three of the most significant of these groups were, Political and Economic Planning, Mass Observation, and the Next Five Years Group.

Like the documentary movement, these groups were non-aligned pressure-groups, which lacked any significant political or mass public base of support. This lack of political or public connection gave them a certain amount of independence, but it also deprived them of any real political and public influence. Hugh Dalton, commenting on the Next Five Years Group, described it as 'like officers without rank and file, better known to each other than to the general public, moving in select and narrow circles, carrying almost no electoral weight.'[27] Dalton's comments applied equally to the documentary movement, which did not attach itself to any political party during the inter-war period, nor to any political movement, such as, for example, the Popular Front, or the Peace Pledge Campaign.

Another feature which these groups, including the documentary movement, had in common, was the middle-class origins of their members and supporters. For example, Political and Economic Planning consisted of around 100 members, who were drawn from the business and professional classes, and the group's twice yearly report was read by people from that same social and class background.[28] Similarly, the three founders of Mass Observation: Humphrey Jennings, Charles Madge, and Tom Harrisson, all came from an Oxbridge background, and the network of 2,000 'mass observers' which these three established also came from middle-class backgrounds. The pamphlets and books which Mass Observation published were also aimed at a middle-class readership,[29] and the same was true of The Next Five Years Group, which was run by middle-class professionals. The group's 1935 manifesto, *The Next Five*

Years, An Essay in Political Agreement, contained the signatures of 150 prominent academics and public figures.[30]

Like these groups, the documentary film movement also consisted of middle-class people, who communicated to a predominantly middle-class audience, and to an almost exclusively middle-class group of supporters. Despite the populist rhetoric which he often employed, Grierson's work and ideas were aimed, consciously or unconsciously, at the middle-class audience who read the minority journals and watched educational or 'interest' films. This posed a contradiction which he was never able to adequately resolve. At the same time that he used a populist rhetoric to describe the documentary movement, he also referred to the 'specialised and discriminating audiences' of the 'specialised' documentary film.[31] In addition, his conception of a specialized distribution and exhibition network implied a predominantly, perhaps exclusively, middle-class audience. Like the other pressure-groups mentioned above, the documentary movement was primarily dedicated to the communication of ideas to governing elites and intellectuals, and although Grierson used a rhetoric of mass communications, the reality behind that rhetoric was that the movement functioned, inevitably, as a means of minority, and not mass communication.

The primary objective of the pressure-groups mentioned above, including the documentary movement, was to promote the development and establishment of a State managerial bureaucracy. This was the context within which the documentary film movement must be viewed. It was a context based on the idea, popular at the time, of a progressive reforming bureaucracy. One of the main reasons why the documentary film movement was treated with suspicion and hostility by a Conservative political establishment, was because it was associated with this movement of centre progressive opinion. It was because of this, and also because the movement contradicted government policy on encouraging industrial combination and reducing State intervention, that it failed to establish itself securely during the inter-war period.

In addition to these factors, another factor also influenced the documentary movement's lack of success, and that was its use of a naturalist representational aesthetic, which was considered to be subversive by the establishment. The impact of the First World War on British society was considerable. One characteristic of that impact was the creation of a demand for information on, and representations of, the social and military events taking place.[32] Newspapers devoted extensive coverage to news from the Front, and the demand for newsreel and other cinema coverage of the war rose considerably. Films such as *The Battle of the Somme* (1916) and *The Battle of the Ancre* (1917), which consisted almost entirely of actuality footage, were very popular, as were the newsreels of Gaumont

British and Pathe.[33] Although the cinema, and popular culture in general, remained dominated by non-naturalist fictional forms, the reportage and naturalist styles which developed during the war had an important cultural influence on British society then, and throughout the inter-war period.

Some elements within the establishment viewed documentary reportage with apprehension. When film footage and press reports first began to arrive back from the Front, the War Office imposed a series of comprehensive restrictions upon their use.[34] When public opinion forced a relaxation of these draconian measures a comprehensive system of censorship was then introduced to control the media and documentary representations of the war. Although the establishment was worried by the media in general, it was particularly worried by the ability of documentary films to represent military and social events in such extensive detail. Film was seen as an unpredictable means of mass communication, which could have unforeseen social consequences.[35]

After 1918, the impact of unemployment and recession, and the growth of a widespread demand for social reconstruction and reform, contributed to the growing influence of a documentary reportage aesthetic. A number of written documentary accounts of the war appeared, including Robert Graves's *Goodbye to all That* (1929), Siegfried Sassoon's *Memoir's of a Foxhunting man* (1928), R. C. Sherriff's *Journey's End* (1929), Ernest Hemingway's *A Farewell to Arms* (1929), and Eric Maria Remarque's *All Quiet on the Western Front* (1929).[36] In addition to these written accounts of the war, a number of films also appeared, which used documentary formats. These included H. Bruce Woolf's *Battle of Jutland* (1921) and *Armaggedon* (1923), Lewis Milestone's *All Quiet on the Western Front* (1929-30) and G. W. Pabst's *Westfront 1918* (1930).

In addition to these documentary accounts of the war, a number of works also appeared which used a documentary format to represent contemporary social problems.[37] These included Walter Greenwood's *Love on the Dole* (1933), J.B. Priestley's *English Journey* (1933), George Orwell's *The Road to Wigan Pier* and Christopher Isherwood's *Goodbye to Berlin* (1936). In these works, the boundaries between reportage and fiction became obscured, as was the case with some of the films of the period, such as John Grierson's *Drifters* (1929-30), Walther Ruttmann's *Berlin* (1927), and G. W. Pabst's *Kameradschaft* (1931).

Because these works were sometimes overtly critical of the status quo, they were often treated with hostility by the establishment. But even when such works contained little or no such criticism, their use of a documentary reportage style was considered as subversive in itself.[38] In a period when only middle-class experience was considered to be worthy of representation in novels and films, positive representations of working-class experience in the arts was often considered to be 'left wing propaganda'.[39] It was partly due to this perception that naturalist styles of aesthetic representation were left wing, that the documentary movement encountered so many problems during the inter-war period. Grierson's *Drifters* was no 'socialist epic', as some discerning critics of the time pointed out,[40] but, at the time, its representation of working-class experience seemed radical in itself.

The establishment view that the documentary movement was a leftist organization was also reinforced by the movement's close association with Russian films. Grierson had been one of the first people in the West to make a close study of Eisenstein's influential *Battleship Potemkin*,[41] and *Drifters* was premièred on the same billing at which *Potemkin* received its British première.[42] In addition, despite the fact that public exhibition of the Soviet films had been banned, Grierson projected them privately at the Imperial Institute cinema from as early as 1928.[43] He also wrote extensively on the Soviet cinema in contemporary journals such as the *Clarion*, the *New Clarion*, and *Everyman*.[44]

This association with Soviet films contributed towards the documentary movement's characterization, in the eyes of the establishment and the film trade, as a leftist organization. Official apprehension over the Russian films must be seen in the context of the political and economic crisis of 1929-31, and against the growing influence of Marxist thought amongst artists and intellectuals, following that crisis.[45] As artists and intellectuals turned towards socialism and Marxism, the Soviet films were particularly influential in providing a model for socially and politically purposive art.[46] As such, they were also a prime target for a political establishment which was becoming increasingly concerned about the growing influence of Marxist thought.

The influence of the Soviet films was due to their success in combining three central concerns of left-oriented artists during the period. These were: (a) the need to develop a documentary reportage aesthetic, (b) the need for political commitment, and (c) the need to develop a modernist and formalist aesthetic.[47]

Naturalist modes of representation were considered to be essential for an adequate representation of working-class experience. Writing in *Left Review* in 1935, Montagu Slater argued that a principal condition for literary advance was: 'knowledge of the ordinary world of people and things, the world of work, the world of everyday economic struggle. Certainly to describe things as they are is a revolutionary act in itself.'[48] Similarly, in 1936, Stephen Spender praised Auden and Isherwood's *The Ascent of F6* for its 'realistic scenes of political reportage,'[49] and, the same year, *Left Review* also criticized Lewis Grassic Gibbon's *Grey Granite* (1935) for its lack of naturalistic detail.[50]

However, although documentary reportage was held up as a means of establishing a radical cultural practice, excessive use of naturalism was unacceptable to the left. Marxist theory had always drawn a distinction between naturalism – which described immediate appearances – and realism – which went beyond immediate appearances to describe more abstract determining realities. Writing in the journal *Fact* in 1937, Storm Jameson argued that reportage must go beyond immediate experience, to reveal underlying realities.[51] Similarly, in 1932, the Workers Theatre Movement argued that:

The naturalistic form, namely that form which endeavours to show a picture on the stage as near to life as possible, is suitable for showing things as they appear on the surface, but does not lend itself to disclosing the reality which lies underneath. And it is just this reality, lying just beneath the surface of capitalist society that the worker's theatre must reveal.[52]

An overly naturalist aesthetic was unacceptable because it could not represent abstract realities, and because it could not offer sufficient scope for social and political comment. It was also unacceptable because it contradicted a central belief of modernist aesthetics: that the work of art was not a reproduction of reality, but a signifying structure which interpreted reality through formal means.[53]

The success of Soviet films such as *Potemkin* and *Earth* was largely due to the fact that they achieved a successful integration of naturalism formalism, and political statement. As such, they became important models from which to construct a radical cultural practice. To a lesser extent the same was also true of the films made by the documentary movement, which were seen in some quarters as having achieved the same synthesis of naturalism, formalism, and social content. For example, Storm Jameson argued that 'Perhaps the nearest equivalent of what is wanted already exists in another form in the documentary film .... We may stumble on the solution in the effort of trying to create the literary equivalent of the documentary film.'[54]

It is clear, therefore, that the documentary film movement's association with Soviet films did not only consist of the instrumental role which the movement played in introducing those films into Britain, but also in the movement being classified, in some quarters, as an example of a politically radical cultural practice, in the same category as the communist epics of Eisenstein, Pudovkin, and Turin. This classification, when combined with the documentary movement's use of a naturalist style which was considered to be politically radical, was sufficient in itself to ensure the hostility of certain groups within the establishment and the film industry.

It is apparent from the above that, in some instances, the documentary movement provided a model for progressive cultural practices in the thirties. Grierson encouraged this by establishing contacts with other contemporary cultural practices. For example, a number of prominent intellectuals worked on films made by the documentary movement. These included Benjamin Britten, W. H. Auden, J. B. Priestley, Humphrey Jennings, Robert Flaherty, Carl Dreyer, Victor Turin, Walter Leigh, Ernst Meyer, Maurice Jaubert and Lionel Wendt. *Chapter and Verse* (1936) also included interviews by T. S. Eliot, Somerset Maugham, Rebecca West, John Masefield, and Julian Huxley. In addition, both during the EMB and GPO periods, Grierson encouraged distinguished people from the arts to see the film units' work, and to join in critical debate over the issues raised. These visitors included H. G. Wells, Julian Huxley, Alistair Cooke, Graham Greene, and Lazio Moholy-Nagy.

This attempt to connect with other cultural movements was also carried out in the house journals of the documentary movement: *Cinema Quarterly* (1932-6), *World Film News* (1936-8) and *Documentary Newsletter* (1940-7). The central aim of these journals was to propagate Grierson's ideas, and the ideas behind the documentary movement, through influencing cultural trends, and through commissioning articles from a range of distinguished intellectuals. Between 1936 and 1937 *World Film News* published papers from authors as diverse as Graham Greene, Ivor Montagu, Frances Klingender, George Bernard Shaw, Somerset Maugham, Aldous Huxley, T. S. Eliot, and Charles Laughton, as well as several by Grierson. The remit of these journals was wide. For example, the July edition of *World Film News* contained an advertisement for a reading of surrealist poetry, an advert for the Imperial Institute Cinema, and regular sections on the development of the official and corporate public relations industry.

The aim of these journals was to provide a forum for debate, and to advance the ideas of their founders. In this respect they can be compared with the literary journals of the period, such as The *Criterion, Scrutiny, The Dial* (in America), *Life and Letters Today* and *New Writing*. The political line of these journals was often very different to that of the documentary movement's journals, but they shared the same emphasis on creating a forum for critical debate. Some journals were closer to the ideals of the documentary movement than others, and *Life and Letters Today* carried several critical reviews of films made by the movement. T.S. Eliot, the editor of *Criterion*, contributed several articles to *World Film News*, and it was Eliot who first published W. H. Auden in 1930. Auden later went on to contribute to two of the documentary movement's most significant films: *Coal Face* (1935), and *Night Mail* (1936). The publication of Eliot's *The Waste Land* in *The Dial* also had an important influence on Grierson, and many of Grierson's formative influences came from his reading of *The Dial* whilst at Glasgow University between 1919 and 1923.

So, there were definite correspondences between the journals of the documentary movement and other periodicals of the period, and these correspondences must be viewed against the context of a cultural climate which was prepared to explore new and different ideas. The documentary movement did not only make films, it propagated an ideology, through films, journalism, lectures, public appearances and other means. In this respect it can be compared with the literary journals mentioned above, and also with a host of other journals which appeared during the period. For example, Grierson contributed papers to the *Clarion, New Clarion, New Britain, Artwork, Cinema, Today's Cinema* and the *Realist,* all of which commissioned papers from a wide range of sources. There was, therefore, a general expansion of critical literature and cultural ideologies during the period, and the documentary movement was associated with that development.

That expansion was influenced by a significant growth in readership and literacy during the period, which was in turn partly caused by the appearance of cheap critical literature aimed at the mass market. The appearance of Penguin in 1937 was a major event in this respect, including works such as R. H. Tawney's *Religion and the Rise of Capitalism* (1936) and Roger Fry's *Vision and Design.* The Left Book Club was also influential in this respect. It was founded in 1936 by Victor Gollancz, and offered a book a month to subscribers who undertook to purchase the monthly choice for a six month minimum period. The price of 2s 6d undercut the average price of 12 or 18 shillings significantly, and this tapped an unexpectedly large market, with monthly sales rising to a peak of 50,000, an unheard of figure for serious works of this type.[55] The Left Book Club produced some outstanding classics, including Edgar Snow's *Red Star Over China* and A. L. Morton's *A People's History of England* (1938). It maintained an average membership of 50,000 and was supported by over 1200 Left Book Club Groups. Together with the examples of the journals mentioned above, the success of the Left Book Club illustrates the extent of the growth of critical readership during the period, and it was to this readership that the rhetoric of the documentary movement was primarily directed.

The origins of this expansion of critical cultural ideologies lay in the climate of intellectual uncertainty which came into being after the First World War. The war, the Depression, and the Russian Revolution all had a profound effect on many liberal intellectuals. Liberal certainties concerning the relation of the individual to society were shaken, and a deeply-felt unease was experienced concerning the nature of the new mass society. In response, intellectuals turned to a variety of ideas and theories in an attempt to come to terms with the new social reality of mass society, mass democracy and monopoly capitalism.

A common theme in many of the writings of the period was a belief that capitalism had failed, and must be transformed or abandoned. In

Christopher Isherwood's *Mr. Norris Changes Trains* (1935), Norris is depicted as an unprincipled capitalist arms dealer, and in George Orwell's *Keep the Aspidistra Flying* (1936) there is an open contempt for capitalist culture.[56] The works of Graham Greene also revolve around the idea of a struggle between individuals and a cruelly exploitative capitalist culture, as in *It's a Battlefield* (1934), *A Gun for Sale* (1936), and *Confidential Agent* (1939).[57] Similarly, J. B. Priestley's *English Journey* (1933) and *Angel Pavement* (1930) also contained clearly articulated outrage at the existence of poverty in the midst of affluence, as did Orwell's archetypal *The Road to Wigan Pier* (1937).

This sense of outrage over capitalist exploitation and the poverty of the Depression can also be found in the works of W. H. Auden, Stephen Spender, Edward Upward, Louis MacNeice, Christopher Isherwood, John Lehmann, and C. Day Lewis, whose works first appeared in the anthologies *New Signatures* (1932) and *New Country* (1933). Another common theme in these works, and in the writings of the authors mentioned above, was the representation of industrial subject matter. In Auden's *The Orators* (1932), the derelict landscape of industrial decay is represented and contrasted with the self-absorbed sensitivity of the traditional intellectual.[58] Auden's early writing was deeply concerned with the social reality of the inter-war period, and with the need for commitment on the part of the artist. These early writings were also affected by his short stay in Germany in the early thirties, when he was influenced by the work of Brecht, the Berlin cabaret, and the German expressionist cinema. These influences can be seen in his first two verse plays: *The Dog Beneath the Skin* (1935) and the *Ascent of F6* (1936), in which foregrounding and cinematic montage effects are used in conjunction with verse and dramatic narrative. These verse plays were written at the same time that Auden worked on *Coal Face* (1935) and *Night Mail* (1936) at the GPO Film Unit. In these films he used similar techniques to those which he used in the verse plays, and the sequences he was responsible for constitute the most interesting parts of both films. Two good examples of this are the sequence in *Night Mail*, in which verse is spoken at an accelerating pace over images of speeding train wheels, and the sequence in *Coal Face*, in which verse and music is used in conjunction with statistics and dramatic photographic imagery of mine working.

Many of the themes found in the work of the writers mentioned above can also be found in the films of the documentary film movement. Criticism of capitalism is most acute in *Coal Face*, but it is also there in *The Face of Britain, Today We Live, Housing Problems*, and *Drifters*. Similarly, an emphasis on industrial subject matter was a foundation stone of the documentary movement's theory and practice, and appeared in virtually all of their films. This emphasis brought with it a certain degree of identification with working-class life and experience. However, this identification was often ambivalent. Liberal intellectuals, sensitive to the inequalities and injustices of capitalism, were also apprehensive about the impersonal nature of mass society. As Raymond Williams has pointed out, the word 'mass' was a new word for 'mob', and many believed that mass society, mass democracy, and mass culture constituted a threat to civilized values, and to culture itself.[59] For some writers, mass society threatened the individual with abstract impersonal forces. In Aldous Huxley's *Brave New World* (1932), mass society is seen as inherently evil and anti-individual, and in much of George Orwell's writing there is a similar anxiety concerning the way that society dominates the individual. Orwell's position left him unable to identify with either capitalism or socialism, and his novels often betray the isolation of the liberal intellectual who has no real contact with the public. A similar liberal unease also affected the work of Auden, Isherwood, Huxley, and others. These writers felt unable to make a direct commitment, and their work frequently reflects a sceptical apprehension concerning mass society.

Grierson and the documentary movement were also influenced by these sceptical ideas concerning the nature of mass society. All the documentary film-makers came from middle-class or upper-middle-class backgrounds, and Grierson had been influenced by elitist ideas from the early twenties. However, there is a difference between Grierson, and Orwell or Huxley, in that Grierson accepted the fact of mass society, and tried to make it work. Whereas Orwell expressed a despair about the effect of society on the individual, Grierson devised a theory and practice which tried to reconcile the contradiction between individual participation and abstract impersonal forces.[60]

So, although Grierson can be grouped alongside the writers mentioned above, who were struggling to define the parameters of a culture more appropriate to contemporary conditions, he is more properly related alongside individuals who reacted more positively to to the new mass society. In this category one must include Charles Madge, Tom Harrisson, and Humphrey Jennings, who started Mass Observation; novelists such as Edward Upward, John Sommerfield, and J.B. Priestley; and others such as Victor Gollancz, Ivor Montagu, Rex Warner, Montagu Slater, and John Lehmann.

However, it would be wrong to make too clear a distinction here, between writers such as Huxley and Orwell, and others such as Madge and Upward. There were no clear demarcations, and many collaborations between all the groups and individuals mentioned above. The context was one of inter-connection between cultural practices, as intellectuals struggled to come to terms with changing circumstances. For example, even though the *Criterion* moved steadily to the right under the editorship of T.S. Eliot, space was always made available for left-wing writers like the Marxist historian A. L. Morton. The same diversity can be found in the pages of the documentary movement's house journals. H. G. Wells and T. S. Eliot may have written for *World Film News*, but so also did Marxists such as Ivor Montagu, Ralph Bond, and Francis Klingender.

Grierson also maintained close contacts with film-making organizations on the left throughout the thirties. In 1929 he launched the London Workers Film Society with Ralph Bond.[61] Other societies were formed elsewhere in Britain, and a Federation of Workers Film Societies was established, with a distribution organization called Atlas Films. After three years the workers film society movement dissolved, and a new company, Kino Films, was established in 1933 to distribute 16 millimetre films to halls and meeting rooms.[62] Kino distributed Russian and German films, and also films made in Britain by the Workers Film and Photo League, which became the Film and Photo League in 1936. Kino also established its own production arm, and included many of the films made by the documentary movement in its exhibition programmes. Bond started work at the GPO Film Unit in 1931, and in 1937 made *Today We Live* for the Strand Film Unit. In 1938 and 1939 he made *Advance Democracy* and *People With a Purpose* at the Realist Film Unit for the London Co-operative Society. In 1937 the Workers Film Association was formed by the Labour Party and the TUC. It generally showed films acquired from Kino, including films made by the documentary movement.

It is apparent from the above that, far from being distanced from these leftist film-making organizations, some of which were directly associated with the Communist Party, the documentary movement maintained strong links with them, and frequently offered them material support. Some of the most significant films to be made on the left during the thirties were made by Ivor Montagu, working under the auspices of the Communist Party. In 1934 Montagu formed the Progressive Film Institute as a producer and distributor for the Communist Party, and in 1936 the PFI sent a unit to Spain to cover the Civil War. The unit included Montagu, Sidney Cole, Thorold Dickinson, Alan Lawson, and Norman McLaren – whom Grierson had sent from the GPO Film Unit. The Unit's first film was *Defence of Madrid* (1936), followed by *News from Spain* (1937), *Crime Against Madrid* (1937), *Spanish ABC* (1938), *Behind the Spanish Lines* (1938), and *Testament of Non-Intervention* (1938). Other films on Spain included *Help Spain* (1938) and *Modern Orphans of the Storm* (1937) both commissioned by the National Joint Committee for Spanish Relief. The first of these was made by James Calvert and distributed by Kino, and the latter was made by Basil Wright and the Realist Film Unit, and also distributed by Kino. Montagu's best film was *Peace and Plenty* (1939), made to promote the policy of the Communist Party. It used animation techniques, puppets and graphics in addition to archive and newly-shot material to criticize the appeasement policies of Chamberlain's National Government.[63] Another important film was *Hell Unlimited* (1936), which was directed by Norman McLaren and distributed by Kino. *Hell Unlimited* was an anti-war film, and used a variety of innovative techniques, some verging on the surrealist, to criticize the arms race.[64] It was after seeing this film, and the slightly earlier *Colour Cocktail* (1936), an exercise in abstract colour and musical configurations, that Grierson offered McLaren a job at the GPO Film Unit.[65]

It has been argued that the strategies employed and films made by these leftist and Marxist organizations were of greater significance than the compromised efforts of the documentary movement. Grierson's strategy involved working within 'the system', and using sponsorship as a framework within which to insert alternative interpretations. This worked sometimes, but, at other times, as Ralph Bond has pointed out, the message was so well hidden that no one but the film-maker knew it was there.[66] On the other hand, the nature of the audience for Kino and the Progressive Film Institute remains open to question. It was probably narrowly defined, and it may be that the films made by Montagu and others had little influence outside of this small, committed audience.

In the circumstances, Grierson's strategy of engaging in cultural struggle within dominant institutions was probably more appropriate. This strategy gave the ideas and films of the documentary movement access to a wider range of opinion than the films made by Kino or the Progressive Film Institute. It also enabled the documentary movement to influence middle opinion in a way that the films made by these other organizations could not. However, it is not necessary to draw distinctions, or apportion merit, between these two approaches to the problem of how to challenge dominant hegemony. The two approaches complemented each other during the period, and, as has been shown, there were many connections between the documentary film movement and these left wing film organizations. Both during the thirties, and during the 1980s, Montagu, Bond and other film-makers have made it clear that they saw themselves as engaged in the same struggle as the documentary movement, and did not see themselves as rivals.

During the inter-war period a process of cultural renewal and experimentation took place, and many intellectuals participated in attempts to define the parameters of an emerging post-*laissez-faire* society. That intellectual and cultural context was in turn determined and mediated by a political and economic context, of the gradual transformation of Britain from an economic liberal to a social-democratic society. The documentary film movement was associated with, and was mediated by, these contexts. The period was one in which ideological and political boundaries became less clearly defined, and this makes it difficult to pinpoint the exact ideological location of the documentary movement in relation to other contemporary ideologies. However, one can make a valid distinction between a dominant Conservative ideology, and an evolving minority culture of socialist and social-democratic reform. The documentary movement was associated with that culture, and had an influence upon it.

8   The influence of idealism

John Grierson's epistemology, and aesthetic and political ideas, were primarily derived from a tradition of philosophical idealism which he encountered in Scotland prior to 1924. This tradition influenced his activities as a producer and administrator, and had a major influence on the development of the documentary film movement during the inter-war period. Neither Grierson's ideas, nor the documentary movement, can be fully understood without reference to idealist philosophy, which was the source of many of the movement's most significant features, as well as the source of many of its most substantial shortcomings.

Idealism was one of a number of radical petty bourgeois ideologies which appeared in the eighteenth and nineteenth centuries, in opposition to *laissez-faire* liberalism. These ideologies appeared throughout Europe, but they achieved their most systematic expression in Germany, where they resulted in that body of thought which is now referred to as classical German philosophy. In Germany, feudalism remained dominant long after it had been replaced by bourgeois capitalist regimes in other western European countries. One result of this was that the liberal philosophy of the Enlightenment scarcely penetrated German intellectual life, which remained closely linked to the intellectual atmosphere and feudal relations of the Middle Ages.[1] The mystical irrationalism of German idealist philosophy reinforced existing feudal political relations, and made Germany a focal point of metaphysical, and anti-materialist, ideologies.

Another factor in the spread of anti-materialist ideologies in Germany, was the alienation of the German intelligentsia from political affairs under the feudal system. This alienation led the intelligentsia into a contemplative insularity, and into an ideal of private, as opposed to public life.[2] This in turn led to the 'spiritualisation' of social and political issues, within an intellectual discourse which regarded the world as inexplicable in rational and material terms. The German intelligentsia turned from socially purposive knowledge, to intuition and metaphysical vision, and although this drift towards irrationalism was a general European phenomenon at the time, it was principally in Germany that it became 'a philosophy of contempt for empirical reality, based on the timeless and the infinite, the eternal and the absolute.'[3]

As was the case with European feudalism in general, German feudalism eventually failed to suppress the expanding productive forces of capitalism. As feudal political and economic relations collapsed, so also did German philosophical idealism, which, under Hegel, had become the representative ideology of Prussian feudalism. However, German idealism was not just a conservative ideology, whose main function was to protect German feudal relations against the encroachments of the bourgeois State. As a consequence of Germany's distance from the centre of bourgeois power in Europe, German intellectuals became conscious of the fact that classical liberalism, which reached its most significant formulation in the economic liberalism of Adam Smith, had transformed the humanist and liberal values of the Enlightenment, into a class ideology which served the interests of the industrial and commercial middle classes.[4] Philosophical idealism, therefore, was both a progressive and a conservative phenomenon, in relation to bourgeois liberalism.

As philosophical idealism declined in Germany, it was imported into Britain, where it developed into an ideology which was strongly critical of unchecked *laissez-faire* capitalism. As such, British idealism was principally a middle-class response to the need for reform of British capitalism. However, given the long history of middle-class governance in England, and the hegemonic nature of liberal ideology, few British idealists were completely anti-capitalist. Most favoured the continuation of a reformed capitalist system which would stabilize social relations and defuse public dissent.[5] The idealist movement combined elements from both right and left into an often contradictory ideology which emphasized social duty, reform, spirituality, and a return to the social relations of pre-industrial England.[6] As a radical middle-class and lower-middle-class response to the social problems created by capitalism, British idealism was both a progressive and a reactionary phenomenon. It was progressive in the sense that it advocated a more equitable distribution of wealth and resources, and it was reactionary in that it was derived from the lower middle class and liberal profession's need to protect their traditional status and social function, from the expansion of corporate capitalism and the organised working class.[7] This need to protect and reproduce the traditional status of the middle strata, led many British idealists to formulate elitist conceptions of democracy.

British idealism reached the zenith of its influence as a cultural and social ideology between 1880 and 1914. After 1914 it experienced a precipitous decline, and many prominent intellectuals alleged that it, and hegelianism in particular, had been a significant factor in causing the outbreak of the First World War.[8] As idealism declined in prestige, it merged into other theories and ideologies which emphasized the need to use the new mass communications media in order to promote social cohesion. There was a direct continuity between idealism, and the emergence of these ideologies. The idealist advocacy of a 'clericsy' of intellectuals who would work closely with politicians, was absorbed into theories which argued that technology could be used to open channels of communication between the State and the public. This was reflected, for example, in Grierson's notion of a society where philosophers, mass communicators and legislators, would work in harmony to engineer social cohesion and development.[9]

These post-war ideas on the socially purposive use of mass communications media were part of a larger debate on post-war reconstruction and reform. After the war, the most extensively supported pre-war reformist consensus, which consisted of a synthesis of radical liberalism and idealism, was superseded by a social-democratic reformist consensus, which emphasized the need for a significantly increased redistribution of social resources. This social-democratic movement became the most extensively supported reform movement of the inter-war period, and, even though the period was marked by considerable industrial unrest, there was no mass support for a socialist transformation of British society.[10]

Idealism did not disappear completely after 1918, as many critics have supposed, but instead continued to influence political and cultural debate throughout the inter-war period. Idealist traditions initially became established in Britain in two main centres, at Glasgow and Oxford Universities, and there was a considerable movement in personnel between these two centres. The first wave of idealists included T. H. Green, F. H. Bradley, Matthew Arnold, Bernard Bosanquet, and John and Edward Caird. A second wave, who were active during the inter-war period, included R. H. Tawney, William Temple, A. D. Lindsay, William Beveridge, J. B. S. Haldane, and John Grierson. Idealist philosophy was taught at these two centres throughout the inter-war period, particularly at Balliol College Oxford, where Joachim, Lindsay, Edward Caird, J. A. Smith, and Collingwood all taught within an idealist tradition.

Many people left Glasgow and Balliol during the inter-war period, and entered professions where they introduced idealist ideas on the social use of culture. Social communication was a central theme within idealist thought, and, after 1918, many idealists became involved in the establishment of a public service role for the new social media of radio and film. John Grierson, from an idealist background at Glasgow, founded the documentary movement, and individuals such as Stephen Tallents and A. C. Cameron of the British Film Institute all came from idealist backgrounds at Oxford. There were also many debates on the educational and social role of film during the period, some of which reached the highest levels of government. Many of these debates were influenced by idealist themes, and idealism played a major part in the development of educational ideologies during the inter-war period.

There was also a considerable involvement from people influenced by idealist ideas at Oxford and Glasgow, in establishing the public service and educational policies of the BBC. Arthur Acland, H.A.L. Fisher, Fred Clarke, Michael Sadler, C. A. Lewis, William Temple, William Beveridge, A. D. Lindsay, Mary Summerville, and many others, were involved in influencing public service broadcasting. A similar influence affected the literary culture of the period. Idealist ideas on the social role of culture, dating from Arnold and Coleridge, influenced many writers and critics throughout the inter-war period, including T. S. Eliot, F. R. Leavis, and others. Although many of these specifically idealist influences became absorbed into social-democratic reformist ideologies during the period, idealism remained a significant force within British culture throughout the inter-war period.

This is the context from which John Grierson emerged. He was not an isolated thinker, but was part of this continuity of idealist thought, which affected many areas of intellectual life from 1918 to 1939, and which merged into various streams of reformist thought after 1918. Grierson's uniqueness lay in the fact that, whilst adapting his ideas to post-war reformist ideologies, he retained idealist philosophy at the centre of his ideas. During his life he returned constantly to the same idealist texts and authors, and to the same central core of idealist themes. His ideas, throughout his life, retained a remarkable consistency and faithfulness to idealist philosophy which sometimes bordered on the obsessive. This was to have both positive and negative consequences for the documentary film movement.

Grierson first gained access to idealist thought through his father, Robert, who introduced him to the works of Carlyle, Coleridge, Byron, and Ruskin. After this, he studied idealist philosophy at Glasgow University, which, from 1880 till at least 1925, was dominated by neo-kantian and neo-hegelian philosophical doctrines, and by the ideas of philosophers such as Bernard Bosanquet, Edward Caird, T. H. Green and F. H. Bradley.[11] Philosophy was Grierson's major subject at university, where he graduated with honours in moral philosophy, logic, and metaphysics.[12] He made frequent reference to idealist philosophers such as Plato, Hegel, Kant, Croce, and Bradley, throughout his life, and often described himself as a 'kantian.'[13]

One of the central ideas in the philosophical idealism taught at Glasgow, and one which had a significant influence on Grierson, was the notion of 'organic' or 'intelligible' unity. Kant believed that, in order to comprehend nature fully, man subsumed particulars within general laws in order to construct a system of interrelated rules. This process was guided by the belief that nature was an intelligible unity. Kant did not believe that there was an intelligible totality, but that man's reflective judgement was such that empirical enquiry into nature depended on him assuming the existence of an organic unity.[14] However, Hegel did believe in the existence of an organic totality, which he called the 'Absolute'. All the individual things of which the world was composed were aspects of the Absolute, and every manifestation of being was intelligible as a particular manifestation of the Absolute.[15]

Grierson's writings during the 1920s reveal an unclear comprehension and use of these kantian and hegelian concepts. For example:

> The mind demands coherence. . . therefore there is a demand for coherence and unity.[16]

> The notion of an ultimate synthesis is a conception of the mind necessary to itself.[17]

These quotations express a kantian conception of totality, but in the following Grierson identified with hegelian Absolute idealism: 'The ultimate. . . is a coherent and dynamic unity which eternally makes itself explicit through and in space and time.'[18]

This conceptual confusion indicates the contradictory quality of Grierson's ideas in the period. Those ideas consisted of a disorganized synthesis of kantian and hegelian themes, and it is an over-simplification to argue, as some critics have, that Grierson was primarily a hegelian. After 1918, hegelianism fell into disrepute.[19] Grierson also subscribed to this view, and, writing in 1922, described hegelianism as 'the old idealism which led to the conservatism of death, and to the atrocities of the Great War.'[20]

At university Grierson was particularly influenced by the philosophers F. H. Bradley and A. D. Lindsay, both of whom combined kantian and hegelian ideas in their philosophies. Bradley believed in a hegelian conception of organic totality, which he called 'the Absolute', and which he believed could be comprehended through intuition or aesthetic experiences. He believed that cognitive reason dissected the Absolute, and, consequently, alienated man from direct experience of underlying unity.[21]

Bradley's philosophy had a fundamental influence on Grierson, but in his later university writings bradleyan ideas were re-interpreted from a kantian perspective. This was influenced by the teachings of Grierson's professor of Moral Philosophy at Glasgow: A. D. Lindsay.22 Unlike Bradley, Lindsay did not believe in the existence of an organic unity, but he shared Bradley's belief in the value of the State and of institutional structures. Bradley's belief in organic totality and the value of noncognitive aesthetic experience, and Lindsay's belief in gradualist reform, constituted the two most significant sources of Grierson's idealism, and his ideas, then and afterwards, consisted of a synthesis of these influences.

The central concept in this synthesis, was that of 'organic totality'. Grierson believed that society consisted of a matrix of interdependent relations, 'Sleeping or waking, we are concerned each day in an interdependency. . . . This is the fact of modern society.'[23] He believed that this matrix of interdependent relations evolved in accordance with the principle of cumulative integration, and he called this objective movement of history the 'continuing reality.'[24] He believed that societies and institutions which had integrated their internal relations to a significant extent, were qualitatively superior to those which had not, and this led him to believe that corporate institutions, and, in particular, the State, were of greater intrinsic value than smaller, unassimilated and unassociated institutions.

These ideas amounted to a corporatist conception of society, in which individual and social phenomena were perceived as being integrated, at different levels, within the social totality. As a consequence of this belief, Grierson argued that ideologies which promoted integration were 'good propaganda', whilst those which promoted division were 'propaganda of the devil.'[25] He believed that social conflict occurred because individuals and institutions were unaware of underlying social inter-dependency, and because they were deceived by a superficial perception of conflict and division. He rejected the idea that there were fundamental and irreducible divisions in society, and believed that it was an ignorance of the underlying 'continuing reality' of evolving inter-dependence which led to such perceptions.

These beliefs led Grierson to see individualism as a potentially negative force, because it expressed the opposite principle to that of integration. Throughout his writings, terms such as 'personal', 'private', 'individualism', 'hedonism', 'disorder', and 'sophistication', were given negative connotations; whereas terms such as 'alliance' 'unity', 'bind', 'pattern', 'structure' 'interdependency', 'co-operative', 'loyalty', and 'duty', were given positive connotations. He also claimed that he was not interested in 'the vulgarities of the private personal life,'[26] but in the social activity of citizens within 'the body politic'. This belief in the intrinsic superiority of social and corporate phenomena led him to argue that the State was the most important agent in society, because it offered the best means of constraining selfish individualism, and of realising the principle of integration: 'The State is the machinery by which the best interests of the people are secured. Since the needs of the State come first, understanding of those needs comes first in education.'[27] According to Grierson, when the State constrained individualism in the interests of social unity, it exercised 'good totalitarianism':

> You can be 'totalitarian' for evil and you can also be 'totalitarian' for good. . . . So the kind of totalitarianism I am thinking of, while it

may apply to the new conditions of society, has as deep a root as any in human tradition. I would call the philosophy of individualism Romantic and say we have been on a spectacular romantic spree for four hundred years. I would maintain that this other 'totalitarian' viewpoint is classical.[28]

Grierson believed that excessive individualism was unacceptable because it contradicted the principle of social integration, and that 'good totalitarianism' was justified because it affirmed the principle of integration. However, he also believed that 'bad totalitarianism' could result from circumstances in which the 'agents of the State' subverted the institutions of the State, for sectional purposes.[29]

This distinction between the agents and institutions of State was important to Grierson. He believed that the institutions of State possessed intrinsic value because they represented the culmination of an evolution towards social integration. Consequently, he believed that artists and communicators must operate within the 'degree of general sanction'[30] legitimated by the institutions of State. Denial of the general sanction, and, by implication, of the institutions of State, represented a rejection in principle of what he called the 'continuing reality' of evolving cumulative integration. Similarly, any radical transformation of the institutions of State also constituted an equivalent rejection of continuing reality. Because of this, Grierson argued that the citizen, and documentary film-maker, must accept constraint within the sphere of discourse legitimated by the 'general sanction'.

But Grierson believed that circumstances could exist in which the agents of State could subvert the institutions of State. In such circumstances he believed that the documentary film-maker should take on a more critical role. However, the ideological base from which that film-maker mounted his/her critique must, according to Grierson, remain the existing structure of society. This ruled out fundamental criticisms of established society, and also ruled out the development of a radical/critical documentary film practice.

The ideas on the nature of reality which are described above, express an almost biological conception of organic unity and integration, which was derived from philosophical idealism. The same was true of Grierson's ideas on epistemology and aesthetics, which were primarily derived from Bradley and Lindsay's synthesis of kantian and hegelian idealism. Grierson was particularly influenced by the kantian belief that the basis of the aesthetic experience lay in the perception of complex unity, and he believed that the human mind sought harmony in the aesthetic experience: 'Art is the prototype of that harmony which the human mind seeks, its proper business is to harmonise the relations of life.'[31] He was also influenced by Bradley's belief that underlying reality could only be experienced intuitively, and that conceptual reason could not comprehend the existential complexity of reality.[32] This implied that, in order to be effective, art and education should use generalized and symbolic, rather than overtly didactic or pedagogic modes of expression. This also applied to the documentary film which, according to Grierson, should not convey didactic factual information, but should use dramatic and symbolic material which: 'strikes out the more useful patterns of modern citizenship. . . and conveys patterns of civic appreciation, civic faith and civic duty'.[33]

This use of symbolic expression to represent social inter-connection was apparent in the final reel of *Drifters* (1929), in which Grierson used over-lapping dissolves to emphasize the ways in which all parts and 'patterns' of the social process of herring fishing were inter-connected. Similar scenes, showing an almost organic inter-connection of social practices, can be found in Basil Wright's *Song of Ceylon* (1933-4), Grierson and Flaherty's *Industrial Britain* (1931), and in other films made by the documentary movement during the inter-war period.

These beliefs on the use of symbolic expression to represent social inter-connection were reinforced when Grierson travelled to America in 1924. In America, he encountered right-wing ideologies which emphasized the public's incapacity for sophisticated rational cognition, or for effective participation within the democratic process. He was particularly influenced by Walter Lippmann's general scepticism concerning democratic values, and by his belief that public cognition was based on generalized subjective judgement.[34] Although Grierson repudiated much of Lippmann's elitist ideology, he was influenced by the latter's belief that the public comprehended the social world in terms of generalized subjective judgement, rather than cognitive rationalism. From this epistemological premiss, he argued that the documentary film should not try to teach the public 'to know everything about everything all the time,'[35] but should instill an understanding of the significant generative forces in society. This reinforced his earlier idealist conviction that generalized intuition, rather than cognitive rationalism, was the best means of comprehending underlying reality.

From these ontological and epistemological premises, Grierson defined the principal function of the documentary film as that of representing the inter-dependence and evolution of social relations in a dramatic and symbolic way. This function was, therefore, both sociological and aesthetic at the same time. It was sociological, in that it involved the representation of inter-dependent social relations; and it was aesthetic, in that it involved the use of imaginative and symbolic means to that end.[36] Examples of such representations can be found in most of the documentary films made by the movement, for example, in *Drifters* and *Song of Ceylon*, as well as in *Night Mail*, in which the poetry of W. H.

Auden is used to add a symbolic dimension to a narrative on how the Royal Mail 'binds' society together through communication. Grierson saw no conflict between the aesthetic and sociological function of the documentary film, which he believed was the ideal medium for 'civic education' because it revealed the underlying inter-dependence of social relations. It was: 'the medium of all media born to express the living nature of inter-dependency,. . . (it). . . outlined the patterns of inter-dependency more distinctively and more deliberately than any other medium whatsoever'.[37] Grierson's first systematic exposition of his theory of documentary film appeared in an EMB memorandum written in 1927, entitled 'Notes for English Producers'.[38] This was divided into two parts. Part I, reasserted many of the ideas which had appeared in his American writings of 1924-26, particularly in *Better Popular Pictures* (1926).[39] However, Part II, entitled 'English Cinema Production and the Naturalistic Tradition', contained his first clearly articulated exposition of the documentary film.

In his report, Grierson postulated two different categories of naturalist film production. The first of these would consist of films seven-to-nine reels in length, which would correspond to his earlier model of epic cinema, and would consist of fictional narratives, film stars, studio locations etc.. The second category, which did not correspond to any previous model elaborated by Grierson, would consist of films one-to-four reels in length, which would have simple plots, and no film stars or studio locations. The principal function of these films would be to represent social interconnection in both primitive cultures and modern industrial society,[40] and Grierson believed that they would mark a 'new phase in cinema production'.[41]

Grierson envisioned that these and other documentary films would play a key role within what he called the 'informational State', in which social inter-dependency and political legislation would be explained to the public, through propaganda, by documentary film-makers. He believed that failure to establish such a State, based on close collaboration between political legislators and mass communicators, would result in social conflict. But such close collaboration raised, and still raises, questions concerning the autonomy and critical independence of the documentary movement. Grierson hoped to resolve these questions by establishing the documentary movement within a semi-independent public corporation, rather than within a government department which was subject to direct State control, as was the case with both the EMB and GPO Film Units. This was why he was so influenced by the examples of the Canadian Motion Picture Bureau and the BBC.

But Grierson's enthusiasm for the public corporation was also influenced by his conception of the State. He conceived of the State, not

as one centralized entity, but as an amalgamation of relatively autonomous corporate entities, in which power was equally distributed. He was
opposed to the over-centralization of power, which he thought could lead
to abuse, and believed that the best means of avoiding such abuse was
through a distribution of power amongst corporate institutions, and
through a voting franchise.

This corporatist conception of the State further emphasized the
importance which Grierson placed upon working within the 'general
sanction', for, in a corporate society, in which semi-autonomous corporate institutions worked through consensus, rather than through
coercive central diktat, it was the framework of assumptions and beliefs
which constituted the 'general sanction' which bound society together.
Any attempt by artists and communicators to bypass that consensus
could lead to either social fragmentation, or to centralized dictatorship.[42]

These ideas were primarily derived from a philosophical idealist
discourse, from which Grierson developed a utopian model of relations
between documentary and the State, and which provided the philosophical basis for his activities as an administrator and theorist. However,
the intimate collaborative relationship between political legislators and
mass communicators which was implied in that utopian model was far
removed from the political realities of British society during the inter-war
period. The period was dominated by Conservative political ideologies,
and the documentary film movement was regarded with mistrust and
apprehension by the establishment, because of its association with
political reformism.

In addition, and contrary to Grierson's hopes, the documentary
movement never achieved the degree of stable autonomy which the
institutional structure of a public corporation would have provided. The
EMB was an executive commission under the political control of the
Dominions and Colonial Secretary of State, and under the financial
control of the Treasury. Similarly, the GPO Film Unit was answerable to
Parliament through the Postmaster General, and was also under the
financial control of the Treasury. This adverse situation was far removed
from the semi-independent autonomy enjoyed by the BBC, and the
documentary movement found itself exposed to pressures from those
within the political establishment and the film trade who were either
opposed to the movement's ideology, or who felt their interests
threatened by the movement's expansion.

When these factors are taken into account it is difficult to imagine how
the documentary film movement could have evolved into the semi-
autonomous, socially purposive instrument which Grierson had
originally envisioned. His ideology contravened too many basic tenets of
dominant Conservatism to prosper. In addition, despite the history of
retrenchment and decline experienced by the State-owned documentary

movement, Grierson continued to depend on an unrealistic utopian model of the relationship between documentary and the State, which he had derived from philosophical idealism, and which was incompatible with existing political circumstances. It is true that the documentary movement expanded outside of the State during the thirties, but private sponsorship was always of secondary importance to Grierson, and he turned to it, primarily, in a context of retrenchment at the EMB and GPO Film Units. Although he was fully conscious of the formidable difficulties which faced the documentary movement, an idealist model continued to pervade his overall ideology, and this contradiction between an impractical utopian model and an adverse political reality was inevitably resolved to the detriment of the documentary movement.

Grierson's own temperament was partly responsible for this. He was obsessively fixated with the idealist philosophy which had influenced him in his youth, and believed that it provided fundamental answers to the contemporary problem of the nature of democracy within mass society. This 'tunnel vision' made him, at one and the same time, both inflexible and opportunistic. His typical response, when reality appeared to contradict his ideas, was to retreat to the small number of well read idealist texts already mentioned in this book. This rather compulsive obsession was also reflected in the dogmatic conviction and certitude with which he expounded his ideology. His ideas did not develop much beyond his youth, and he compulsively re-stated them thereafter, ignoring, ridiculing, or dealing superficially with arguments which contradicted his own.

In addition to being materially responsible for the documentary movement's decline, philosophical idealism was also the source of several questionable features of Grierson's ideology. His *a priori* acceptance of the 'institutions of State', and of the need for film-makers to work within the 'general sanction', led to the production of documentary films which were of minimal critical value. In *Housing Problems* and *Drifters*, for example, problematic social and political issues were depicted as being totally resolvable. His theory of documentary film also implied a centralized and hierarchical practice of social ideology production, in which social communication was passed down from a bureaucratic elite to the public, and never vice-versa. Similarly, his conception of a society managed by mandarins and public relations experts can only be characterized as 'democratic' with some difficulty. Beneath the rhetoric of 'democracy' there was an underlying rhetoric, of a self-perpetuating bureaucratic elite.

But if philosophical idealism was partly responsible for the documentary movement's decline, and for authoritarian elements in Grierson's ideology, it also provided the movement with a degree of ideological coherence, and was a principal source of Grierson's reformism. Idealism was not an exclusively right-wing political phenomenon. When it appeared in Britain in the nineteenth century, it was premissed on a belief in State regulation of capitalism in the interests of civil society. In the twentieth century, it developed into right wing and fascist ideologies, premissed on State control of capitalism and civil society. But it also developed into liberal and leftist ideologies which advocated State regulation of capitalism within a democratic franchise, as, for example, in the Independent Labour Party, and in A. D. Lindsay's constitutional reformism, both of which influenced Grierson. The fact that Grierson was influenced by idealism, does not, therefore, entail that he was a totalitarian, even though his ideology contained totalitarian elements. These elements were a legacy of idealism, but they were also a product of centre progressive 'middle way' opinion in Britain during the inter-war period.[43] Grierson's emphasis on the management of society by bureaucratic elites was characteristic of middle way opinion, which questioned the idea of participatory democracy, and emphasized the need for efficient management within a corporate, technocratic society based on universal franchise.[44] Beliefs in the need for elitist leadership were, therefore, common to ideologies across the political spectrum, and this must be borne in mind when relating Grierson's authoritarianism to other ideological trends of the period.[45]

The type of corporate society advocated by Grierson and others during the 1930s, was opposed by the left, who feared that it might develop into a form of corporate fascism, like that which had appeared in Italy under Mussolini. The Marxist theorist John Strachey argued that a British New Deal could lead to fascism, whilst the Labour Party activist Stafford Cripps argued that Lloyd George's Economic Commission was similar to fascist institutions in Italy and Germany.[46] But comparison of the American New Deal with European fascism was mistaken, and the establishment of a corporate, centre progressive State in Britain, would have constituted an advance on existing *laissez-faire* and corporate Conservatism. Similarly, it can be argued that Grierson and the documentary movement were a progressive and reformist phenomenon, in relation to the dominant Conservatism of the inter-war period.

Notes

Introduction

1 Forsyth Hardy, H., *John Grierson, A Documentary Biography* (London, Faber & Faber, 1979), p.17.
2 ibid., p.44.
3 ibid., p.214.
4 First Meeting of the EMB Film Conference, 1 February 1927. PRO CO/760/37.
5 Forsyth Hardy, op. cit., p.54
6 EMB Film Committee, *The Cinema Activities of the EMB* (12 December 1932), PRO CO/760/37.
7 ibid.
8 EMB Film Committee, *Non-Theatrical Distribution* (19 March 1932), PRO CO/760/37/EMB/C/71.
9 These statistics are not totally reliable, they will be discussed in detail in the section of the chapter dealing with the EMB Film Unit.
10 Low, Rachel, *History of the British Film, Volume Four: 1919-1929* (London, Allen & Unwin, 1971), p.103.
11 Lee, J. M., 'The Dissolution of the EMB' *Journal of Imperial and Commonwealth History*, vol. 1, no. 1 (October, 1972), p.54.
12 Rotha, Paul, *Documentary Diary* (London, Hill & Wang, 1973), p.114.
13 ibid., p.124.
14 Forsyth Hardy, op. cit., pp.61-2.
15 Rotha, op. cit., p.46.
16 Orbanz, Eva, (ed.) *Journey to a Legend and Back, The British Realist Film* (Berlin, Edition Volker Spiess, 1977), p.177.
17 Sherman, John, 'The Grierson Influence', *Undercut*, no. 9 (Summer, 1983) pp. 16-17.
18 Forman, Denis, Interview in *Orbanz* op. cit., pp. 110-16.
19 'The Grierson Influence', conference held at Canada House Cultural Centre, March 1983; and 'John Grierson, 1898-1972', conference held at University of Stirling, October 1977.
20 In particular, Rotha op. cit., chapters 2, 3, 5, and 'Afterthought'.
21 Nichols, Bill, 'Documentary Theory and Practice', in *Screen*, vol. 17, no. 4 (Winter 1976-7), p.35.
22 Barnouw, Erik, *Documentary, A History of the Non-Fiction Film* (London, Oxford University Press, 1974), p.240.
23 Nichols, op. cit., p.34.
24 Grierson, John, *I Derive My Authority From Moses* (Grierson Archive Papers, University of Stirling, 1957-72), G7A.9.1.p.3.
25 For further elaboration see chapters Four and Five of this Book.

26 Willemen, Paul, 'Presentation', in Macpherson D. (ed.) *British Cinema, Traditions of Independence* (London, British Film Institute, 1980), p.1.

27 Lovell, Alan, in Macpherson (ed.), op. cit., p.18.

28 Lejeune, C. A., the *Observer*, 21 August, 1932.

29 Johnston, Claire, in Macpherson (ed.), op. cit., p.18.

30 ibid.

31 Johnston, Claire, in *Undercut* op. cit., p.12.

32 Montagu, Ivor, in *Undercut* op. cit., pp.13-15.

33 Grierson, John, 'The Challenge of Peace', in Hardy, Forsyth, H. (ed.) *Grierson On Documentary* (London, Faber & Faber, 1946), p.172.

34 Hood, Stuart, 'A Cool Look at the Legend', in Orbanz, op. cit., p.150.

35 Wollen, Peter, *Signs and Meanings in the Cinema* (London, Secker & Warburg, 1969), pp.116-17.

36 Willemen, Paul, 'Editorial', in *Cinema Semiotics and the Work of Christian Metz* (*Screen*, vol. 14., nos 1/2 Spring/Summer, 1973), p.2.

37 ibid.

38 Nichols, op. cit.

39 Tudor, Andrew, *Theories of Film* (London, Secker & Warburg, 1974), p.75.

40 ibid.

41 Lovell, in *Undercut* op. cit.

42 Kuhn, Annette, 'Recontextualising a Film Movement', in Macpherson (ed.), op. cit.

43 Interviews with Alberto Cavalcanti, Paris, 1983; and Basil Wright, England, 1987.

44 Grierson, John, *I Remember, I Remember* (Grierson Archive Papers 1957-72), G7.17.2. pp.10-11.

45 Hillier, John, and Lovell, Alan, *Studies in Documentary* (London, Secker & Warburg, 1972), p.20.

46 Passmore, John, A Hundred Years of Philosophy (London, Duckworth, 1957), p.60.

47 Copleston, F., *A History of Philosophy Volume Eight: Bentham to Russell* (London, Search Press, 1966), p.164.

48 Hillier and Lovell, op. cit., p.23.

49 ibid., p.24.

50 Grierson, John, 'First Principles of Documentary', in Hardy (1946) op. cit., pp.39-42.

51 Swann, Paul, *The British Documentary Film Movement 1926-1945* (PhD Thesis for the University of Leeds, 1979), pp.121-3.

52 Robinson, F. P., Letter to Stephen Tallents, 19 December, 1934. PRO T160/742, F13860/03/2.

53 Treasury to Post Office, 24 July, 1939. POST 33 5199 P16682/37. File No.6. Post Office Archive.

54 Morris, Peter, 'Re-thinking Grierson: The Ideology of John Grierson', in P. Verronneau, M. Dorland and F. Feldman (eds) *Dialogue Canadian and Quebec Cinema* (Montreal, Mediatexte, 1987), pp.24–56.

1 John Grierson

1 Dickson, Tony, *Scottish Capitalism* (London, Lawrence & Wishart, 1980), p.254.

2 ibid., p.190.

3 Ferguson, W., 'Scotland, 1689 to the present', in *The Edinburgh History of Scotland*, vol. 4 (Edinburgh Oliver & Boyd, 1968), p.330.

4 ibid., p.354.

5 ibid., p.364.

6 Glover, Janet, *The Story of Scotland* (London, Faber & Faber, 1960), p.360.

7 ibid., p.85.

8 Dickson, op cit., p.258.

9 ibid., p.264.

10 Glover, op. cit., p.362.

11 Dickson, op. cit., p.286.

12 Glover, op. cit., p.364.

13 Ferguson, op. cit., p.335.

14 Mackie, J. D., *A History of Scotland* (London, Penguin, 1964), p.362.

15 Dickson, op. cit., p.264.

16 Gray, R. Q., 'Religious Culture and Social Class in Late 19th and Early 20th Century Edinburgh', in Crossick (ed.), *The Lower Middle Class in Britain* (London, Croom Helm, 1977), pp.144-6.

17 Dickson, op. cit., p.206.

18 Hobsbawm, E. J., *The Age of Capital 1848-1875* (London, Weidenfeld & Nicholson, 1975), p.289.

19 Dickson, op. cit., p.206.

20 Copleston, Frederick, *A History of Philosophy Volume VIII, Bentham to Russell* (London, Search Press, 1966), p.13.

21 ibid., p.15.

22 Mill, J. S., *On Liberty* (Oxford, Blackwell, 1946), p.9.

23 ibid., p.50.

24 Copleston, op. cit., p.43.

25 Thompson, E. P., *The Making of the English Working Class* (London, Gollancz, 1963); Weber, Max, *The Protestant Ethic and the Spirit of Capitalism* (1930); Tawney, R. H., *Religion and the Rise of Capitalism* (London, John Murray, 1936).

26 Glover, op. cit., p.379.

27 ibid., p.381.

28 Ferguson, op. cit., p.336.

29 Williams, Raymond, *Culture and Society* (London, Chatto & Windus, 1958), p.167.

30 Lacey, A. R., *A Dictionary of Philosophy* (London, Routledge & Kegan Paul, 1976), p.86.

31 ibid., p.86.

32 Ferguson, op. cit., p.338.

33 Forsyth Hardy, H., *John Grierson, A Documentary Biography* (Faber & Faber, London, 1979), p.12.

34 Grierson, John, 'Everyman His Own Stevenson', in *Scotland* (Edinburgh, November, 1950).

35 Interview with Forsyth Hardy, Edinburgh, 1 October, 1985.

36 Interview with Marion Taylor, Edinburgh, 5 October, 1985.

37 Mackie, op. cit., pp.348-51.

38 Interview with Forsyth Hardy, op. cit.

39 Forsyth Hardy, op. cit., p.12.

40 ibid.

41 Grierson, John, 'My Father was a Teacher', in *The Land*, vol. 2, no.3., (1942-3).

42 Interview with Marion Taylor, op. cit.

43 ibid.

44 Forsyth Hardy, op. cit., p.12.

45 Grierson, John, letter to Anthony Grierson, Sarasota, Florida, June 1942. Cited in Forsyth Hardy, op. cit.

46 Cole, G.D.H., and Postgate, Raymond, *A History of the Common People, 1746-1936* (London, Methuen, 1938), p.408.

47 ibid., p.412.

48 Glover, op. cit., p.365.
49 Interview with Forsyth Hardy, op. cit.
50 ibid.
51 Interview with Marion Taylor, op. cit.
52 Grierson, John, in *The Land* op. cit.
53 ibid.
54 Copleston, op. cit., p.148.
55 Grierson, John, *Man and the State* (Grierson Archive Papers, University of Stirling, 1898-1927), G1.2.2, p.7.
56 ibid., p.6.
57 Lacey, op. cit., p.86.
58 Grierson, John, A paper on Cornford's 'From Religion to Philosophy' (Grierson Archive Papers, 1898-1927), G1.2.1, p.23.
59 Copleston, op. cit., p.156.
60 Williams, op. cit., p.81.
61 ibid., p.84.
62 Interview with Forsyth Hardy, op. cit.
63 Forsyth Hardy, op. cit., p.15.
64 Grierson, John, *The Nature and Value of Philosophical Enquiry, With Reference to Carlyle's 'Characteristics'* (Grierson Archive Papers 1898-1927), G1.2.87, p.9.
65 Grierson, John, *Contribution of Poetry to Religion* (Grierson Archive Papers 1898-1927), 15 February 1920, G1.5.2. p.3.
66 Ruskin, John, *Stones of Venice* (London, Smith & Elder, 1899), pp.163-5.
67 Grierson, John, *The Utilitarian Position* (Grierson Archive Papers 1898-1927), G1.2.4, p.6.
68 ibid., p.7.
69 Williams, Raymond, op. cit., p.84.
70 ibid., p.115.
71 Arnold, Matthew, *Culture and Anarchy* (London, Murray, 1867), p.70.
72 ibid., p.xi.
73 Grierson, G1.2.4, op. cit., p.6.
74 ibid., p.3.
75 Mill, J. S., op. cit., p.50.
76 Grierson, G1.2.2, op. cit., p.2.
77 Grierson, G1.2.4, op. cit., p.6.
78 Grierson, G1.2.2, op. cit., p.4.
79 Interview with Marion Taylor, op. cit.
80 Mackie, op. cit., p.361.
81 Grierson, John, *The character of an Ultimate Synthesis* (Grierson Archive Papers 1889-1927), G1.2.6, p.11.
82 ibid., p.12.
83 Interview with Marion Taylor, op. cit.
84 Grierson, in *The Land*, op. cit.
85 Forsyth Hardy, op. cit., p.19.
86 ibid., p.21.
87 Grierson, John, Letter to Frances Strauss, 7 September 1927 (Grierson Archive Papers, Grierson-Strauss Correspondence, 1927-34), G21A.
88 Grierson, John, *Background for the Use of Film by Rehabilitation Officers* (15 February 1945).
89 Interview with Forsyth Hardy, op. cit.
90 Grierson, John, *When is a Highlandsman* (Council of Scottish Clan Societies, 8 September, 1962).

91 Interview with Forsyth Hardy, op. cit.
92 Grierson, John, *Byron and his Age* (Grierson Archive Papers 1898-1927), G1.2.10, p.16.
93 Grierson, G1.2.2, op. cit., p.5.
94 ibid.
95 Mowat, C. L., *Britain Between the Wars* (London, Methuen, 1955), p.1.
96 Grierson, 15 February 1945, op. cit.
97 Ferguson, op. cit., p.363.
98 ibid., p.354.
99 Middlemas, Keith, *The Clydesiders* (London, Hutchinson, 1965), p.97.
100 Forsyth Hardy, op. cit., p.24.
101 Grierson, 15 February 1945, op. cit.
102 Gallacher, William, *Revolt on the Clyde* (London, Lawrence & Wishart, 1936), p.213.
103 ibid., p.210.
104 Dickson, op. cit., p.275.
105 Oakley, C. A., letter to the author, November 1985.
106 Forsyth Hardy, op. cit., p.23.
107 Letter from Charles Dand to Professor Jack Ellis, in *Cinema Journal*, no.xii, (Spring, 1973).
108 Grierson, John, Preface to *Documentary Film* by Rotha, Paul, Griffith, Richard, and Road, Sinclair, (Faber & Faber, London, 1952), pp.22-3.
109 Dickson, op. cit., p.342.
110 Cole and Postgate, op. cit., pp.568-70.
111 Middlemas, op. cit., p.30.
112 Dickson, op. cit., p.276.
113 Middlemas, op. cit., p.276.
114 Cole and Postgate, op. cit., p.554.
115 Grierson, John, 'Searchlight on Democracy', *Grierson on Documentary* (London, Faber & Faber, 1946), pp 99-100.
116 Middlemas, op. cit., p.112.
117 Kirkwood, David, quoted in Shinwell, Manny, *Conflict Without Malice* (London, Oldhams Press, 1955).
118 Interview with Forsyth Hardy, op. cit.
119 Russell, Bertrand, *Principles of Social Reconstruction* (London, Allen & Unwin, 1916), p.18.
120 ibid., p.205.
121 ibid., p.245.
122 ibid., p.254.
123 ibid., p.255.
124 Russell, Bertrand, *Roads to Freedom* (London, Allen & Unwin, 1918), p.209.
125 Russell, (1916), op. cit., p.205.
126 Grierson, John, G1.2.8., op. cit., p.6.
127 ibid., p.7.
128 ibid., p.5.
129 Grierson, John, notes from a lecture given by A. D. Lindsay, entitled *Politics of Aristotle* (Grierson Archive Papers 1898-1927), G1.3.12.
130 Russell, (1918), op. cit., p.140.
131 Grierson, G1.2.2., op. cit., p.7.
132 Forsyth Hardy, op. cit., p.17.
133 Morgan, Alexander, *Scottish University Studies* (Edinburgh and London, Oliver Boyd, 1933), p.87.

134 ibid., p.90.
135 Mackie, op. cit., p.355.
136 Letter from Michael S. Moss, University Archivist, Glasgow University, to the author, 8 November 1985.
137 ibid.
138 Letter from J. William Hess, Associate Director, Rockefeller Archive Centre, to the author. 17 June 1985.
139 Mackie, J. D., *The University of Glasgow* (Glasgow, Jackson, Son & Co., 1954) p.220.
140 Copleston, op. cit., p.164.
141 Mackie, (1954), op. cit., p.225.
142 Passmore, John, *A Hundred Years of Philosophy* (London Duckworth, 1957), pp.55-6.
143 Richter, M., *The Politics of Conscience, T. H. Green and his Age* (London, Wiedenfeld & Nicolson, 1964), p.13.
144 Green, T. H., Review of John Caird's *Introduction to the Philosophy of Religion* (London, 1880).
145 Passmore, op. cit., p.57.
146 Russell, Bertrand, *A History of Western Philosophy* (London, Allen & Unwin, 1946), p.675.
147 Lacey, op. cit., p.20.
148 Kemp, John, *The Philosophy of Kant* (London, Oxford University Press, 1968), p.38.
149 Copleston, Frederick, *A History of Philosophy, Volume Six: Wolff to Kant* (London, Search Press, 1960), p.38.
150 Kolakowski, Leszek, *Main Currents of Marxism, Volume One: The Founders* (London, Oxford University Press, 1978), p.45-7.
151 Kant, Immanuel, *Critique of Judgement* (1790), LV1 BD p.40.
152 Copleston, (1960), op. cit., p.356.
153 Kant, op. cit., p.197.
154 White, Morton, *The Age of Analysis* (New York, Mentor, 1955), p.14.
155 Kolakowski, op. cit., p.48.
156 Copleston, op. cit., p.240.
157 Grierson, G1.2.7, op. cit., p.7.
158 Grierson, G1.2.6, op. cit., p.6.
159 Grierson, G1.2.7, op. cit., p.8.
160 ibid., p.1.
161 ibid.
162 ibid., p.8.
163 Grierson, G1.2.6, op. cit., p.14.
164 Interview with Marion Taylor, op. cit.
165 Copleston, (1966), op. cit., p.218.
166 Bradley, F. H., *Essays on Truth and Reality* (London, Clarendon Press, 1914), p.188.
167 Bradley, F.H., *Appearance and Reality* (London, Swann & Co., 1893), p.80.
168 Bradley, (1914), op. cit., p.202.
169 Mukerji, A. C., 'British Idealism', in *A Dictionary of Eastern and Western Philosophy* (London, Allen & Unwin, 1953), p.308.
170 Passmore, op. cit., pp.62-5.
171 Bradley, (1914), op. cit., p.223.
172 Passmore, op. cit., p.66.
173 Copleston, (1966), op. cit., p.188.

174 Bradley, (1914), op. cit., p.174.
175 ibid., p.175.
176 Passmore, op. cit., p.69.
177 Bradley, F. H., *Ethical Studies* (London, H. S. King & Co., 1876), p.166.
178 ibid., pp.190-200.
179 ibid., p.166.
180 ibid., p.192.
181 ibid.
182 Wollheim, R., *Bradley* (London, Harmondsworth, 1959), p.14.
183 ibid., p.279.
184 Grierson, G1.2.7, op. cit., p.7.
185 Grierson, G1.2.6, op. cit., p.5.
186 ibid., p.7.
187 ibid., p.12.
188 Grierson, G1.2.5, op. cit., p.7.
189 Grierson, G1.2.7, op. cit., p.8.
190 Grierson, G1.5.2, op. cit., p.2.
191 Lovell and Hillier, op. cit., pp.21-2.
192 Grierson, John, 'Education and the New Order', in the *Democracy and Citizenship Series*, Pamphlet no. 7, 1941. Published by the Canadian Association for Adult Education
193 ibid.
194 ibid.
195 Grierson, G1.2.6, op. cit., p.15.
196 Grierson, G1.2.10, op. cit., p.9.
197 Letter from Charles Oakley to the author, 30 October 1985.
198 Scott, D., *A. D. Lindsay* (Oxford, Blackwell, 1971), p.102.
199 ibid., p.100.
200 ibid., p.403.
201 ibid., p.405.
202 ibid., p.406.
203 ibid., p.50.
204 ibid., p.57.
205 Grierson, G1.2.6, op. cit., p.12.

2 John Grierson and the influence of American Scientific naturalism, 1924–7

1 Moss, Michael, S., Glasgow University Archivist, letter to the author, 8 November 1985. Including a copy of John Grierson's graduation report.
2 Interview with Forsyth Hardy, Edinburgh, Tuesday 8 May, 1986.
3 Hess, J. William, letter to Forsyth Hardy, 7 April 1976; and Grierson's Fellowship Summary, Laura Spellman Rockefeller Memorial, series 3, box 51, folder 547.
4 Hardy, Forsyth, H., *John Grierson, A Documentary Biography* (London, Faber & Faber, 1979), p.31.
5 Rockefeller Fellowship Summary, op. cit.
6 ibid.
7 Marshall, John, Interview with Forsyth Hardy, Wilton, Connecticut, 3 December 1976, in Forsyth Hardy (1979), op. cit.
8 Purcell, A. E., 'The Undermining of Democratic Theory: Naturalism and Objectivism in the Social Sciences', in *The Crisis of Democratic Theory:*

Scientific Naturalism and the Problem of Value (Kentucky, University Press of Kentucky, 1973), pp.15-45.

9 Extracts from Glasgow University Library records of books borrowed by John and Agnes Grierson, 1915-24. Photocopies from Glasgow University Library, and from the John Grierson Archive, University of Stirling.

10 See chapter four of this Book.

11 Interview with Forsyth Hardy, May 1986.

12 Grierson, John, 'Art and Revolution', in *Today's Revolution in the Arts*, North Carolina, April 1962 (Grierson Archive Papers, University of Stirling), G7.56.6. p.2.

13 Burke and Howe, *American Authors and Books* (New York, Crown, 1972).

14 Grierson, G7.56.6., op. cit., p.2.

15 ibid., p.3.

16 Novack, George, *Pragmatism Versus Marxism: An Appraisal of John Dewey's Philosophy* (New York, Pathfinder Press, 1975), p.55.

17 Swingewood, A., *A Short History of Social Thought* (London, Macmillan, 1974), p.55.

18 Hobsbawm, E. J., *The Age of Revolution* (London, Weidenfeld & Nicolson, 1962), p.295.

19 Novack, op. cit., p.60.

20 Swingewood, op. cit., p.47.

21 Purcell, op. cit., p.3.

22 Curti, Merle, *The Growth of American Thought* (New York, Harper & Bros., 1943), p.560.

23 James, William, *Pragmatism* (New York, Longmans, 1907), p. 47.

24 Purcell, op. cit., p.10.

25 ibid., p.11.

26 Merriam, C. E., *Political Power* (Chicago, University of Chicago Press, 1934), p.96.

27 Lasswell, H. D., *Politics: Who Gets What, When How* (New York, McGraw Hill, 1936), p.13.

28 Purcell, op. cit., p.96.

29 Encyclopedia of the Social Sciences, *War and Reorientation* (New York, McGraw Hill, 1930), p.189.

30 Curti, op. cit., p.556.

31 English, H. B., and English, A. C., *A Comprehensive Dictionary of Psychological and Psychoanalytic terms* (New York, Longman, 1958), p.62.

32 Copleston, Frederick, *A History of Philosophy Volume Eight: Bentham to Russell* (London, Search Press, 1966), p.390.

33 Russell, Bertrand, *History of Western Philosophy* (London, Allen & Unwin, 1946), p. 741.

34 Kallen, M., Horace, *Behaviourism* (New York, McGraw Hill, 1930), p.2,498.

35 Hayes, Samuel, *The Response to Industrialism* (Chicago, University of Chicago Press, 1957), p.95.

36 Curti, op. cit., p.570.

37 Lippmann, Walter, *Public Opinion* (New York, and London, Allen & Unwin, 1922), pp.78-9.

38 ibid., p.13.

39 ibid., p.146.

40 ibid., p.106.

41 Dewey, John, 'Public Opinion: A Review of Walter Lippmann's Book', *New Republic* no. 30, 3 May 1922, p.288.

42 Purcell, op. cit., p.105.
43 Lasswell, Harold, *Psychoanalysis and Politics* (Chicago, University of Chicago Press, 1930), p.74.
44 Purcell, op. cit., p.108.
45 ibid., p.101.
46 Shepherd, W. J., President of the American Political Science Association, *Democracy in Transition*, American Political Science Review, 29 February 1935.
47 See chapter Four of this Book.
48 Grierson, John, letter to Renwick.
49 Definition of the term 'objectivist': a belief in the objective existence of things and truths independent of the human mind, Lacey, A. R., *A Dictionary of Philosophy* (London, Routledge & Kegan Paul, 1976), p.209. Purcell uses the term to refer to the school of American thought which believed that only scientific, empirical investigation could yield true knowledge. Purcell, op. cit., p.4.
50 Beritz, Lauren, *The Servants of Power* (New York, 1960), p. 49.
51 Keppel, F. P., *Philanthropy and Learning* (New York, 1936), p.23.
52 Purcell, op. cit. p.28.
53 ibid., p.11.
54 Laura Spellman Rockefeller Memorial, series 3, box 51, folder 547.
55 ibid.
56 Park, R. E., *The City As a Social Laboratory* (Chicago, University of Chicago Press, 1927).
57 Giddings, F. H., 'The Scientific Scrutiny of Social Facts', *Journal of Social Forces*, 1 September, 1928. p.509.
58 Rockefeller Memorial, op. cit.
59 Glasgow University Library records, op. cit.
60 Grierson, John, G1A.5.4., op. cit., p.10.
61 Grierson, John, *On Education* (Grierson Archive Papers 1939-45), G4.19.21, p.3.
62 ibid., p.4.
63 Grierson, John, letter to Renwick, op. cit.
64 Novack, op. cit., p. 14.
65 ibid., p.40.
66 Hayes, op. cit., p.97.
67 Russell, Bertrand, (1946), op. cit., p.775.
68 Dewey, John, *Democracy And Education* (New York, Macmillan, 1916), p.255.
69 Novack, op. cit., p.211.
70 Grierson, John, *Man and the State* (Grierson Archive Papers 1898-1927), G1.2.2.
71 Passmore, John, *A Hundred Years of Philosophy,* (London, Duckworth, 1957), p. 115.
72 Grierson, G4.19.9, op. cit. p.6.
73 Grierson, G4.19.21., op. cit., p.3.
74 Dewey, John, *Human Nature and Conduct* (New York, 1922), p. 170.
75 Dewey, John, *Reconstruction in Philosophy* (New York, Allen & Unwin, 1920), p. 160.
76 Ellwood, C. A., 'Scholarship in the Social Sciences', in *Social Science* no, 7, 1932.
77 Purcell, op. cit., p.45.
78 Ellwood, C. A., *Cultural Evolution, A Study of Social Origins and Development* (New York and London, Century Social Science Series, 1927), p. 255.
79 ibid.
80 ibid., p.258.
81 Grierson, John, *Plato in the Light of Higher Criticism* (Grierson Archive Papers 1898-1927), G1A.3.5.

82 Grierson, John, *Saving Modern Art From its Friends* (Grierson Archive papers 1898-1927), G1A.3.12; and *Sermon*, 1920, G1A.5.4.

83 Grierson, John, G1A.3.12., op. cit., and *The Nature and Value of Philosophical Enquiry, With Reference to Carlyle's Characteristics* (Grierson Archive Papers 1898-1927), G1.2.8. p.9.

84 Grierson, G4.19.21, op. cit., p.1.

85 ibid., p.2.

86 Grierson, G7.56.6, op. cit., p.8.

87 ibid.

88 Grierson, John, *Byron and his Age* (Grierson Archive papers 1898- 1927), G1.2.10, p.5.

89 Scott, D., *A. D. Lindsay* (Oxford, Blackwell, 1971), p.406.

90 Grierson, G4.19.19, op. cit., p.1.

91 Grierson, G4.19.21, op. cit., p.2.

3 Grierson's aesthetic 1924–7

1 Grierson, John, interview conducted by Canadian Radio and Television Council, 11 April 1969 (Grierson Archive Papers, University of Stirling), G7a.54. p.9.

2 Laura Spellman Rockefeller Memorial, series 3, box 51, folder 547, (Rockefeller Archive Papers, New York).

3 Chicago Evening Post articles on modern painting. Photocopies from Basil Wright. Held at the John Grierson Archive, University of Stirling. G1A.3.1 – G1A.3.10.

4 Grierson, John, 'Art and Revolution', in *Today's Revolution in the Arts*, North Carolina, April 1962. (Grierson Archive Papers), G7.56.6, p.2.

5 Forsyth Hardy H., interview with the author, Edinburgh, 8 May 1986.

6 Grierson, John, *Of Whistler and a Light that Failed*, (Grierson Archive Papers, 1924-7), G1A.3.3.

7 Kant, Immanuel (1724-1804), *Critique of Pure Reason* (London, Macmillan, 1963) Bradley, F. H. (1846-1924), *Essays on Truth and Reality* (Oxford, Clarendon Press, 1914), p.188.; and Hegel, G. W. F. (1770-1830), *Philosophy of History* (Stuttgart, Samtliche Werke, Band 6, 1927).

8 Grierson, John, *The Character of an Ultimate Synthesis* (Grierson Archive Papers 1918-1924), G1.2.6, p.15. See also *Vorticism Brought to Serve Drama*, G1A.3.10,

9 Grierson, John, G1A.3.10, op. cit., and 'Better Popular Pictures', in *Transactions of the Society of Motion Picture Engineers*, vol. xi, no. 29, August, 1927 p.234.

10 Grierson, John, *The B. B. Lollipop Company Incorporated* (Grierson Archive Papers 1898-1927), G1A.3.1.

11 Grierson, John, *Saving Modern Art From Its Friends* (Grierson Archive Papers 1898-1927), G1A.3.12.

12 Grierson, G1A.3.10, op. cit.

13 Grierson, John, G1A.3.3, op cit.

14 ibid.

15 Grierson, John, *Finding in Plato a Key to Modern Art* (Grierson Archive Papers 1898-1927), G1A.3.9.

16 ibid.

17 Grierson, John, *The Personality Behind the Paint* (Grierson Archive Papers 1898-1927), G1A.3.2.

18 Grierson, G1A.3.12, op. cit.

19 Grierson, G1A.3.2, op. cit.

20 Grierson, G1A.3.3, op. cit.

21 Grierson, G1A.3.2, op. cit.

22 Grierson, John, *Plato in the Light of Higher Criticism* (Grierson Archive Papers 1898-1927), G1A.3.5.
23 Instrumentalist: meaning to use art for a particular or general purpose. Realist: meaning to use art in order to record as objectively as possible.
24 Grierson, G1A.3.12, op. cit.
25 Grierson, John, *Byron and his Age* (Grierson Archive Papers 1898-1927), G1.2.10. p.5.
26 Grierson, G1A.3.12, op. cit.
27 ibid.
28 Wyndham Lewis, 'Blast, A Review of the Great English Vortex', (Catalogue of the Wyndham Lewis Retrospective, The Tate Gallery, London, 1956), in *The Phaidon Dictionary of Twentieth Century Art* (London, Plaidon 1973), p.401.
29 Grierson, G1A.3.10., op. cit.
30 Grierson, G7.56.6, op. cit.
31 ibid.
32 Grierson, G1A.3.12, op. cit.
33 ibid.
34 Grierson, G1A.3.10, op. cit.
35 Grierson, G1A.3.12, op. cit.
36 ibid.
37 Grierson, John, letter to Professor W. L. Renwick, 22 December 1925.
38 Grierson, G1.2.10, op. cit., p.5.
39 Grierson, letter to Renwick.
40 Grierson, John, *On Education* (Grierson Archive Papers 1939-1945), G4.19.21, p.3.
41 ibid.
42 Schudson, Michael, *Discovering the News* (New York, Basic Books, 1978), p.96.
43 Hayes, Samuel, P., *The Response to Industrialism 1885-1914* (Chicago, University of Chicago Publications, 1957), p.75.
44 Lafaber, Walter, and Polenberg, Richard, *The American Century: A History of the United States Since the 1890s* (New York, Wiley, 1975), p.33.
45 Hayes, op. cit., p.51.
46 Lafaber and Polenberg, op. cit., p.37.
47 Schudson, op. cit., p.102.
48 ibid., p.106.
49 Grierson, letter to Renwick.
50 ibid.
51 Grierson, John, *Propaganda and Education* (An address before the Winnipeg Canadian Club, 19 October 1943), cited in Forsyth Hardy, H., *Grierson On Documentary* (London, Faber & Faber, 1946), p. 151.
52 ibid.
53 Grierson, G7A.54, op. cit., pp.9-14.
54 Laura Spellman Rockefeller Memorial, series 3, box 51, folder 547.
55 Forsyth Hardy, H., *John Grierson, A Documentary Biography* (London, Faber & Faber, 1979), p.35.
56 Balio, Tino, *The American Film Industry* (University of Wisconsin Press, 1976), p.302.
57 ibid., p.218.
58 Forsyth Hardy, (1979), op. cit., p.35.
59 The mechanics are unclear. Grierson may have sent copies of the article to a number of film companies, or he may have been directed to FPL by Lippmann.
60 Balio, op. cit., p.148.

61 Everson, W., *American Silent Films* (Oxford University Press, 1978), p.111.
62 Hampton, Benjamin, *History of the American Film Industry* (New York and London, Noel Douglas, 1931), p.222.
63 Grierson, in Forsyth Hardy (1946), op. cit., p.151.
64 Rosenberg, Bernard, and Silverstein, Harry, *The Real Tinsel* (London, Macmillan, 1970), p.82.
65 Lasky, Jesse, L., *I Blow My Own Trumpet* (London, Gollancz, 1957), pp.134-5.
66 Rosenberg and Silverstein, op. cit., p.83.
67 Grierson, Letter to Renwick, op. cit.
68 Grierson, John, *The Product of Hollywood* (Motion Picture News, 27 November 1926), (Grierson Archive Papers 1898-1927), G1A.5.1.
69 ibid.
70 ibid.
71 Grierson, John, 'Putting Punch in a Picture', *Motion Picture News*, 27 November 1926, (Grierson Archive Papers 1898-1927), G1A.5.4.
72 Grierson, John, 'Putting Atmosphere in a Picture', *Motion Picture News*, 4 December 1926, (Grierson Archive Papers 1898-1927), G1A.5.5.
73 Cine-verité theorists: Dai Vaughan in England; Richard Leacock, and Robert Drew in America. See Jacobs, Lewis (ed.) *The Documentary Tradition* (Canada and USA, Hopkinson and Blake, 1971).
74 Grierson, G1A.5.5, op. cit.
75 Grierson, G4.19.21, op. cit., p.4.
76 Grierson, G7.56.6, op. cit., p.4.
77 ibid.
78 Grierson, John, 'What Makes A Special', *Motion Picture News*, 20 November 1926 (Grierson Archive Papers 1898-1927), G1A.5.3.
79 Grierson, G1A.5.4, op. cit.
80 Grierson, G1A.5.5, op. cit.
81 ibid.
82 Grierson, John, 'Better Popular Pictures', *Transactions of the Society of Motion Picture Engineers*, vol. xi, no. 29, (USA, August 1927), p.243.
83 ibid., p.240.
84 Grierson, G1.2.10, op. cit., p.15.
85 ibid., p.7.
86 Trotsky, Leon, 'The Formalist School of Poetry and Marxism' (1920), in Trotsky, Leon, *Literature And Revolution* (Michigan, Ann Arbor Paperbacks, University of Michigan Press, 1960).
87 Plekhanov, Georgei, 'On Art for Art's Sake', in *Unaddressed Letters – Art and Social Life* (Moscow, Foreign Languages Publishing House, 1957).
88 Dand, letter to Forsyth Hardy, 24 August 1976.
89 Plekhanov, Georgei, 'On Art for Art's Sake' and 'On the Social Basis of Style', in Craig, David, *Marxists on Literature, An Anthology* (London, Penguin, 1975), pp.76-95 and pp.272-82.
90 ibid., p.230.
91 ibid., p.230 and p.240.
92 Cornforth, Maurice, 'Materialism and Idealism', in *Dialectical Materialism, An Introduction, Volume One, Materialism and the Dialectical Method* (London, Lawrence & Wishart, 1952), pp.17-19.
93 Grierson, G1A.5.3, op. cit.
94 Political and Economic Planning, *The British Film Industry* (Political and Economic Planning, London, 1952), pp.32-45.

95 Klingender, F., and Legg, Stuart, *Money Behind the Screen* (Lawrence & Wishart, London, 1937), p.48.

96 Poulantzas, Nicos, *Classes in Contemporary Capitalism* (London, New Left Books, 1975), p.46.

97 Grierson, G1A.5.1, op. cit.

98 Everson, op. cit., p.112.

99 Hampton, op. cit., p.222.

100 Grierson, G1A.5.3, op. cit.

101 Grierson, G7.56.6, op. cit., p.3.

102 Lacey, A. R., *A Dictionary of Philosophy* (London, Routledge & Kegan Paul, 1976), p.121.

103 Grierson, G7.56.6, op. cit., p.4.

104 Hobsbawm, E.J., *Industry and Empire* (London, Weidenfeld and Nicolson, 1968), p.149.

105 Mandel, Ernest, *Marxist Economic Theory* (London, Merlin Press, 1962), pp.158-9.

106 Emery, Edwin, *The Press and America* (New York, Prentice Hall, 1954), pp.442-50.

107 Tedlow, Richard S., *Keeping the Corporate Image, Public Relations and Business 1900-1950* (London, Jaicon Press, 1979), p.6.

108 Leyda, Jay, *Kino, A History of the Russian Soviet Film* (London, Allen & Unwin, 1960), p.146.

109 Grierson, John, *Personal Memories of the Early Russian Cinema* (DDR Film Archive, 1967), pp.1-2.

110 Nettl, J.P., *The Soviet Achievement* (London, Thames & Hudson, 1967), p.29.

111 Barna, Yon, *Eisenstein* (London Secker & Warburg, 1973), p.91.

112 Mayakovsky, Vladimir, Speech given at the Sovkino Conference, 15 October, 1927.

113 Barna, op. cit., p.111.

114 Seton, Marie, *Sergei M. Eisenstein* (London, Bodley Head, 1952), p.87.

115 Grierson, DDR Film Archive, op. cit., p.2.

116 Grierson, G1A.5.5., op. cit.

117 ibid.

118 Grierson, John, 'Eisenstein and Documentary', in *Eisenstein 1898-1948* (Society for Better Cultural Relations with the USSR, London, 1948).

119 Eisenstein, Sergei, M., 'The Cinematic Principle and the Ideogram', in Jay Leyda, (ed. and translator) *Film Form, Essays in Film Theory* (London, Dennis Dobson, 1951), p.37.

120 Eisenstein, op. cit., p.45.

121 Barna, op. cit., p.96.

122 Grierson, DDR Film Archive, op. cit.

123 Barna, op. cit., p.95.

124 Grierson, in *Transactions of the Society of Motion Picture Engineers* (SMPE), op. cit., p.230.

125 Grierson, John, 'Flaherty', in *Artwork* (August, 1931).

126 Grierson, in *Transactions of the SMPE*, op. cit. pp.236-7.

127 Grierson, *Artwork*, op. cit.

128 Grierson, John, 'The Russian Example', in the *Clarion* (November, 1930).

129 Grierson, *Transactions of the SMPE*, op. cit., 245.

130 ibid., p.239.

131 Grierson, the *Clarion*, 1930, op. cit.

132 ibid., p.3.

133 Grierson, DDR Film Archive, op. cit., p.5.
134 Grierson, John, 'Cinema', *Artwork* (Winter, 1930).
135 ibid.
136 Montagu, Ivor, 'An Obituary Article on Dovzhenko', *Sight and Sound* (Summer, 1957).
137 Leyda, op. cit., p.275.
138 Nettl, op. cit., p.119-21.
139 Montagu, op. cit. (1957).
140 Grierson, DDR Film Archive, op. cit.
141 ibid.
142 Flaherty, Frances, Hubbard, *The Odyssey of a Film Maker* (New York, Arno Press and the New York Times, 1972), pp.12-14.
143 Barnouw, Erik, *Documentary, A History of the Non-Fiction Film* (London, Oxford University Press, 1974), pp.41-2.
144 Flaherty, op. cit., pp.22-3.
145 Grierson, *Transactions of the SMPE*, op. cit., p.232.
146 Flaherty, op. cit., p.19.
147 *Motion Picture News* (20 November 1926).
148 Grierson, *Transactions of the SMPE*, op. cit., p.232.
149 Grierson, G1A.5.5, op. cit.
150 Grierson, John, 'Flaherty's Poetic *Moana*', *New York Sun* (8 February, 1926). Grierson signed the article under the pseudonym of 'The Moviegoer'.
151 Calder-Marshall, Arthur, *The Innocent Eye, The Life of Robert J. Flaherty* (London, W. H. Allen, 1963), p.119.
152 Ellis, Jack, 'The Young Grierson in America, 1924-1927', *Cinema Journal*, vol. viii (Fall, 1968), p.17.
153 Grierson, *Artwork*, (1931), op. cit.
154 Grierson, *Transactions of the SMPE*, op. cit., p.242.
155 Grierson, G7.56.6, op. cit., p.4.
156 Grierson, *Transactions of the SMPE*, op. cit., p.242.
157 Grierson, *New York Sun*, op. cit.
158 Canudo, Riccioto, 'L'Usine aux Images', in Jacobs, Lewis, op. cit., pp.25-7.
159 Grierson, *Transactions of the SMPE*, op. cit., p.232.
160 Grierson, the *Clarion* (August 1930), op. cit.
161 Grierson, *Artwork* (Autumn, 1931), op. cit.
162 Grierson, 'Drifters', the *Clarion* (October, 1929).
163 Grierson, G1A.5.2, op. cit.
164 Grierson, G1A.5.3, op. cit.
165 Grierson, G1A.5.2, op. cit.
166 Grierson, John, *Propaganda and Education* (An address before the Winnipeg Canadian Club, 19 October, 1943).
167 Grierson, *Transactions of the SMPE*, op. cit., 229.
168 Grierson, G1A.5.2, op. cit.
169 Grierson, G1A.5.4, op. cit.
170 Grierson, G1A.5.3, op. cit.
171 Hampton, op. cit., p.222.
172 Purcell, op. cit., pp.1-32. For Purcell's analysis and definition of the terms 'objectivist' and 'scientific'.
173 Grierson, G1A.5.3, op. cit.
174 Lippmann, op. cit., p.13.
175 Grierson, G1A.5.4, op. cit.
176 Grierson, John, 'Address to the Paramount Theatre Manager's School',

Exhibitor's Herald (26 September, 1925), p.32.

177 Grierson, G1A.5.4, op. cit.
178 Grierson, G1A.5.3, op. cit.
179 ibid.
180 Grierson, G1A.5.1, op. cit.
181 ibid.
182 ibid.
183 Grierson, *Transactions of the SMPE*, op. cit., p.248.
184 ibid., p.234.
185 ibid., p.233.
186 Grierson, G1A.5.4, op. cit
187 Grierson, John, 'The Seven Obstacles to Progress', *Motion Picture News* (4 December, 1926).
188 Grierson, *Transactions of the SMPE*, op. cit., p.236.
189 ibid., p.248.
190 Grierson, G1A.5.1, op. cit.
191 Grierson, *Transactions of the SMPE*, op. cit., p.247.
192 ibid., p.248.
193 Grierson, John, 'Robert Flaherty', *The Reporter* (16 October 1951).
194 Grierson, G1A.5.3, op. cit.
195 ibid.
196 Grierson, John, 'Filming the Gospel, A Dangerous Policy', *World Film News* (May, 1936).
197 For further biographical material on these three Soviet directors see Schitzner, Luda, Schitzner, Jean, and Martin, Marcel (eds) *Cinema in Revolution, The Heroic Age of the Soviet Film* (London, Secker & Warburg, Cinema Two Series, 1973).
198 Grierson, John, 'Cinema', *Artwork* (Winter 1930).
199 Leyda, op. cit., pp.248-9.
200 Rotha (1930), op. cit., pp.236-7.
201 Grierson, G2.16.4, op cit. This article examines the development of the realist feature film, with particular reference to the Soviet film makers and to Flaherty.
202 Leyda, op. cit., p.260.
203 Rotha, (1930), op. cit., p.250.
204 Turkin, Valentin, *Lessons of Turksib* (Sovietskaya Ekran, 11 June 1929). Cited in Leyda, op. cit.
205 Turkin, Valentin, (1887-1958), Journalist, scenarist and scriptwriter. Further biographical details available in *Cinema in Revolution*.
206 Grierson, DDR Film Archive, 1967, op. cit.
207 Interview with Forsyth Hardy, H., May 1986.
208 Grierson, John, 'Review of the Year's Films', *Artwork* (Winter, 1931).
209 Grierson, G1A.5.6, op. cit.
210 Grierson, G1A.5.7, op. cit.
211 ibid.
212 ibid.
213 Grierson, John, *The Seven Obstacles to Progress*, Parts One and Two: G1A.5.6, and G1A.5.7. The Grierson Archive has in fact misfiled these two parts; and G1A.5.7. actually precedes G1A.5.6.
214 Lenin, Vladimir Ilich (1870-1924), 'Party Organization and Party Literature', *Lenin on Literature and Art* (Moscow, Progress Publishers, 1970). Originally published in *Novaya zhizn*. 13 November, 1905.
215 Grierson, *Artwork* (Autumn, 1931), op. cit.

216 'The Film in the USSR-1937', Report of an ACT delegation to the USSR, in *The Cine Technician*, (May 1937), pp.95-111.
217 Brewster, Ben, 'The Soviet State, The Communist Party and the Arts' (Red Letters, no.3).
218 Leyda, op. cit., p.121.

4 John Grierson, the Empire Marketing Board Film Unit, and the documentary film movement, 1927-33

1 Grierson, John, Transcript of an interview with John Grierson, for the Canadian Television and Radio Commission. 11 April 1969 (Grierson Archive Papers 1957-72), G7A.5.4, p.10.
2 Hardy, Forsyth, H., *John Grierson, A Documentary Biography* (London, Faber & Faber, 1979), p.44.
3 Swann, Paul, *The British Documentary Film Movement 1926-1945* (PhD Thesis, University of Leeds, 1979), p.30.
4 Nichols, Robert, *The Times* (August-September, 1925); in particular: 'An Art in Bondage', *The Times* Saturday 5 September, 1925), p.11.
5 Tallents, Stephen, 'The Birth of British Documentary', *Journal of the University Film Association*, vol.20, no.1., (1968), p.17.
6 ibid.
7 Lee, J. M., 'The Dissolution of the EMB', *The Journal of Imperial and Commonwealth History*, vol.1, no.1. (October, 1972), p.51.
8 ibid., p.50.
9 Benham, F., *Great Britain Under Protectionism* (New York, Macmillan, 1941), p.73.
10 Boothby, Robert and Macmillan, Harold, *Industry and the State, A Conservative View* (London, Macmillan, 1927), p.126.
11 Saxon Mills, *There is a Tide* (London, Heinemann, 1954), p.129.
12 Mowat, C. L., *Britain Between the Wars 1918-1940* (London, Methuen, 1955), p.190.
13 Middlemas, K., and Barnes, A. J., *Baldwin, A Biography* (London, Weidenfeld & Nicolson, 1969), p.287.
14 Amery, Leo, *My Political Life* (London, Hutchinson, 1953), p.346.
15 Willert, Arthur, KBE, and Long, B. K., *The Empire and the World: A Study in Leadership and Reconstruction* (London, Oxford University Press, 1937), p.159.
16 Lee, op. cit., p.50.
17 Constantine, Stephen, 'Bringing the Empire Alive', in Mackenzie, John (ed.), *Imperialism and Popular Culture*, (Manchester University Press, 1986), p.199.
18 ibid.
19 Tallents, Stephen, *Man and Boy* (London, Faber & Faber 1943), p.234.
20 ibid., p.247.
21 Amery, op. cit., p.347.
22 Ramsden, J. A., 'Baldwin and the Film', in Pronay, N. (ed.) *Politics, Propaganda and Film* (London, Macmillan, 1982), p.133.
23 Amery, op. cit., p.347.
24 The most important of these was William Crawford: Member, Publicity Advisory Committee, Ministry of Health, 1926; Member, Imperial Economic Conference, 1925-6; Member, EMB, 1926-31; Vice Chairman, Post Office Publicity Committee, 1933-8.
25 Huxley, Gervas, *Both Hands* (London, Chatto & Windus, 1970), p.129.

26 Lee, op. cit., p.51.
27 Huxley, op. cit., p.130.
28 Amery, op. cit., p.352.
29 Taylor, P. M., *The Projection of Britain* (Cambridge, Cambridge University Press, 1981), p.253.
30 Memorandum of the British Poster Advertising Association, 9 December 1929, PRO CO 760/22, EMB/PC/126.
31 ibid., cited in Swann, op. cit., p. 34.
32 Nevett, T. R., *Advertising in Britain: A History* (London, Heinemann, 1974), pp.110-37.
33 Crawford, W., *How to Succeed in Advertising* (London, World's Press News, 1931).
34 Nevett, op. cit., p.93.
35 Taylor and Sanders, *British Propaganda During World War One* (London, Macmillan, 1982), p.30.
36 *The Battle of the Somme* (1916), silent, in five parts, 77 minutes duration.
37 This subject is further elaborated in chapter Two of this Book.
38 i.e., Swann, Forsyth Hardy, Rotha, Grierson, Wright, etc.
39 Summary of Proceedings of the 1926 Imperial Conference, Cmd. 2768, vol. xi, 545., *Exhibition of Films Within the Empire* p.597. OPL. BL.
40 Thirteenth Report of a General Economic Sub-Committee, Cmd. 2709, 1926, p.1009., OPL. BL.
41 ibid., p.1,102.
42 EMB Film Committee memorandum, 28 January, 1927. PRO CO 760/37 EMB/C/1.
43 *Proposal For the Preparation of a Film Under the Auspices of the EMB*. PRO CO 760/37 EMB/C/1, 28 January 1927.
44 First Meeting of the EMB Film Committee Conference, PRO CO 760/37, 1 February, 1927.
45 ibid.
46 Tallents, (1968), op. cit., p.17.
47 Grierson, John, 'Notes for English Producers', Memorandum to the EMB Film Committee (April 1927), PRO BT 64/86 6880.
48 Grierson, John, 'Better Popular Pictures', in *Transactions of the Society of Motion Picture Engineers*, vol. xi., no. 29 (August 1926), pp.227-49. (British Library, Science Reference Library, Shelf Mark: (P)QR 30-E(6), Acc. No. S062663003).
49 Grierson, PRO BT 64/86 6880, op. cit., p.2.
50 ibid., p.3.
51 ibid., p.4.
52 ibid., p.3.
53 ibid., p.5.
54 ibid., p.6.
55 ibid., p.8.
56 ibid., p.9.
57 ibid., p.13.
58 ibid., p.14.
59 ibid., p.15.
60 ibid., p.18.
61 ibid., p.21.
62 ibid.
63 ibid.
64 ibid., p.22.

65 ibid.
66 ibid.
67 Letter from L. S. Amery to Philip Cunliffe Lister, 5 May, 1927. PRO BT 64/86 EMB/C/2.
68 Buchan, John, to Elliot, Walter, 26 May, 1927, PRO CO 760/37 EMB/C/3.
69 Tallents (1968), op. cit., pp.17-18.
70 Grierson, John, 'Further Notes on Cinema Production', EMB Film Committee Memorandum (28th July, 1927), PRO CO 760/37 EMB/C/4., p.1
71 ibid., p.7.
72 ibid., p.8.
73 ibid., p.10.
74 ibid., p.12.
75 ibid.
76 ibid., p.13.
77 ibid.
78 ibid., p.16.
79 'The Empire Marketing Board and the Cinema' EMB Film Committee Memorandum (1st March 1928), PRO CO 760/37 EMB/C/9.
80 Forsyth Hardy, op. cit., and Swann, op. cit
81 PRO CO 760/37 EMB/C/9, op. cit., p.8.
82 ibid., p.10.
83 ibid.
84 Huxley, op. cit., p.148.
85 Tallents (1968), op. cit., p.20
86 Grierson, John, letter to Frances Strauss, 21 February, 1928 (The Grierson-Strauss correspondence: Letters from John and Marion Grierson to Frances Strauss 1927-34), G2A.1.
87 Forsyth Hardy, op. cit., p.53. Hardy claims that the rushes were 20,000 feet. There is some dispute over the correct figure.
88 ibid., p.54.
89 Ellis, Jack, C., John Grierson, A Guide to References and Resources (Boston, 1986), p.29.
90 Forsyth Hardy, op cit. p.51.
91 Film Society Programme No.33 (Grierson Archive Papers 1927-33), G2.1.2.
92 Grierson, John, 'English Cinema Production and the Naturalistic Tradition', in 'Notes for English Producers', PRO BT 64/86 6880, pp.13-22.
93 ibid., pp.20-1.
94 Forsyth Hardy (1979) op. cit. Hillier, John, and Lovell, Alan, Studies in Documentary (London, Secker & Warburg, 1972), Parsons (1978).
95 Low, Rachel, History of the British Film, Vol.3., 1918-1929 (London, Allen & Unwin, 1971), p.296.; and Hood, Stuart, 'The Grierson Influence', Undercut no.9. (Summer, 1983), p.16.
96 Potamkin, Harry, Allen, 'Grierson's Drifters', Close Up (October, 1930).
97 Grierson, John, Notes on the Scenario (Grierson Archive Papers 1927-33), G2.1.17.
98 Author's analysis of Reel One of Drifters.
99 ibid.
100 Draft titles for Drifters, typed manuscript by John Grierson, undated (Grierson Archive Papers 1927-33), G2.1.11.
101 ibid.
102 Musical suggestions for Drifters, typed manuscript by John Grierson. Undated (Grierson Archive Papers 1898-1927), G1.2.3.

103 Ellis (1986), *op cit.* p.33. There is some question as to whether it was Fingal's Cave. Hardy says it may have been Prokofiev, but it is more likely to have been Mendelssohn, as Prokofiev is not mentioned in any of the draft scenarios.

104 Draft music score for *Drifters* (Grierson Archive Papers 1898-1927), undated, G1.2.4.

105 Hood, Stuart, 'John Grierson and the Documentary Film Movement', in Porter, Vincent and Curran, James, (ed.), *British Cinema History* (London, Weidenfeld & Nicolson, 1984), p.106.

106 ibid.

107 ibid.

108 Grierson, John, untitled essay on documentary, undated (Grierson Archive Papers 1927-33), G2.16.3, p.1.

109 ibid.

110 Grierson, John, untitled undated article beginning 'Against this background some sort of indication of the part of cinema is possible', (Grierson Archive Papers 1927-33), G2.8.7. p.1.

111 Extract from the Book Withdrawal Register, Glasgow University Library (Grierson Archive Papers 1898-1927), G1A.1.1.

112 Bradley, F. H., *Essays on Truth and Reality* (London, Clarendon Press, 1914), p.175.

113 Kemp, John, *The Philosophy of Kant* (London, Oxford University Press, 1968), p.38.

114 Grierson, John, *Kant's Aesthetic*, G1.2.7, and *The Character of an Ultimate Synthesis*, G1.2.6, (Grierson Archive Papers 1898-1927).

115 Grierson, John, 'Vorticism Brought to Serve Drama', *Chicago Evening Post* (1925-6) (Grierson Archive Papers 1898-1927, photocopies from Basil Wright), G1A.3.10.

116 Grierson, John, in *Transactions of the Society of Motion Picture Engineers* op. cit., p.234.

117 Grierson, John, *New Worlds for Cinema* (Typescript for an unpublished manuscript on the use of film in education, and by the Church; Grierson Archive Papers 1927-1933), G2.21.5. p.3.

118 Grierson, John, G7.17.2, op. cit. p.11.

119 Grierson, John, G2.21.5, op. cit., p.16.

120 Grierson, John, 'Drifters', the *Clarion* (October, 1929).

121 Grierson, John, 'Propaganda Film Technique', *Kinematograph Weekly* (18 December, 1930).

122 Grierson, the *Clarion* op cit.

123 Grierson, John, 'Silver Scales, but not the Scales of Justice', *Tit Bits* (1 February, 1930), p.647.

124 Cited in Calinescu, Matei, *Faces of Modernity* (London, Bloomington, 1977), p.138.

125 ibid.

126 Bradbury, Malcolm, and McFarlane, James, *Modernism* (London, Penguin, 1974), p.78.

127 Bergman, 'Essay on Time and Free Will' (1889), cited in Passmore, John, *A Hundred Years of Philosophy* (London, Pelican, 1957), p.105.

128 Hughes, Stuart, *Consciousness and Society* (London, MacGibbon & Kee, 1959), p.176.

129 Eliot, T. S., 'Ulysses, Order and Myth', *The Dial*, no.75 (New York, 1923), pp.480-3. Grierson read this article in 1923.

130 Bullock, Allen, 'The Double Image', in Bradbury and McFarlane, op. cit., p.66.

131 Lacey, A. R., *A Dictionary of Philosophy* (London, Routledge & Kegan Paul, 1976), p.30.
132 Hughes, op. cit., p.184.
133 McFarlane, James, 'Mind and Nature of Modernism', in Bradbury and McFarlane, op. cit., pp.79-80.
134 Pike, Christopher, *The Futurists, The Formalists and the Marxist Critique* (London, Ink Links Ltd., 1979), p.22.
135 Gestalt: a pattern or structure, perceived as a whole, rather than as a collection of parts, *Collins English Dictionary* (London, Collins, 1982), p.467.
136 Pike, op. cit., p.22.
137 Conventionalism: Any doctrine according to which any hypothesis depends on convention, rather than on a relation to reality (Lacey, op. cit., p.43). The doctrine that all languages of observation and experience are theory impregnated; normally associated with the work of Thomas Khun (Lovell, Terry, *Pictures of Reality* (London, BFI, 1983), p.15).
138 Grierson, G2.8.7, op. cit., p.1.
139 Grierson, John, 'Art and Revolution', in *Today's Revolution in the Arts* (North Carolina, April 1962, Grierson Archive Papers 1957-72), G7.56.6, p.1.
140 ibid., p.2.
141 Grierson, John, articles in the *Chicago Evening Post*, 1925-6, (Grierson Archive Papers 1898-1927), G1A.3.
142 Grierson, G7.56.6, op. cit., p.2.
143 Andrew, Dudley, J., *The Major Film Theories* (London, Oxford University Press, 1976), p.12.
144 Balazs, Bela, *Der Sichtbare Mensche oder Der Kultur Des Films* (Wien, Leipzig, Deutsch-Osterreichischer Verlag, 1924).
145 *Harrap's Standard English-German Dictionary* (Oxford, Oxford University Press, 1977), pp.77-8.
146 English and English, *A Comprehensive Dictionary of Psychological and Psychoanalytic Terms* (London, Longmans, 1958), p.225.
147 Andrew, op. cit., p.37.
148 Arnheim, Rudolph, *Art and Visual Perception,* (USA, Berkeley, UCL Press, 1967), p.vi.
149 ibid., p.37.
150 Andrew, op. cit., p.37.
151 ibid., p.31.
152 ibid., pp.39-40.
153 ibid., p.79. The line from neo-kantianism to Gestalt psychology is not a direct one however – as Andrew has pointed out.
154 Grierson, John, *Rudolph Arnheim's 'Film'* (Unpublished review of Arnheim's 1932 book. Grierson Archive Papers 1927-1933), G2.19.7. p.2.
155 ibid., p.3.
156 ibid., p.4.
157 ibid.
158 Shklovsky, Victor, 'Art and Technique', in *Russian Formalist Criticism, Four Essays* Leman, Lee, and Reis, Martin (trans.) (USA, 1965).
159 Eichenbaum, B. M., 'Theory of the Formal Method', in L. Matejka and K.Pomorska, *Readings in Russian Poetics: Formalist and Structuralist Views,* (Michigan, Ann Arbor 1971), p.35.
160 Mukarovsky, Jan, 'Standard Language and Poetic Language', in *Prague School Reader in Aesthetics: Literary Structure and Style* translated by Garvin, Paul. R, Washington, Georgetown University Press, 1964, p.19.

161 Grierson, John, 'Of Whistler and a Light that Failed', *Chicago Evening Post* December 1925 (Grierson Archive Papers 1898-1927), G1A.3.8.

162 Grierson, John, *A Working Plan for 16mm Film* (Grierson Archive Papers 1927-33), G2.17.1, p.6.

163 Grierson, G7.15.5, op. cit., p.6.

164 Grierson, John, 'First Principles of Documentary', in Forsyth Hardy (1946), op. cit., p.40.

165 Wright, Basil, interview with the Author, Little Adam Farm, Frieth, High Wycombe, 9th March 1987.

166 Interview with Basil Wright, (1987) op. cit.

167 Balazs, Bela, 'Hungarian Letter', *The Dial* (April, 1923).

168 Balazs, Bela, *Theory of Film, Character and Growth of a New Art* (London, Dobson, 1952), p.189.

169 Andrew, op. cit., p.91.

170 Balazs (1952) op. cit., p.108.

171 Vaughan James, C., *Soviet Socialist Realism, Origins and Theory,* (London, Macmillan, 1973, p.89.

172 Balazs. op. cit., p.162.

173 Balazs, (1924), op. cit.

174 ibid., p.40.

175 ibid., p.41.

176 Grierson, John, 'Flaherty, Naturalism and the Problem of the English Cinema', *Artwork* (Autumn, 1931), p.214.

177 Andrew, op. cit., p.100.

178 ibid., p.101.

179 Grierson, 'First Principles of Documentary', in Forsyth Hardy (1946), op. cit., p.42.

180 Grierson, PRO CO 760/37 EMB/C/9., op. cit.

181 'Creation of a Small Empire Marketing Board Producing and Editing Unit' (EMB Film Committee Memorandum, 28 April, 1930), PRO CO 760/37 EMB/C/39.

182 Forsyth Hardy, (1979), op. cit., p.58.

183 Tallents, (1968), op. cit., p.27.

184 Swann, op. cit., p.53.

185 Rotha, op. cit., p.49.

186 ibid., p.51.

187 Grierson, John, various writings held at the Grierson Archive (Grierson Archive Papers 1927-33), G2.8 – G2.15.

188 Forsyth Hardy, op. cit., pp.61-2.

189 Rotha, op. cit., p.46.

190 Forsyth Hardy, op. cit., p.61.

191 Extract from the Proceedings of the Imperial Conference of 1930, PRO CO 760/37 EMB/C/54. 6 January, 1931.

192 Proceedings of the 1930 Imperial Conference, Cmd. 3717, p.52. Cited in Swann, op. cit., p.54.

193 *The Extension of the Board's Publicity Arrangements* (EMB Film Committee Memorandum, 18 July, 1931), PRO CO 760/37 EMB/C/59.

194 Rotha, op. cit., p.50.

195 ibid.

196 Forsyth Hardy, op. cit., p.65.

197 Rotha, op. cit., p.61.

198 Low, (1971), op. cit., p.43.

199 Swann, op. cit., p.45.

200 Lejeune, C. A., the *Observer* (21 August, 1932).
201 'Future Activities and Resources' (EMB Film Committee Memorandum, 12 December 1931), PRO CO 760/37 EMB/C/68.
202 'Programme of Work 1932-3 (EMB Film Committee Memorandum, 27 April, 1932), PRO CO 760/37 EMB/C/74.
203 Estimates for First Six Months of Financial Year 1933-4, (EMB Film Committee Memorandum, 9 December, 1932), PRO CO 760/37 EMB/C/79.
204 Grierson, John, *Report on a Visit to America* (EMB Film Committee Memorandum, 9 May, 1931), PRO CO 760/37 EMB/C/57.
205 Badgley, Frank, *Report of Activities of the Canadian Government Motion Picture Bureau* (EMB Film Committee memorandum, 24 August, 1928), PRO CO 760/37 EMB/C/14.
206 See chapter Six of this Book for further elaboration.
207 Untitled paper compiled by John Grierson on Government film services in the Soviet Union, 12 September, 1928, PRO CO 760/37 EMB/C/19.
208 'The Cinema Activities of the EMB' (EMB Film Committee Memorandum, 12 December, 1932), PRO CO 760/37 EMB/C/82.
209 Political and Economic Planning, *The British Film Industry* (London, PEP, 1952), pp.53-4.
210 Grierson, John, PRO BT 64/86 6880, op. cit., p.22.
211 Political and Economic Planning (1952), op. cit., p.54.
212 Low (1971), op. cit., p.103.
213 Forsyth Hardy, op. cit., p.65.
214 PRO CO 760/37 EMB/C/82., op cit.
215 'Non-Theatrical Distribution' (EMB Film Committee Memorandum, 19 March, 1932), PRO CO 760/37 EMB/C/71.

5 The General Post Office Film Unit, 1933–9

1 Lee, J. M., 'The Dissolution of the EMB', *The Journal of Imperial and Commonwealth History* vol. 1, no.1, (October, 1972), p.55.
2 Swann, Paul, *The British Documentary Film Movement, 1926-1945* (PhD Thesis for the University of Leeds, 1979), p.69.
3 Rotha, Paul, *Documentary Diary* (London, Hill & Wang, 1973), p.114.
4 Swann, op cit., p.77.
5 Rotha, op. cit., p.114.
6 ibid., p.73.
7 Cavalcanti, Alberto, interview with Emil Rodregues Monegal, in *Quarterly Journal of Film Radio and Television* (Summer, 1955), p.342.
8 Wright, Basil, in Orbanz, Eva (ed.) *Journey to a Legend and Back, The British Realistic Film* (Edition Volker Spiess, Berlin, 1977), p.135.
9 Cavalcanti, Alberto, Interview with the author, Paris, May 1983.
10 Wright, in Orbanz, op. cit., p.135.
11 Rotha, op. cit., p.124.
12 Hardy, Forsyth, H., *John Grierson, A Documentary Biography* (London, Faber & Faber, 1979), p.77.
13 ibid., p.78.
14 ibid.
15 Greene, Grahame, *The Spectator* 2 August 1935.
16 Swann, (1979), op. cit., p.79.
17 Commons Select Committee Report on Expenditure, 'Government Cinematograph Films' (HMSO, 2 July 1934), pp. 9-15.

18 Rotha, op. cit., p.116.
19 Report of the Select Committee on Estimates, 2 July 1934 (GPO Archive POST 33 5199/P16682/ 1937), file no.2, p.9,: 'Government Cinematograph Films.'
20 ibid.
21 Treasury Minute, 16 November 1934, POST 33 5199/P16682/37.
22 Interim Report of the Post Office Film Unit Committee, 24 December, 1934, POST 33 5199/P16682/37.
23 Letter from the Treasury to the Post Office Accountant General's Department, 17 December 1934, POST 33 5199/P16682/37 File No.2.
24 ibid.
25 Letter from the Treasury to the Post Office, 21 January 1935, POST 33 5199/P16682/37.
26 Letter from the Treasury to the Post Office, 6 February 1935, POST 33 5199/P16682/37.
27 Alberto Cavalcanti, interview, op. cit.
28 Robinson, F. P., to Tallents, S. G., 19 December 1934, PRO T160/742/F13860/ 03/2.
29 GPO Film Committee Memorandum, 'Making Films for Outside Bodies', 1936, POST 33 5089/P18036/36, file no.6.
30 Swann, Paul, 'John Grierson and the GPO Film Unit 1933-1939', *Historical Journal of Film Radio and Television* 1984, p.30.
31 Swann, (1979), op. cit., pp.119-20.
32 POST 33 5089 P18036/36, file no. 6, op. cit.
33 Rotha, op. cit., p.142.
34 ibid., p.68.
35 Cavalcanti, interview, op. cit.
36 Rotha, op. cit. p.144.
37 ibid., p.147.
38 *The Times* (17 July, 1937).
39 Rotha, op. cit., p.155.
40 Bond, Ralph, in Orbanz, (ed.) op. cit., p.125.
41 Rotha, op. cit., p.159.
42 Cavalcanti, interview, op. cit.
43 Post Office Film Committee Memorandum, reorganization of Composition and Control, POST 33 P16682/37.
44 Alberto Cavalcanti, interview, op. cit.; and Harry Watt, in Orbanz, Eva (ed.) *Journey to a Legend and Back, The British Realistic Film* (Berlin, Edition Volker Spiess, 1977), p.80.
45 Letter from the House of Lords to the Post Office, 12 July 1937, POST 33 5199/P16682/37.
46 Letter from the Post Office to the Treasury, 14 June 1939, POST 33 5199/ P16682/37.
47 Letter from the Treasury to the Post Office, 24 July 1939, POST 33 5199/P16682/37.
48 Mowat, op. cit., chapter Eleven.
49 Rotha, op. cit., p.131.
50 ibid., p.274.
51 Wright, in Orbanz (ed.) op. cit., p.135.
52 Cavalcanti, interview, op. cit.
53 Watt, Harry, in Orbanz (ed.) op. cit., p.80.
54 ibid.
55 Swann, (1979), op. cit., p.109.

56 Letter from the Accountant General's Department to the Treasury, 12 August 1939. POST 33 5199 P16682/37, file no.6.
57 Transfer of Film Unit to the Ministry of Information, POST 33 5555 1939-42, P11692/1940, file no.7.
58 Letter from the Treasury to the Accountant General's Department, 9 October 1939, POST 33 5555 1939-42, P11692/1940.

6 Public relations, propaganda, and documentary film, 1900–39

1 Hobsbawm, E.J., *Industry and Empire* (London, Penguin, 1968), p.149.
2 Hayes, Samuel, P., *The Response to Industrialism, 1885–1914* (Chicago, University of Chicago Press, 1957), p.49.
3 ibid., p.50.
4 ibid. p.51.
5 Tedlow, Richard, S., *Keeping the Corporate Image: Public Relations and Business, 1900-1950* (London, Jaicon Press, 1979), p.36.
6 Hayes, op. cit., p.70.
7 ibid.
8 Lloyd, Herbert, *Public Relations* (London, English Universities Press, 1960), p.3.
9 ibid., p.4.
10 ibid., p.53.
11 Tedlow, op. cit., p.9.
12 Fitzgerald, Patrick, *Industrial Combination in England* (London, Pitman & Sons,1927), p.158.
13 ibid., p.199.
14 Wickwar, W. H., *The Public Services* (London, Cobden-Sanderson, 1938), p.126.
15 Crawford, W., *How To Succeed in Advertising* (London, World's Press News, 1931), p.10.
16 Nevett, T. R., *Advertising in Britain: A History* (London, Heinemann, 1974), pp.110-37.
17 Low, Rachel, *History of the British Film, Volume Two : 1906-1914* (London, Allen & Unwin, 1948), p.169.
18 ibid., p.146.
19 ibid., p.31.
20 Medlicott, W. N., *Contemporary England, 1914-1964* (London, Longmans, 1967), p.16.
21 Marwick, Arthur, *The Deluge* (London, Macmillan,1965), Introduction.
22 Taylor, P., and Sanders, M., *British Propaganda During World War One* (London, Macmillan, 1982), p.15.
23 Marwick (1968), op. cit., Introduction.
24 Taylor and Sanders, op. cit., p.20.
25 ibid., p.30.
26 ibid., pp. 30-32.
27 ibid., p.39.
28 ibid., p.78.
29 ibid., p.53.
30 ibid.
31 ibid., p.54.
32 ibid., p.75.
33 ibid., p.82.

34 ibid., pp.94-7.
35 Low, Rachel, *The History of the British Film, Volume Three, 1914-1918* (London, Allen & Unwin, 1948), pp.151-2.
36 Reeves, N. A., *Official British Film Propaganda During the First World War* (London, Croom Helm 1986), p.156.
37 Taylor and Sanders, op. cit., p.124.
38 Reeves, op. cit., p.124.
39 ibid., p.126.
40 Low, op. cit., p.36.
41 ibid pp. 167-73.
42 ibid., p.173.
43 ibid., p.174.
44 ibid., p.173.
45 ibid., p.174.
46 ibid.
47 ibid., p.179.
48 ibid., p.233.
49 Taylor and Sanders, op. cit., p.126.
50 Stuart, Campbell, *Secrets of Crewe House* (London, Hodder & Stoughton, 1920), p.90.
51 Mowat, C. L., *Britain Between the Wars* (London, Methuen, 1955), p.28.
52 Political and Economic Planning, *The British Social Services* (London, Politic and Economic Planning, 1937), p.59.
53 Balfour Committee on Industry and Trade, *Survey of Industries, Volume One* (London, HMSO 1929).
54 Political and Economic Planning, *Industrial Trade Associations* (London, Politic and Economic Planning, 1957), p.13.
55 ibid.
56 Aldcroft, D. H., *The British Economy Between the Wars* (Oxford, Philip Allen, 1983), p.53.
57 Mowat, op. cit., p.27.
58 Taylor, op. cit., p.58.
59 ibid., pp.86-7.
60 ibid., p.53.
61 ibid., p.87.
62 Aldcroft, op. cit., p.12.
63 Mowat, op. cit., p.129.
64 ibid., p.130.
65 Taylor, op. cit., p.89.
66 Nevett, op. cit., p.145.
67 Crawford, W. S., *How to Succeed in Advertising* (London, World's Press News, 1931).
68 Nevett, op. cit., p.150.
69 Taylor, and Sanders op. cit., p.87.
70 ibid. p.88.
71 ibid.
72 ibid., p.57.
73 ibid.
74 Low, Rachel, *History of the British Film, Volume Four, 1919-1929* (London, Allen & Unwin, 1971), 129.
75 ibid., p.93.
76 Cinematograph Films Act HMSO, London, 1927.

77 Report of a Departmental Committee Appointed to Consider the Position of the Textile Trades after the war (London, HMSO, 1918).
78 Stevenson, John, and Cook, Chris, *The Slump* (London, Cape, 1977), p.270.
79 Addison, Paul, *The Road to 1945* (London, Quartet, 1977), p.24.
80 Stevenson and Cook, op. cit., p.54.
81 Addison, op. cit., p.35.
82 'Government Competition with the Trade', *Kinematograph Weekly* (23 November, 1933).
83 Kearney, M., Neville, Secretary of the Film Producers Group and Director of the Film Industries Department, Federation of British Industries, in *Sight and Sound* no.2 (1934), pp.117-18
84 Aldcroft, op. cit., p.308.
85 Addison, op. cit., p.32.
86 Aldcroft, op. cit., p.309.

7 Documentary film and reform

1 Mowat, C.L., *Britain Between the Wars* (London, Methuen, 1955), pp.547-8.
2 Grierson, John, *Art and Revolution* (Grierson Archive Papers 1957-72, University of Stirling), G7.56.6, p.8.
3 Grierson, John, *Byron and his Age* (Grierson Archive Papers 1898-1927), G1.2.10, p.5.
4 Lippmann, Walter, *A Preface to Politics* (New York, and London, T. Fisher Unwin, 1913), p.100.
5 Grierson, John, 'Education and the New Order', in Forsyth Hardy, H. (ed.), *Grierson on Documentary* (London, Faber & Faber, 1946), p.127.
6 Grierson, John, *Man and the State* (Grierson Archive Papers 1898-1927), G1.2.2, p.5.
7 Addison, Paul, *The Road to 1945* (London, Quartet, 1977), p.29.
8 Grierson, John, 'Notes for English Producers' (Memorandum to the EMB Film Committee, April 1927), PRO BT 64/86 6880.
9 Marwick, Arthur, 'Middle Opinion in the Thirties', *English Historical Review* vol. 79 (1964), p.296.
10 Stevenson John, and Cook, Chris, *The Slump* (London, Cape, 1977), p.281.
11 Addison, op. cit., p.36.
12 Pimlott, Ben, *Labour and the Left in the 1930s* (Cambridge, Cambridge University Press, 1977), p.39.
13 ibid., p.38.
14 Grierson, John, *The Social Relationship of Cinema* (Grierson Archive Papers 1933-9), G3.9.4, p.1.
15 *Collected Writings of John Maynard Keynes* vol. ix, p.297.
16 ibid., p.258.
17 Grierson, John, *The Projection of Britain* (Transcript of a BBC TV programme, November 1954).
18 Morrison, Herbert (1888-1965), Minister of Transport 1929-31, Minister of Supply 1940, Foreign Secretary 1951.
19 Wickwar, W. H., *The Public Services* (London, Cobden Sanderson, 1938), p.33.
20 Grierson, John, 'Answers to a Cambridge Questionaire', *Granta* (1967).
21 ibid., p.6.
22 *Cinematograph Films Act* (London, HMSO, 1927).
23 Swann, Paul, *The British Documentary Film Movement 1926-1945* (PhD thesis, University of Leeds, 1979), pp.72-3.

24 Grierson, John, *I Derive My Authority from Moses* (Grierson Archive Papers 1957-72), G7A.9.1.

25 Cited in Addison, op. cit., p.43.

26 Hardy, Forsyth, H., *John Grierson, A Documentary Biography* (London, Faber & Faber, 1979), p.29.

27 Pimlott, op. cit., p.147.

28 Marwick (1964), op. cit., p.287.

29 Calder, Angus, 'Introduction', *Britain by Mass Observation* (London, Cresset, 1986), p.xiii.

30 Next Five Years Group, *An Essay in Political Agreement* (London, Macmillan, 1935).

31 Grierson, John, 'Further Notes on Cinema Production' (Memorandum to the EMB Film Committee, 28 July, 1927), PRO CO 760/37 EMB/C/4.

32 Stevenson, John, *British Society 1914-1945* (London, Penguin, 1984), p.414.

33 Reeves, N. A., *Official British Film Propaganda During the First World War* (Unpublished PhD Thesis, University of London, 1981), p.233.

34 Taylor and Sanders, *British Propaganda During World War One* (London, Macmillan, 1982), p.124.

35 ibid.

36 Mowat, op. cit., p.537.

37 Laing, Stuart, 'Presenting Things as They Are', in Gloversmith (ed.), *Class, Culture and Social Change* (London, Harvester, 1980), p.142.

38 Lehmann, John, *New Writing in Europe* (London, Penguin, 1940), p.25.

39 Laing, op. cit., p.147.

40 Potamkin, Harry Allen, 'Grierson's *Drifters*', *Close Up* (October, 1930); and Schrire, David, 'Evasive Documentary', *Cinema Quarterly* (1934), vol. III, no.1.

41 See chapter Six of this Book for further details.

42 Film Society Programme no. 33, 10 November, 1929, Tivoli Palace, Strand, London (Grierson Archive Papers 1927-33), G2.1.2.

43 Tallents, Stephen, *Exhibition of Films at the Imperial Institute* (EMB Film Committee minute, 12 September, 1927 PRO CO 760/37 EMB/C/3).

44 Grierson, (Grierson Archive Papers 1927-1933), G2.8.15.

45 Widdowson, Peter, 'Between the Acts? English Fiction in the 1930s', in Clark (ed.), *Culture and Crisis in Britain in the 1930s* (London, Lawrence and Wishart, 1979), pp.133-6.

46 Lehmann, op. cit., p.20.

47 Laing, op. cit., p.145.

48 Slater, Montagu, *Left Review* (May, 1935), pp.364-5.

49 Spender, Stephen, *Left Review* (November 1936), p.779.

50 *Left Review* (February 1936).

51 Jameson, Storm, *Fact* no.4 (1937), p.11.

52 Cited in Laing, op. cit., p.158.

53 McFarlane, James, 'The Mind of Modernism', in Bradbury M. and McFarlane, J. (eds), *Modernism 1890-1930* (London, Penguin, 1974), pp.79-80.

54 Jameson, Storm, op. cit., p.18.

55 Branson, Noreen and Heinemann, Margot, *Britain in the Nineteen Thirties* (London, Panther, 1973), p. 301.

56 Widdowson, Peter, in Clark (ed.), op. cit. p.149.

57 ibid., p.152.

58 Branson and Heinemann, op. cit., p.295.

59 Williams, Raymond, *Culture and Society 1780-1950* (London, Chatto & Windus, 1958), p. 287.

60 LeMahieu, D. L., *A Culture for Democracy* (Oxford, Clarendon, 1988), p.3.
61 Bond, Ralph, 'Cinema in the Thirties: Documentary Film and the Labour Movement', in Clark and Heinemann (eds), op. cit., p.246.
62 ibid., p.248.
63 ibid., p.254.
64 Hogenkamp, Bert, 'Making Films With a Purpose: Film-making and the Working Class', in Clark and Heinemann (eds), op. cit., p.151.
65 Hardy, Forsyth, H. op. cit., p.83.
66 Bond, Ralph, in Clark (ed.), op. cit., p.252.

8 The influence of idealism

1 Hauser, Arnold, *Rococo, Classicism and Romanticism, The Social History of Art*, Vol 3 (London, Routledge & Kegan Paul, 1951), p.94.
2 ibid., p.99.
3 ibid., p.105.
4 Hobsbawm, Eric, *The Age of Revolution* (London, Cardinal, 1962), p.296.
5 Williams, Raymond, *Culture and Society 1780-1950* (London, Chatto & Windus, 1958), pp.123-8.
6 Hobsbawm, op. cit., pp.299-305.
7 ibid., p.299.
8 Hobhouse, L. T., *The Metaphysical Theory of the State* (London, Allen & Unwin, 1918).
9 Grierson, John, *Kant's Aesthetic* (Grierson Archive Papers 1898-1927), G1.2.7, p.7.
10 Stevenson, John, and Cook, Chris, *The Slump* (London, Cape, 1977), p.265.
11 Copleston, Frederick, *A History of Philosophy, Volume VIII: Bentham to Russell* (London, Search Press, 1966), p.164.
12 Moss, Michael, S., University Archivist, Glasgow University, letter to the author, 8 November 1985.
13 Hardy, Forsyth, H., interview with the author, Edinburgh, May 1985.
14 Kolakowski, Leszek, *Main Currents in Marxism, Volume 1: The Founders* (Oxford University Press, 1978), pp.45-7.
15 ibid., p.48.
16 Grierson, John, G1.2.7, op. cit., p.7.
17 Grierson, John, *The Character of an Ultimate Synthesis* (Grierson Archive Papers 1898-1927), G1.2.6, p.6.
18 Grierson, G1.2.7, op. cit., p.8.
19 Hobhouse, op. cit.
20 Grierson, G1.2.6, op. cit., p.12.
21 Mukerji, A. C., 'British Idealism', in Radhakrishnan, S. and Ruttonjiwadia, R. (eds) *A Dictionary of Eastern and Western Philosophy* (London, Allen & Unwin, 1953), p.308.
22 Oakley, Charles, letter to the author, 30 October 1985.
23 Grierson, John, 'The Challenge to Peace', in Forsyth, Hardy, H. (ed.), *Grierson on Documentary* (London, Faber & Faber, 1946), p.176.
24 Grierson, John, 'Preface', in Rotha, Paul, *Documentary Film* (London, Faber & Faber, 1939), and G3.14.4, op. cit., p.2.
25 ibid.
26 Grierson, John, 'I Derive my Authority from Moses', *Take One*, 2, no.9 (January–February 1970).

27 Grierson, John, 'Education and the Total Order', in Forsyth Hardy (ed.) (1946), op. cit., p.139.
28 Grierson, John, in Hardy (ed.), (1946), op. cit., p.130.
29 Grierson, John, *Byron and his Age* (Grierson Archive Papers 1898-1927), G1.2.10. p.9.
30 Grierson, John, 'The Challenge of Peace', in Hardy (ed.) (1946), op. cit., p.172.
31 Grierson, John, *The Social Relationships of Cinema* (Grierson Archive Papers 1933-9), G3.9.4, p.1.
32 Grierson, John, *The Contribution of Poetry to Religion* (Grierson Archive Papers 1898-1927), G1.5.2.
33 Grierson, John, 'The Challenge of Peace', in Hardy (ed.), (1946), op. cit., p.174.
34 Lippmann, Walter, *Public Opinion* (New York and London, Allen & Unwin, 1922), pp.78-9.
35 Grierson, John, *On Education* (Grierson Archive Papers 1939-1945), G4.19.21 p.3.
36 Grierson, John, 'Answers to a Cambridge Questionnaire', *Granta* (Cambridge, Cambridge University Press, 1967).
37 Grierson, John, 'The Challenge to Peace', in Hardy (ed.) (1946), op. cit., p.178.
38 Grierson, John, 'Notes for English Producers' (Public Records Office, Board of Trade, 1927, 64/86 6880).
39 Grierson, John, 'Better Popular Pictures', *Transactions of the Society of Motion Picture Engineers*, vol. xi, no.29 (New York, August 1926), pp.249-79.
40 Grierson, John, PRO BT 64/86 6880, op. cit., p.21.
41 ibid., p.22.
42 Grierson, John, *Granta*, op. cit., p.10.
43 Marwick, Arthur, 'Middle Opinion in the Thirties', *English Historical Review* vol.79 (1964).
44 Addison, Paul, op. cit., p.50.
45 As in, Morris, Peter, 'Re-thinking Grierson: The Ideology of John Grierson', in Verronneau, Dorland and Feldman (eds), *Dialogue Canadian and Quebec Cinema* (Montreal, Mediatexte, 1987).
46 Pimlott, Ben, *Labour and the Left in the 1930s* (London, Cambridge University Press, 1977), pp.64-5.

Bibliography

Manuscript and archive sources

The John Grierson archive, University of Stirling

G1: 26 April 1898 – January 1927

G1.1 – G1.6: Papers relating to the period of Grierson's career at Glasgow University, 1919-23, and at Armstrong College, University of Durham, 1923-4.

G1.1. – G1.4: Collections of notes and articles on philosophy. G1.5. – G1.6: Sermons and other papers. G1.7. – G1.10: Papers from Grierson's period in America as a Rockefeller Research Fellow, 1924-7.

G1.7. – G1.9: Miscellaneous papers. G1.10: Article for *Motion Picture News* (4 December 1926).

G1.A.1. – G1A.5: Miscellaneous papers, including, Grierson's prose from Glasgow University Magazine, extracts from Chicago newspapers, extracts from *Motion Picture News*, and review of Flaherty's *Moana*

G2: February 1927 – September 1933

G2.1. – G2.4: Papers relating to the Empire Marketing Board, including notes on *Drifters* and other films, and miscellaneous EMB papers. G2.5. – G2.7: Papers relating to the League of Nations and international film activity. G2.8. – G2.21: Writings by John Grierson, including articles in the *Clarion*, *New Clarion*, *Everyman*, *New Britain*, *Artwork*, *Cinema Quarterly*, *Kinematograph Weekly, John Bull, Tit-bits*, and typescript for unpublished book entitled *New Worlds for Cinema*. G2.22. – G2.28: Miscellaneous papers, including correspondence, press cuttings and various articles on film and the EMB.

G2A.1. – G2A.4: The Grierson-Strauss Correspondence, official papers relating to the EMB Film Unit, and press cuttings and articles by Grierson.

G3: 1 October 1933 – 17 October 1939

G3.1 – G3.4: Scripts and material relating to the GPO Film Unit.

G3.9. – G3.14: Writings by John Grierson, including articles on documentary film, and reviews in *Cinema Quarterly, The Listener, Daily Herald*, the *Fortnightly, Fortnightly Review*, and the Preface to Paul Rotha's *Documentary Film* (2nd ed. 1938).

G3.15 – G3.18: Miscellaneous papers, including correspondence, press cuttings, and *First Report of the Cinematograph Films Council*, 1939.
G3A.1 – G3A.4: Papers relating to the GPO Film Unit.

G4.: 18 October 1939 – 7 November 1945

G4.18. – G4.22: Writings by John Grierson, including articles on documentary film and propaganda in *The Land, Food for Thought, Art in Action, The Nation*, and others; and various unpublished articles.
G4.23. – G4.30: Correspondence with Stephen Tallents and others.
G4.P2. – G4.P3: Publications, *The Spectator*, 5858 (4 October 1940), and *The Land* (1942-3), including 'My Father was a Teacher', pp.188-90.

G5: 8 November 1945 – 31 December 1950

G5.8. – G5.10: Writings by John Grierson, including *The Voice of the State*, unpublished manuscript, 102 pp. Various articles on education and documentary film, including article on Eisenstein, 2 May 1948.
G5.P1 – G5.P5: Publications, including *The Public's Progress* (London, Contact Books, 1947, with Basil Wright and Paul Rotha.
G5A.2: *Documentary 1947*, discussion between Basil Wright and John Grierson on the Edinburgh Film Festival, (31 August 1947).

G6: 1 January 1951 – 10 October 1957

G6.33 – G6.34: Writings by John Grierson, various articles, including *Films and Universities*, with Basil Wright.
G6.P1 – G6.P76: Publications. Works cited, in *Cine Technician, Sight and Sound, Film Forum*, and *Scotland*

G7: October 1957 – February 1972

G7.14 – G7.22: Writings by John Grierson. Including, 'The Relationship Between the Political Power and the Cinema', Edinburgh International Film Festival Celebrity Lecture (1968); 'Personal Memories of the Russian Cinema', Leipzig Film Festival (1967), 'Answers to a Cambridge Questionnaire', *Granta* (1967), and other articles.
G7.23 – G7.34: General correspondence, including correspondence with Paul Rotha, Stephen Tallents, John Amiss, Arthur Elton, and others.
G7.35 – G7.39: Writings by authors other than John Grierson.
G7.40. – G7.57: Items relating to organizations connected with film-making, and programmes and papers relating to film festivals and film publicity.
G7.P1 – G7.P39: Publications, including *Scotland, Japan Motion Picture Almanac, The Living Cinema, Sight and Sound, Film Quarterly, Journal of the Society of Film and Television Arts*, and others.
G7A.1. – G7A.10: Scripts for programmes featuring John Grierson on radio and television, and reviews by John Grierson. Including interviews with the Canadian Television and Radio Commission, 1969.

General Post Office Archive, London

POST 33: Post Office Film Unit 1934-42

POST 33 4483 (1933): Information on films used by Post Office, supplied to Select Committee on Estimates.

POST 33 4927 (1933-4): Transfer of Film Unit and library from Empire Marketing Board to Post Office.

POST 33 4928 (1935-48): Post Office Films. Distribution for outside showing by British Film Distributors.

POST 33 4930 (1934-8): British Institute. Grants from Cinematograph Fund.

POST 33 4951 (1934-5): Post Office Film Unit. Invitation to tender for operational services.

POST 33 5089 (1936-9): Post Office Film Unit and Library. Committee to examine cost of productions.

POST 33 5199 (1937-9): Post Office Film Unit. Reorganization of composition and control. Report of Committee of Enquiry, 1936.

POST 33 5259 (1937): GPO Film Unit. Administration to be under new post of Controller of Publicity.

POST 33 5421 (1935-8): Post Office Film Unit. Proposed film on Anglo-Swiss telephone service.

POST 33 5454 (1936-9): Post Office Film Unit. Staff on contractors' books, alteration to pay, personnel, pay, etc.

POST 33 5470 (1939): Post Office Film Unit. Lease of Sound Recording Apparatus from RCA Limited.

POST 33 5498 (1939): GPO Film Unit. Production of air raid precaution film for the Home Office.

POST 33 5511 (1935-6): GPO Film Unit. Awards gained at International Film Festival, Brussels.

POST 33 5555 (1939-42): GPO Film Unit. Administrative and financial control transferred to the Ministry of Information.

National Film Archive, London

Holdings of documentary films by Grierson and the documentary film movement, 1930-9.

Imperial War Museum, London

Department of Film. Holdings of films from the First World War and Second World War. Correspondence, scripts and other material.

British Film Institute

Library, London. Manuscript material, correspondence, press cuttings, and literature on and by the documentary film movement. Periodical holdings and microfilm holdings.

Public Records Office, London

PRO CO 760/37: Minutes, correspondence, and memoranda of the Empire Marketing Board Film Committee.

PRO T 160: Treasury Correspondence and memoranda on government film activities.

PRO T 161: Treasury correspondence and memoranda on Imperial film propaganda

PRO BT 61: Minutes and memoranda of the Inter-departmental Committee on Trade Propaganda and Advertising.

PRO BT 64: Board of Trade Industries and Manufactures Department, correspondence and memoranda on the British film industry, and minutes and memoranda of the Cinematograph Films Council.

PRO BT 64/88: Memorandum on the Moyne Committee.

PRO BT 64,93/6488 39: *First Annual Report of the Cinematograph Films Council* (1939).

PRO BT 64/86 6880: EMB Film Committee Memorandum by John Grierson, entitled 'Notes for English Producers' (1927).

PRO INF 1: Ministry of Information Planning Committee minutes, and correspondence and memoranda of the Ministry of Information Films Division.

PRO INF 5: Correspondence and memoranda on production of films for the Ministry of Information Films Division.

PRO INF 5/55: Foreign Distribution of *North Sea*.

PRO INF 6/294: Shooting Script for *North Sea*.

PRO BT 55: Minutes and memoranda of the Moyne Committee.

Government publications

Cinematograph Act, 1909 (London, HMSO, 1909).

Proceedings of the Imperial Conference, 1926, (London, HMSO, 1926), CMD 2768.

Thirteenth Report of a General Economic Sub-committee (London, HMSO, 1926), CMD 2709.

Cinematograph Films Act 1927 (London, HMSO, 1927).

First and Second Reports of a Select Committee on Estimates (London, HMSO, 1928).

Report of the Select Committee on National Expenditure, the May Committee (London, HMSO, 1930-1). CMD 3920.

Minority Report to the May Committee Report (London, HMSO, 1930-1), CMD 3920.

Proceedings of the Imperial Conference, 1930 (London, HMSO, 1930), CMD 3718.

Report of the Imperial Committee on Economic Consultation and Co-operation the Skelton Committee (London, HMSO, 1933), CMD 4335.

Report of the Select Committee on Estimates (London, HMSO, 1934).

Report of the Select Committee on Estimates (London, HMSO, 1938).

Biographies and memoirs

Amery, L. S., *My Political Life* (London, Hutchinson, 1953).
Beveridge, James, *John Grierson, Film Maker* (London, Macmillan, 1979).
Boyle, A., *Only The Wind Will Listen, The Life and Work of John Reith*, (London, Hutchinson, 1972).
Calder-Marshall, Arthur, *The Innocent Eye*, The Life of Robert J. Flaherty (London, W. H. Allen, 1963).
Forsyth, Hardy, H., *John Grierson, A Documentary Biography* (London, Faber & Faber, 1979).
Huxley, Gervas, *Both Hands* (London, Chatto & Windus, 1970).
Rotha, Paul, *Documentary Diary* (London, Secker & Warburg, 1973).
Saxon Mills, G. H., *There is a Tide, The Life and Work of Sir William Crawford* (London, Heinemann, 1954).
Tallents, Stephen, *Man and Boy* (London, 1943).
Watt, Harry, *Don't Look at the Camera* (London, Elek Books, 1974).

Secondary sources

Abrams, Philip, *The Origins of British Sociology* (Chicago and London, University of Chicago Press, 1968).
Addison, Paul, *The Road to 1945* (London, Quartet, 1977).
Albig, William, *Public Opinion* (London, McGraw Hill, 1939).
Aldcroft, D. H., *The Inter-war Economy* (London, Batsford, 1970).
Aldcroft, D. H., *The British Economy Between the Wars* (Oxford, Philip Allen, 1983).
Allen, G. C., *British Industries and Their Organisation* (London, Longmans, 1959).
Althusser, Louis, *Lenin and Philosophy and other Essays* (London, New Life Books, 1971).
—— *For Marx* (Paris, 1965).
Amery, Leo, *Empire and Prosperity* (London, Faber & Faber, 1930).
Anderson, Perry, 'The Antinomies of Antonio Gramsci', *New Left Review* (November 1976–January 1977).
—— *Arguments Within English Marxism* (London, 1980).
Andrew, Dudley, *The Major Film Theories, An Introduction* (London, Oxford University Press, 1976).
—— *Concepts in Film Theory* (London, Oxford University Press, 1984).
Armes, Roy, *A Critical History of British Cinema* (London, Secker & Warburg, 1978).
Arronovitch, S., *Monopoly, A Study of British Monopoly Capitalism* (London, Lawrence & Wishart, 1955).
Arts Enquiry, *The Factual Film* (London, Oxford University Press, 1947).
Ayer, A. J., *The Problem of Knowledge* (London, Penguin, 1956).
—— *Philosophy in the Twentieth Century* (London, Counterpoint, 1982).
Balazs, Bella, *Theory of the Film* (London, Dobson, 1945).
—— *Der Sichtbare Mensch oder Der Kultur des Films* (Wien, Leipzig, Deutsch-Osterreichischer Verlag, 1924).
Balcon, Michael, *Twenty Years of British Films 1925-1945* (London, Falcon Press, 1947).

Balio, Tino, *The American Film Industry* (Madison, Wisconsin, University of Wisconsin Press, 1976).

Barna, Yon, *Eisenstein* (London, Secker & Warburg, 1973).

Barnouw, Erik, *Documentary* (London, Oxford University Press, 1974).

Bartlett, F. C., *Political Propaganda* (London, Cambridge University Press, 1940).

Barton, Paul, *Corporate Public Relations* (New York, 1966).

Bell, Elaine, 'The Origins of British TV Documentary, the BBC 1946-1955', in Corner, J. and Richardson, K. (eds.), *Documentary in the Mass Media* (London, Edward Arnold, 1986).

Bell, Thomas, *Pioneering Days* (London, Lawrence & Wishart, 1941).

—— *John Mclean* (Glasgow, Communist Party of Great Britain, Scottish Committee, 1944).

Benham, F., *Great Britain Under Protectionism* (New York, Macmillan, 1941).

Beritz, Lauren, *The Servants of Power* (New York, 1960).

Bernays, E. L., *Crystalizing Public Opinion* (New York, Boni & Liverweight, 1923).

—— *Propaganda* (New York, Boni & Liverweight, 1928).

—— *Public Relations* (Oklahoma, University of Oklahoma Press, 1952).

—— *The Engineering of Consent* (New York, 1955).

Blackburn, Robin (ed.), *Ideology in Social Science, Readings in Critical Social Theory* (London, Fontana, 1972).

Bobbio, Norberto, 'Gramsci and the Conception of Civil Society', in *Gramsci and Marxist Theory* (Mouffe, London Routledge, 1979).

Boggs, Carl, *Gramsci's Marxism* (London, Pluto, 1976).

Bond, Ralph, 'Cinema in the Thirties', in *Culture and Crisis in Britain in the 1930s*, Clark (ed.) (London, Lawrence & Wishart, 1979).

Boothby, Robert and Macmillan, Harold, *Industry and the State, A Conservative View* (London, Macmillan, 1927).

Bottomore, T. B., *Classes in Modern Society* (New York and London, Ampersand, 1965).

Bradbury, Malcolm, and McFarlane, J. (eds) *Modernism 1890-1930* (London, Penguin, 1974).

Bradley, F. H., *Essays on Truth and Reality* (London, Clarendon Press, 1914).

—— *Appearance and Reality* (London, Swann & Co., 1893).

—— *Ethical Studies* (London, H.S. King & Co., 1876).

Branson, Noreen, and Heinemann, Margot, *Britain in the 1930s* (London, Panther, 1973.

—— *Britain in the 1920s* (London, Weidenfeld & Nicolson, 1975).

Brewster, Ben, 'The Soviet State, the Communist Party and the Arts', London, Red Letters no.3.

British Film Institute, *The Film in National Life* (London, British Film Institute, 1943).

Buchanan, Andrew, *The Art of Film Production* (London, Pitman, 1936).

Bullock, Allen, 'The Double Image', in Bradbury, (ed.) *Modernism* London, Penguin, 1974).

Calder, Angus, 'Introduction', in *Britain by Mass Observation* (London, Cresset, 1986).

Calinescu, Matei, *Faces of Modernity* (London, Bloomington, 1977).

Campbell, C. A., *Scepticism and Construction* (London, Cambridge University Press, 1931).

Carr, E. H., *What is History* (London, Macmillan, 1961).

Cine Technician, *Report of an ACT Delegation to the USSR* (Cine Technician, May 1937).

Clark, John, *Culture and Crisis in Britain in the 1930s* (London, Lawrence & Wishart, 1979).

Clarke, Peter, *Liberals and Social Democrats* (London, Cambridge University Press, 1978).

Clubbe, John, *Carlyle and his Contemporaries* (USA, Duke University Press, 1976).

Cockburn, Claud, *The Devil's Decade* (London, Sidgwick & Jackson, 1973).

Cohen, G. A., *Karl Marx's Theory of History, A Defence* (Oxford, Clarendon Press, 1978).

Cole, G. D. H., 'Guild Socialism', Fabian Tract no.192 (1919).

Cole, G.D.H., and Postgate, Raymond, *A History of the Common People 1746-1946* (London, Methuen, 1938).

Collins, Richard, 'Seeing is Believing, The Ideology of Naturalism', in Corner, J. (ed.), *Documentary in the Mass Media* (London, Edward Arnold, 1986).

Copleston, Frederick, *A History of Philosophy*, vols 1-9 (New York, Doubleday, 1946-66).

Corner, John, and Richardson, Kay, 'Documentary Meaning and the Discourse of Interpretation', in Corner, John (ed.), *Documentary in the Mass Media* (London, Edward Arnold, 1986).

Corner, John, 'Preface', in *Documentary in the Mass Media* Corner, (ed.), (London, Edward Arnold, 1986).

Cornforth, Maurice, *Materialism and the Dialectical Method* (London, Lawrence & Wishart, 1952).

—— *Theory of Knowledge* (London, Lawrence & Wishart, 1954).

Craig, David, (ed.) *Marxists on Literature, An Anthology*, (London, Pelican, 1975).

Crawford, William, *How to Succeed in Advertising* (London, World's Press News, 1931).

Crossick, Geoffrey, 'The Emergence of the Lower Middle Class in Britain', in *The Lower Middle Class in Britain*, Crossick Geoffrey (ed.) (London, 1977).

Curti, Merle, *The Growth of American Thought* (New York, Harper & Bros., 1943).

Dewey, John, *Human Nature and Conduct* (USA and London, Allen & Unwin, 1922).

—— *Reconstruction in Philosophy* (New York, Allen & Unwin, 1920).

—— *Democracy and Education* (USA, Macmillan, 1916).

Dickson, Tony, *Scottish Capitalism* (London, Lawrence & Wishart, 1980).

Donaldson, G., *Scotland, Church and Nation Through Sixteen Centuries* (London, SCM Press, 1960).

Eichenbaum, B. M., 'Theory of the Formal Method', in *Readings in Russian Poetics, Formalist and Structuralist Views* (USA, Ann Arbor, 1971).

Eisenstein, Sergei, *Film Form*, Leyda, Jay (trans.) (London, Dennis Dobson, MCMLI).

Eliot, T. S., 'Ulysses, Order and Myth', in *The Dial*, no.75 (New York, 1923).

Ellis, Jack, C., *John Grierson, A Guide to References and Resources* (Boston, Boston University Press, 1986).

—— 'The Young Grierson in America 1924-1927', *Cinema Journal*, viii, no.17 (Fall, 1968).

—— 'Grierson at University', *Cinema Journal*, xii, 2, no. 41, (Spring, 1973).

Ellwood, C. A., *Cultural Evolution, A Study of Social Origins and Development*

(New York and London, Century Social Science Series, 1927).

Emery, Edwin, *The Press and America* (New York, Prentice Hall, 1954).

Engels, Friedrich, 'Letter to Margaret Harkness', in *Marx and Engels Selected Correspondence* (Moscow, Progress Publishers, 1955).

Everson, W., *American Silent Films* (London and New York, Oxford University Press, 1978).

Fitzgerald, Patrick, *Industrial Combination in England* (London, Pitman & Sons, 1927).

Forsyth Hardy, H., *John Grierson, A Documentary Biography* (London, Faber & Faber, 1979).

—— *Grierson on Documentary* (London, Faber & Faber, 1946).

—— *Grierson on the Movies* (London, Faber & Faber, 1981).

Gallacher, William, *Revolt on the Clyde* (London, Lawrence & Wishart, 1936).

Gasset, Y, Ortega, *The Revolt of the Masses* (London, Allen & Unwin, 1932).

Glover, Janet, *The Story of Scotland* (London, Faber & Faber, 1960).

Gloversmith, Frank (ed.), *Class Culture and Social Change* (London, Harvester Press, 1980).

Gordon, L., *The Public Corporation in Great Britain* (London, Oxford University Press, 1938).

Green, T. H., Review of *Introduction to the Philosophy of Religion* (London, Caird, John, 1880).

Grey, R.Q., 'Religious Culture and Social Class in Late 19th and Early 20th Century Edinburgh', in Crossick, G., (ed.), *The Lower Middle Class in Britain* (London, 1977).

Grierson, John 'Preface' in Rotha (2nd edn) *Documentary Film* (London, Faber & Faber, 1952).

Hampton, Benjamin, *History of the American Film Industry* (New York and London, Noel Douglas, 1932).

Hauser, Arnold, *The Social History of Art*, Vol.3., (London, RKP, 1951).

Hayes, Samuel, P., *The Response to Industrialism 1885-1914* (USA, University of Chicago, 1957).

Henderson, G.D., *Presbyterianism* (Aberdeen University Press, 1954).

Higham, Charles, *Looking Forward* (London, Nisbet and Co., 1920).

Hillier, J., and Lovell, A., *Studies in Documentary* (London, Secker and Warburg, 1972).

Hobhouse, L.T., *The Metaphysical Theory of the State* (London, Allen and Unwin, 1918).

Hobsbawm, E.J., *Industry and Empire, An Economic History of Britain since 1750* (London, Weidenfeld and Nicolson, 1968).

—— *The Age of Revolution, Europe, 1789-1848* (London, Cardinal, 1962).

—— *The Age of Capital, 1848-1875* (London, Weidenfeld and Nicolson, 1975).

Hogenkamp, Bert, 'Making Films with a Purpose, Film making and the Working Class', in Clark and Heinemann (eds), *Culture and Crisis in Britain in the 1930s* (London, Lawrence and Wishart, 1979).

Hollins, T. S., 'The Conservative Party Between the Wars', *English Historical Review* (1981).

Hood, Stuart, 'A Cool Look at the Legend', in Orbanz E. (ed.), *Journey to a Legend and Back, The British Realistic Film* (Berlin, Edition Volker Spiess, 1977).

—— 'John Grierson and the British Documentary Film Movement', in Porter, Vincent, and Curran, James, (eds) *British Cinema History* (London, Weidenfeld & Nicolson, 1983).

Hood, Stuart, in *Undercut*, no.9 (Summer 1983).

Hughes, Stuart, *Consciousness and Society, The Reorientation of European Social Thought 1890-1930* (London, MacGibbon & Kee, 1959).

Huxley, Gervas, *Both Hands* (London, Chatto & Windus, 1970).

Irwin, W., *Propaganda and the News* (New York, McGraw Hill, 1936).

Jacobs, Lewis, (ed.), *The Documentary Tradition* (New York, Hopkinson & Blake, 1971).

James, William, *Pragmatism* (New York and London, Longmans, 1907).

Johnston, Claire, 'Independence and the Thirties', in Macpherson, D., (ed.) *British Cinema, Traditions of Independence* (London, BFI, 1980).

Johnston, Claire, in *Undercut* no.9 (Summer, 1983).

Jones, Herbert, 'The Social Organism', in *Essays in Philosophical Criticism* (London, 1888).

Katz and Lazarsfeld, *Personal Influence* (New York, Macmillan, 1955).

Kemp, John, *The Philosophy of Kant* (London, Oxford University Press, 1968).

Klingender, F. and Legg, S. L., *Money Behind the Screen* (London, Lawrence & Wishart, 1936).

Klugmann, James, *History of the Communist Party of Great Britain* (London, Lawrence & Wishart, 1969).

Kolakowski, Leszek, *Main Currents of Marxism, Volume One, The Founders* (Oxford, Oxford University Press, 1978).

—— *Main Currents of Marxism, Volume Three, The Breakdown* (Oxford, Oxford University Press, 1978).

Kracauer, Siegfried, *Theory of Film, The Redemption of Physical Reality* (Oxford, Oxford University Press, 1960).

Kuhn, Annette, 'British Documentary in the 1930s and Independence, Recontextualising a Film Movement', in Macpherson, D. (ed.) *British Cinema, Traditions of Independence* (London, British Film Institute, 1980).

Kuhn, T. S., *The Structure of Scientific Revolutions* (Chicago, University of Chicago Press, 1970).

Lacey, A. R., *A Dictionary of Philosophy,* (London, Routledge & Kegan Paul, 1976).

Lafaber, Walter, and Polenberg, Richard, *The American Century, A History of the United States Since the 1890s* (New York, Wiley, 1975).

Laing, Stuart, 'Presenting Things as they Are', in Gloversmith, F. (ed.), *Class Culture and Social Change* (London, Harvester Press, 1980).

Lambert, Richard, S., *Propaganda* (London, Thomas Nelson & Sons, 1938).

Lasky, Jesse, L, *I Blow my own Trumpet* (London, Gollancz, 1957).

Lasswell, Harold, *Psychoanalysis and Politics* (Chicago, University of Chicago Press, 1930).

Lee, J. M., 'The Dissolution of the EMB', *Journal of Imperial and Commonwealth History*, vol. 1, no.1 (1972).

Lehmann, John, *New Writing in Europe* (London, Penguin, 1940).

LeMahieu, D. L., *A Culture for Democracy* (Oxford, Clarendon, 1988).

Lenin, V. I., 'Left Wing Communism an Infantile Disorder' in *Left Wing Communism in Great Britain* (UK, Communist Party of Great Britain, 1920).

—— 'Party Organisation and Party Literature', in *Lenin on Literature and Art* (Moscow, Progress Publishers, 1970).

—— *Materialism and Empirico-criticism* (Peking, Foreign Language Press, 1972, originally published in 1918).

Lenman, B., *An Economic History of Modern Scotland 1660-1976* (London, Batsford, 1977).

Lessnoff, Michael, *The Structure of Social Science* (London, Allen & Unwin, 1974).

Leyda, Jay, *Kino, A History of the Rusian and Soviet Film* (London, Allen & Unwin, 1960).

Lichtheim, George, *Marxism* (London, Routledge and Kegan Paul, 1961).

Lindsay, Vachel, *The Art of the Motion Pictures* (New York, Macmillan, 1915).

Lippmann, Walter, *A Preface to Politics* (London and New York, T. Fisher Unwin, 1913).

—— *Public Opinion* (New York and London, Allen & Unwin, 1922).

—— *The Phantom Public, A Sequal to Public Opinion* (New York, Macmillan, 1930).

—— *Liberty and the News* (New York, Harcourt, 1920).

Lloyd, Herbert, *Public Relations* (London, English Universities Press, 1960).

Lovell, Terry, *Pictures of Reality* (London, British Film Institute, 1983).

Low, Rachel, *History of the British Film*, (Six Volumes) (London, Allen & Unwin), *Volume 1, 1896-1906*, (1948); *Volume 2, 1906-1914* (1948); *Volume 3, 1914-1918* (1950); *Volume 4, 1918-1929* (1971); *Volume 5, Documentary and Educational Films of the 1930s* (1979); *Volume 6, Films of Comment and Persuasion in the 1930s* (1979).

Lukacs, Georg, *Writer and Critic* (Kahn, A. (trans.) (London, Merlin, 1978).

Mackenzie, A. J., *Propaganda Boom* (London, Gifford, 1938).

Mackie, John, Duncan, *A History of Scotland* (Edinburgh and London, Harmondsworth, 1964).

—— *The University of Glasgow* (Glasgow, Jackson, Son & Co., 1954).

Mandel, Ernest, *Marxist Economic Theory* (London, Merlin, 1962).

—— *An Introduction to Marxist Economic Theory* (New York, Pathfinder, 1969).

Margolies, David, 'Left Review and Left Literary Theory', in Gloversmith, G., (ed.), *Class Culture and Social Change* (London, Harvester Press, 1980).

Marwick, Arthur, 'Middle Opinion in the Thirties', in *English Historical Review*, vol. 79 (1964).

—— *The Deluge, British Society and the First World War* (London, Bodley Head, 1965).

—— *Britain in the Century of Total War, War Peace and Social Change 1900-1967* (London, Bodley Head, 1968).

McFarlane, James, 'Mind and Nature of Modernism', in Bradbury, M. and McFarlane, J. (eds), *Modernism* (London, Penguin, 1974).

McLellan, David, *Marx Before Marxism* (London, Macmillan, 1970).

McLennan, Gregor, *Marxism and the Methodologies of History* (London, Verso, 1981).

McShane, Harry, *No Mean Fighter* (London, Pluto, 1978).

Medlicott, W. N., *Contemporary England 1914-1964* (London, Longmans, 1967).

Mepham, J., and Ruben, D. H., *Issues in Marxist Philosophy* (Brighton, Harvester Press, 1979).

Meram, Barsam, Richard, *Non-fiction Film, A Critical History* (London, Allen & Unwin, 1974).

Metz, Christian, *Film Language, A Semiotics of the Cinema* (New York, Oxford University Press, 1974).

Middlemas, R. K., *The Clydesiders* (London, Hutchinson, 1965).

Middlemas, K., and Barnes, A. J. *Baldwin, A Biography* (London, Weidenfeld & Nicolson, 1969).

Miliband, Ralph, *The State in Capitalist Society* (London, Quartet, 1973).

Montagu, Ivor, *Film World* (London, Penguin, 1964).
—— in *Undercut* no.9. (Summer, 1983).
Morgan, Alexander, *Scottish University Studies* (Edinburgh and London, Oliver Boyd, 1933).
Mouffe, Chantal, *Gramsci and Marxist Theory* (London, Routledge & Kegan Paul, 1979).
Mowat, C. L., *Britain Between the Wars, 1918-1940* (London, Methuen, 1955).
Mukerji, A. C., 'British Idealism', in *History of Philosophy, Eastern and Western, Vol. Two* (London, Allen & Unwin, 1953).
Mukarovsky, Jan, 'Standard Language and Poetic Language', in Garvin, Paul, (trans.), *Prague School Reader in Aesthetics, Literary Structure and Style* (Washington, Georgetown University Press, 1964).
Mulhern, Francis, *The Moment of Scrutiny* (London, New Left Books, 1979).
Nettl, J. P., *The Soviet Achievement* (London, Thames & Hudson, 1967).
Nevett, T. R., *Advertising in Britain: A History* (London, Heinemann, 1974).
Next Five Years Group, *An Essay in Political Agreement* (London, Macmillan, 1935).
Nichols, Bill, 'Documentary Theory and Practice', in *Screen* vol. 17, no.4, (Winter 1976-7).
Nichols, Robert, 'An Art in Bondage', in *The Times* (5 September, 1925).
Nochlin, Linda, *Realism, Style and Civilization* (London, Penguin, 1971).
Novack, George, *Pragmatism Versus Marxism* (New York, Pathfinder, 1975).
O'Brien, T. H., *British Experiments in Public Ownership and Control* (London, Allen & Unwin, 1937).
O'Conner, D. J., *A Critical History of Western Philosophy* (London, Macmillan, 1964).
Orbanz, Eva (ed.), *Journey to a Legend and Back, The British Realistic Film* (Berlin, Edition Volker Spiess, 1977).
Orwell, George, *Inside the Whale* (London Gollancz, 1940).
—— *The Road to Wigan Pier* (London, Gollancz, 1937).
Passmore, John, *A Hundred Years of Philosophy* (London, Pelican, 1957).
Perkins, V. F., *Film as Film* (London, Pelican, 1972).
Pike, Christopher, *The Futurists, the Formalists, and the Marxist Critique* (London, Ink Links Ltd., 1979).
Pimlott, Ben, *Labour and the Left in the 1930s* (London, Cambridge University Press, 1977).
Plekhanov, Georgei, 'On Art for Art's Sake', *Unaddressed Letters on Art and Social Life* (Moscow, Foreign Languages Publishing House 1957).
—— 'On the Social Basis of Style', *Unaddressed Letters on Art and Social Life* (Moscow, 1957).
Poggi, Leonardo, 'Gramsci's General Theory of Marxism', in Mouffe, C. (ed.), *Gramsci and Marxist Theory* (London, Routledge & Kegan Paul, 1979).
Political and Economic Planning, *The British Film Industry* (London, Political and Economic Planning, 1952).
—— *The British Social Services* (London, Political and Economic Planning, 1937).
—— *Industrial Trade Associations* (London, PEP, 1957).
Pollard, Sidney, *The Idea of Progress* (London, Penguin, 1968).
—— *The Development of the British Economy 1914-1950* (London, Edward Arnold, 1962).
Ponsonby, A., *Lies and Falsehood in Wartime* (London, Allen & Unwin, 1928).

Porter, Bernard, *The Lion's Share, A Short History of British Imperialism 1850-1970* (London, Longmans, 1975).

Potamkin, Harry, A., 'Grierson's *Drifters*', in *Close Up* (October, 1930).

Poulantzas, Nicos, *Political Power and Social Classes* (London, NLB, 1975).

Priestley, J. B., *English Journey* (London, Heinemann, 1934).

Pronay, Nicholas, 'The Political Censorship of Film in Britain Between the Wars', Pronay, N. and Spring, D. W. (eds), *Propaganda, Politics and Film* (London, Macmillan, 1982).

Purcell, A. E., *The Crisis of Democratic Theory, Scientific Naturalism and the Problem of Value* (USA, University of Kentucky, 1973).

Rader, Melvin, *Marx's Theory of History* (New York, Oxford University Press, 1979).

Reeves, N. A., *Official British Film Propaganda During the First World War* (Unpublished PhD thesis, University of London, 1981).

Richter, Melvin, *The Politics of Conscience, T.H.Green and his Age* (London, Weidenfeld & Nicolson, 1964).

Ridley, F. A., and Arand, V. S., *James Maxton and British Socialism* (London, Medusa Press, 1970).

Rotha, Paul, *The Film Till Now, A Survey of World Cinema* (London, Cape, 1930).

—— *Rotha on the Film* (London, Faber & Faber, 1958).

—— *Documentary Film* (London, Faber & Faber, 1936).

Russell, Bertrand, *History of Western Philosophy* (London, Allen & Unwin, 1946).

—— *Roads to Freedom* (London, Allen & Unwin, 1918).

—— *Principles of Social Reconstruction* (London, Allen & Unwin, 1916).

—— *Education and the Social Order* (London, Allen & Unwin, 1932).

Samuel, Raphael, 'The Middle Class Between the Wars', *New Socialist* (January, February, and March 1983).

Schudson, Michael, *Discovering the News* (New York, Basic Books, 1978).

Scott, D., *A. D. Lindsay* (Oxford, Blackwell, 1971).

Seton, Marie, *Sergei M., Eisenstein* (London, Bodley Head, 1952).

Shlovsky, Victor, 'Art and Technique', in Leman and Reis (eds), *Russian Formalist Criticism, Four Essays* (USA, 1965).

Steadman Jones, Gareth, 'History, the Poverty of Empiricism', in Blackburn (ed.), *Ideology in Social Science, Readings in Critical Social Theory* (London, Fontana, 1972).

Stevenson, John, and Cook, Chris, *The Slump* (London, Cape, 1977).

Stevenson, John, *British Society 1914-1945* (London, Penguin, 1984).

Stuart, Campbell, *Secrets of Crewe House* (London, Hodder & Stoughton, 1920).

Sussex, Elizabeth, *The Rise and Fall of the British Documentary Movement* (London, University of California Press, 1975).

Swann, Paul, 'John Grierson and the GPO Film Unit 1933-1939', *Historical Journal of Film Radio and Television*, vol.3, no.1 (1983).

—— 'The Selling of the Empire, The Imperial Film Unit 1926-1933', *Historical Journal of Film Radio and Television* (1984).

—— *The British Documentary Film Movement 1926-1945* (Unpublished PhD thesis, University of Leeds, 1979).

Swingewood, A., *A Short History of Social Thought* (London, Macmillan, 1984).

Symons, Julien, *The Thirties* (London, Faber & Faber, 1960).

Tallents, Stephen, *The Projection of England* (London, Faber & Faber, 1932).

—— *Post Office Publicity* (London, General Post Office, 1935).

—— 'The Birth of British Documentary', *Journal of the University Film Association* vol.20, no.1,(USA, 1968).

Taylor, A. J. P., *English History 1914-1945* (London and Oxford, Clarendon, 1965).

Taylor, P. M., *The Projection of Britain* (Cambridge, Cambridge University Press, 1981).

Taylor, P. M., and Sanders, M. *British Propaganda During World War One* (London, Macmillan, 1982).

Tedlow, Richard, S., *Keeping the Corporate Image, Public Relations and Business 1900-1950*, (USA, JAI Press, 1979).

Thompson, E. P., *The Poverty of Theory* (London, Merlin, 1978).

—— *The Making of the English Working Class* (London, Gollancz, 1963).

Tudor, Andrew, *Theories of Film* (London, Secker & Warburg, 1974).

Vaughan, Dai, 'Notes on the Ascent of a Fictitious Mountain', in Corner (ed.), *Documentary in the Mass Media* (London, Edward Arnold, 1986).

Wallas, Graham, *The Great Society, A Psychological Analysis* (London, Macmillan, 1914).

White, Merton, *The Age of Analysis* (USA, Mentor, 1955).

Wickwar, W. H., *The Public Services* (London, Cobden-Sanderson, 1938).

Widdowson, Peter, 'Between the Acts? English Fiction in the 1930s', in Clark, Heinemann etc. (eds), *Culture and Crisis in Britain in the Thirties* (London, Lawrence & Wishart, 1979).

Willemen, Paul, 'Editorial', in *Screen*, vol.14., nos 1/2, (Spring/Summer).

—— 'Presentation', in Macpherson, D. (ed.), *British Cinema, Traditions of Independence* (London, British Film Institute, 1980)

Willert, Arthur, and Long, B., *The Empire in the World, A Study in Leadership and Reconstruction* (Oxford, Oxford University Press, 1937).

Williams, Raymond, *Culture and Society 1780-1950* (London, Chatto & Windus, 1958).

—— *The Long Revolution* (London, Chatto & Windus, 1961).

Wollen, Peter, *Signs and Meanings in the Cinema* (London, Secker & Warburg, 1969).

Wollheim, Richard, *Bradley* (London, Harmondsworth, 1959).

Wright, Basil, *Use of the Film* (London, Bodley Head, 1948).

—— *The Long View* (London, Secker & Warburg,1974).

Wright, Ian, 'F. R. Leavis, The Scrutiny Movement and the Crisis', in Clark, Heinemann etc. (eds), *Culture and Crisis in Britain in the Thirties* (London, Lawrence & Wishart, 1979).

Newspapers and trade magazines

Chicago Evening Post (1925-6).
the *Daily Express*
the *Daily Film Renter.*
the *Daily Herald* (1930-4).
Exhibitors Herald (1925-6).
the *Glasgow Herald* (1930-3).
Kinematograph Weekly (1919-39).
The Listener (1930-9).
Manchester Guardian (1930-2).
Motion Picture News (1926).

The Newcastle Chronicle (1930-3).
New York Sun (1926).
New York Times.
New York World.
the *Observer* (1929-34).
the *Scotsman* (1930-4).
The Times (1923-7).
the *Yorkshire Post* (1930-4).

Periodicals

Artwork (1930-1).
Cinema (1929-32).
Cinema Quarterly (1932-6).
Cine Technician (1954-5).
the *Clarion* (1929-32).
The Dial (1919-24).
Documentary Newsletter (1940-7).
the *New Clarion* (1929-32).
Everyman (1931-2).
Films and Filming (1955-64).
Film Forum (1954-6).
Film Quarterly (1960).
Granta (1967).
John Bull (1931).
Journal of Imperial and Commonwealth History (1972).
Journal of the University Film Association (1968).
The Land (1942-3).
Life and Letters Today (1930-3).
Marketing (1932).
New Britain (1933-4).
Quarterly of Film Radio and Television (1954).
The Realist (1929).
Saturday Review (1955-7).
Sight and Sound (1932-68).
Scottish Life and Letters (1966).
Scotland (1954-60).
Screenwriter (1966).
Tit-bits (1930).
Todays Cinema (1929-32).
Worker's Cinema (1930).
World Film News (1936-38).

Press cuttings collections

British Film Institute, Library and Information Department, London.
John Grierson Archive, University of Stirling.
Post Office Archive Department, London.

Correspondence

Charles Dand, university friend of Grierson; Alberto Cavalcanti, documentary film-maker; Basil Wright, documentary film-maker; H. Forsyth Hardy, colleague of Grierson; Michael S. Moss, Archivist, University of Glasgow; J.William Hess, Associate Director, Rockefeller Archive Centre.

Interviews

Alberto Cavalcanti, Paris, May, 1983.
H. Forsyth Hardy, Edinburgh, 1 October, 1985.
Marion Taylor, Edinburgh, 5 October, 1985.
H. Forsyth Hardy, Edinburgh, 8 May, 1986.
Basil Wright, High Wycombe, 9 March, 1987.

Index